YAHWEH:
THE DIVINE
NAME
IN THE
BIBLE

יהוה

YAHWEH:
THE DIVINE
NAME
IN THE
BIBLE

G.H.Parke-Taylor

WILFRID LAURIER UNIVERSITY PRESS
WATERLOO, ONTARIO

TABLE OF CONTENTS

PREFACE

For many years I have been fascinated by the Tetragrammaton, while at the same time I have shared with many others a sense of being overwhelmed by the diverse views put forward as to the origin, pronunciation and theological meaning of the divine name in the Old Testament. The literature on the subject, mainly in the form of articles in the journals, is immense, and shows no signs of diminishing, perhaps because no single view has yet found the full support of scholars. The nature of the evidence, biblical and extra-biblical, leads inevitably to speculation and hypothesis.

In spite of the vast literature that has been produced, very few book length monographs have been written. In Helsinki, 1952, the Finnish Oriental Society published A. Murtonen's, *A Philological and Literary Treatise on the Old Testament Divine Names*. In this study, Murtonen has drawn together much of the material relating to the subject and has reached conclusions of interest regarding various terms for deity and names of God, *'ēl, ʾᵉlôah, ʾᵉlōhîm*, and most importantly, the Tetragrammaton, consisting of the four letters *YHWH* (usually pronunced *YAHWEH*, although there is uncertainty regarding the precise vocalization). The bibliography (pp. 10-22) is comprehensive and particularly useful. In an earlier work, *The Tegragrammaton* (West Ewell, England, 1948), published privately by Norman Walker, the claim is made that the Tetragrammaton is a modified form of Egyptian *Yah-weᶜ*, "Moon-One." a thesis which has not won many adherents. Dr. Max Reisel, *Observations on 'ehyeh ʾᵃsher 'ehyeh (Ex. III.14), hw'h' (D.S.D. VIII.13) and shem hammᵉphôrāsh* (Assen: Van Gorcum & Comp. N.V., 1957), sets forth views regarding the phrase *'ehyeh ʾᵃsher 'ehyeh* (I AM WHO I AM) in Exod.3:14, together with an investigation of the five-lettered term used in the Manual of Discipline (which contains the rule of life of an ancient Jewish community, the Qumran covenanters, at a monastery located near the Dead Sea), and a discussion of the divine name in Rabbinic and mystical Kabbalistic literature.

As is well known, studies of major importance regarding various aspects of the significance of the Tetragrammaton have been made by W. F. Albright, H. H. Rowley, O. Eissfeldt, H. G. May, F. M. Cross, Jr., J. P. Hyatt, G. R. Driver, G. Quell and R. de Vaux, among many others. The bibliography included in this present study, although far from exhaustive, will serve as a guide to those who may wish to engage in a fresh examination of the relevant literature.

Unless otherwise indicated, biblical quotations are from the Revised Standard Version. The letter H is used whenever a verse reference in the Massoretic text differs from that of English versions of the Bible; the letter A indicates that a text is in Aramaic. YHWH has been employed generally for the Tetragrammaton and in Scriptural quotations (where RSV renders, "the LORD").

I wish to express my appreciation and thanks to the Principal, Dr. J. Morden, and to the Board of Huron College, for granting me a period of sabbatical leave in 1971, during which I was able to undertake the necessary research for this study.

My grateful thanks go to Dr. John Wevers, of the Near Eastern Studies Department at the University of Toronto, for a careful reading of the initial manuscript and for valuable suggestions. I must not hold him responsible, however, for the views expressed in this study. I am indebted to Dr. Ronald J. Williams and Professor John van Seters, also of the Near Eastern Studies Department at the University of Toronto, for helpful conversations and wise counsel.

Finally, I wish to record my thanks to the late Dr. John Henderson, Librarian of Huron College, for assistance in obtaining books, and to Catherine E. Pell, for accurate typing and secretarial competence.

The book has been published with the help of a grant from the Humanities Research Council of Canada, using funds provided by the Canada Council. I am most grateful for this assistance.

G. H. Parke-Taylor
January, 1975

ABBREVIATIONS

AJSL	*American Journal of Semitic Languages.*
AJT	*The American Journal of Theology*
ASTI	*Annual of the Swedish Theological Institute in Jerusalem*
BDB	F. Brown; S. R. Driver; and C. A. Briggs, *A Hebrew and English Lexicon of the Old Testament* (Oxford: Clarendon Press, 1906).
BASOR	*Bulletin of the American Schools of Oriental Research*
BJRL	*Bulletin of the John Rylands Library*
BWANT	Beiträge zur Wissenschaft vom Alten und Neuen Testament
BZAW	Beihefte zur Zeitschrift für die alttestamentliche Wissenschaft
CBQ	*Catholic Biblical Quarterly*
FRLANT	Forschungen zur Religion und Literatur des Alten und Neuen Testaments
GK	Gesenius-Kautzsch, *Hebrew Grammar*, trans. by G. W. Collins and revised by A. E. Cowley, 2nd English ed. (Oxford: Clarendon Press, 1910).
HTR	*Harvard Theological Review*
HUCA	*Hebrew Union College Annual*
IB	*The Interpreter's Bible*, ed. G. A. Buttrick, 1952-57
ICC	The International Critical Commentary
IDB	*The Interpreter's Dictionary of the Bible*, ed. G. A. Buttrick, 1962
JBL	*Journal of Biblical Literature*
JBR	*The Journal of Bible and Religion*
JNES	*Journal of Near Eastern Studies*
JQR	*The Jewish Quarterly Review*
JSS	*Journal of Semitic Studies*
JTS	*The Journal of Theological Studies*
LXX	The Septuagint
MT	The Masoretic Text
OTL	Old Testament Library
OTS	*Oudtestamentische Studiën*
RB	*Revue Biblique*
RHR	*Revue de l'Histoire des Religions*
SBT	Studies in Biblical Theology
TWNT	*Theologisches Wörterbuch zum Neuen Testament*
VT	*Vetus Testamentum*
ZAW	*Zeitschrift für die alttestamentliche Wissenschaft*

I

THE NAME OF GOD

Names were profoundly significant in the ancient Semitic world. The opening words of the Babylonian Epic of Creation, *Enuma Elish*, refer to a time before the cosmos existed: "When on high the heaven had not been named,/Firm ground below had not been called by name."[1] Without a name there is no real existence.[2]

In Egypt, near the beginning of the second millenium B.C., powerful curses were directed against foreign enemies. In these Egyptian execration texts of the Middle Kingdom period, curses were inscribed on pottery bowls in which the names of hostile Asiatic princes were specifically mentioned. The ritual smashing of these vessels was more than symbolic. The names of the rebels represented their actuality: the magical potency of the curses was believed to take effect when the bowls bearing their names were smashed. To destroy the names was to destroy the enemy rulers themselves.[3]

The Egyptian Book of the Dead contains in chapter 17 an account of the self-creation of Atum, the cosmic "All," from whom came into existence four pairs of deities, as he named parts of his body. These nine deities constituted the Ennead, the sun-god, together with the members of his council. John A. Wilson brings out the significance of the naming of the subordinate deities by Atum. "The name is a thing of individuality and of power; the act of speaking a new name is an act of creation. Thus we have the picture of the creator squatting on his tiny island and inventing names for eight parts of his body—of four pairs of parts—with each utterance bringing a new god into existence."[4]

In much the same way, the Hebrews also attached special importance to the concept of names. In the Yahwistic account of the garden of Eden, "The man gave names to all cattle, and to the birds of the air and to every beast of the field" (Gen.2:20). This implies ownership and control, and is the counterpart of the statement in the Priestly account of creation (Gen.1:26), in which man is

---

[1]Translated by E. A. Speiser in *Ancient Near Eastern Texts*, ed. J. B. Pritchard (Princeton, N.J.: Princeton Univ. Press, 1955), 2nd ed., p. 60.

[2]Cf. U. Cassuto, *A Commentary on the Book of Exodus*, trans. by I. Abrahams (Jerusalem: The Magnes Press, The Hebrew University, 1967), p. 37, "Whatever is without an appellation does not exist, but whatever has a denomination has existence."

[3]H. and H. A. Frankfort, John A. Wilson and Thorkild Jacobsen, in *Before Philosophy* (Harmondsworth, Middlesex: Penguin Books, 1949), pp. 21,22. For application to the exegesis of Amos, chs. 1-2, see A. Bentzen, "The Ritual Background of Amos, 1.2-2.6," *Oudtestamentische Studien*, VIII (1950): 85-99; H. G. Reventlow, *Das Amt des Propheten bei Amos* (Göttingen: Vandenhoeck & Ruprecht, 1962), pp. 62, 63.

[4]John A. Wilson, *op. cit.*, pp. 62-63.

given domination over all living creatures.[5]

The Hebrew word, *shēm*, name, occurs over eight hundred times in the Old Testament. The essential character of a man is concentrated in his name, as for example in Gen.27:36, where by a word-play the name "Jacob" is understood to mean "supplanter," "cheater."[6] J. Pedersen, the Danish scholar, states succinctly, "To know the name of a man is the same as to know his essence"; indeed, "the name is the soul."[7]

Names are frequently symbolic. Isaiah of Jerusalem has a son named "Shear-jashub," "a remnant shall return."[8] Another son a named "Maher-shalal-hash-baz," "The spoil speeds, the prey hastes" (Isa.8:3), referring to the imminent spoliation of Judah by Assyria. So also, Isaiah announces to Ahaz that a son will be born to a young woman (Isa.7:14), who will call his name "Immanu-el," "God with us."[9] Likewise, Hosea's wife, Gomer, bore children who were given symbolic names, "Jezreel," "God sows"; "Lo-ruhamah," "Not pitied"; "Lo-cammi," "Not my people."[10]

Name also implies reputation, renown, fame. Raymond Abba draws attention to the way in which this meaning develops. "When the character and achievements of a person become widely known, he gains a reputation. There is, as it were, an extension of his personality."[11] Abram received the divine promise that his name would be made great (Gen.12:2). David had outstanding success as a warrior, "so that his name was highly esteemed" (I Sam.18:30). A good name is preferable to great riches or precious ointment (Prov.22:1; Eccles.7:1). The *hybris* or arrogant pride of those who built the tower of Babel

---

[5]See G. von Rad, *Genesis: A Commentary*, OTL, trans. by John H. Marks (London: S.C.M. Press Ltd., 1961), p. 81, "name-giving in the ancient Orient was primarily an exercise of sovereignty, of command." Cf. also B. Vawter, *A Path Through Genesis* (London: Sheed and Ward, 1957), Stagbook edition, 1964, p. 59. The sovereignty of God over the stars, which he calls by name, is implied in Isa.40:26.

[6]The popular etymology, as von Rad points out, *op. cit.*, p. 273, is found also in Hosea 12:4 and Jer.9:4 (H 3).

[7]J. Pedersen, *Israel I-II*, 1926, repr. (London: Geoffrey Cumberlege, 1946), p. 245.

[8]Isa.7:3. See William L. Holladay, *The Root Šûbh in the Old Testament* (Leiden: E. J. Brill, 1958), p. 146. The name conveys some measure of hope for the future and contains the seed of a theology of a faithful Remnant; at the same time, the name is ominous, for "only a remnant of them will return" (Isa.10:22).

[9]The use of the feminine form of the adjective, *hārâh*, "pregnant," indicates that the birth of the child with the symbolic name will take place in the near future.

[10]Hos.1:4,6,9, where the meaning of the names is given. The allegorical application in Hosea 2 draws out the significance of the names. Apostate Israel, unfaithful in the covenant relationship, stands under divine judgment. The passage ends on a note of hope in 2:21-23, where the names lose their negative connotation. See James M. Ward, *Hosea: A Theological Commentary* (N.Y.: Harper & Row, 1966), Chap. 2.

[11]R. Abba, article: "Name" in *IDB*, III (N.Y.: Abingdon Press, 1962), p. 502.

consists in their desire to make a name for themselves (Gen.11:4).[12]

A change in name means a change of character. Folk etymology attempts to set forth the original meaning of names, as popularly understood, and sometimes provides an aetiology or explanation. In a narrative containing a number of aetiological elements, Jacob's name is changed to Israel (Gen.32:28), after he has wrestled at the ford of the Jabbok. The meaning of the new name, Israel, "He who strives with God" or "God strives," represents a popular etymology.[13] Nevertheless, there is a significant change in the character of the crafty Jacob from this time forward. According to M. Reisel, the bestowing of a new name was meant to influence not only the character of the recipient, but his future.[14] Solomon, for example, is given the name Jedidiah, "Beloved of Yah," by Nathan the prophet (2 Sam.12:25). This theophorous name correctly interprets the statement "YHWH loved him" (2 Sam.12:24),[15] and becomes prophetic of the future. Although Solomon is David's tenth son, he succeeds his father on the throne and prospers. The name Noah is interpreted in Gen.5:29 as if derived from the root n-h-m (Pi'el, "to comfort") and is regarded as declaring his future role. Gen.5:29, "Out of the ground which the Lord has cursed this one shall bring us relief from our work and from the toil of our hands," seems to provide a link between Gen.3:17-19, in which the ground is cursed, and Gen.9:20, where Noah's planting of a vineyard is symbolic of the restoration of the fertile land after the deluge.[16] So also, the names given to Isaiah's children are charged with prophetic meaning (Isa.7:3; 8:3), so far as the future of Judah is concerned.

The Old Testament contains about one thousand four hundred different proper names of individuals. More than half of them consist of two parts, one of which is the name or designation of a deity.[17] These theophorous names

---

[12]W. F. Albright claims that shēm in this context means not "fame" but "an (inscribed) monument." See Yahweh and the Gods of Canaan (London: The Athlone Press, 1968), p. 88.

[13]Cf. Gen.35:10. According to W. F. Albright, "The Names 'Israel' and 'Judah' with an Excursus on the Etymology of Todah and Torah," JBL, XLVI (1927): 151-185, the most probable derivation is from the verb yāsar, which with 'ēl means "God heals" (pp. 167, 168). For a full treatment of the name Israel, see G. A. Danell, Studies in the Name of Israel in the Old Testament (Uppsala, 1946). Danell equates the name Israel with Jeshurun and Asher. In Haldar's opinion, the most probable derivation is from the root 'sr, "successful," "happy"; "Israel, Names and Associations of." IDB II (N.Y.: Abingdon Press, 1962), p. 765.

[14]M. Reisel, Observations on 'Ehyeh ᵃsher 'ehyeh, hw'h' and shem hammᵉphôrash (Assen: Van Gorcum & Comp. N.V. 1957), p. 2. In subsequent references this work will be referred to as Observations.

[15]M. Noth, Die israelitischen Personennamen im Rahmen der Gemeinsemitischen Namengebung, BWANT, III.10 (Stuttgart: W. Kohlhammer, 1928), p. 149.

[16]These passages are all attributed to the Yahwist by E. A. Speiser, Genesis, The Anchor Bible (N.Y.: Doubleday, 1964), pp. 21, 41, 60-61.

[17]L. Köhler, Hebrew Man, trans. Peter R. Ackroyd (London: S.C.M. Press Ltd., 1956), pp. 63-65.

indicate how closely human life and destiny are related to divine activity and control.

Since names assigned to human beings are regarded as significant in what they declare about the character and influence of individuals, we are justified in expecting divine names to carry specific meaning. Walther Eichrodt emphasizes the importance of this expectation in his treatment of the name of the covenant God, YHWH, "If the saying *nomina sunt realia* is valid in any context, it is surely that of the divine name in the ancient world. The question, therefore, of what kind of name the God of Israel bore is no idle one, but can be the means of arriving at an important insight into Israel's religious thought."[18] Yet, the quest to discover the precise significance of the various names and titles for God which occur in the Old Testament has not led to universally accepted conclusions. The purpose of this present study is to investigate the subject once more and in particular to point to the areas of future research which may prove to be most profitable for a theological understanding of YHWH, the divine name *par excellence*.

The Old Testament contains various titles and surrogates for God, such as El Shaddai, El Elyon, Haqqadosh (The Holy One), and Adonai. In chapter three, consideration will be given to names ascribed to God in the patriarchal period. Gerhard von Rad reminds us that these names became secondary after the name YHWH had been known to Israel, for "these rudimentary names which derive from old traditions, and from the oldest of them, never had the function of extending the name so as to stand alongside the name Jahweh to serve as fuller forms of address; rather, they were occasionally made use of in place of the name Jahweh."[19] In this respect YHWH stands in contrast to the principal deities of the Babylonians and the Egyptians. "Jahweh had only one name; Marduk had fifty with which his praises as victor over Tiamat were sung in hymns. Similarly, the Egyptian Re is the god with many names."[20]

In addition to the name YHWH, the designation for God which occurs with greatest frequency is the word Elohim. The noun Elohim[21] occurs 2,570 times in the Old Testament,[22] often with the definite article. The plural ending has

---

[18]W. Eichrodt, *Theology of the Old Testament*, I, trans. by J. A. Baker (Philadelphia: The Westminster Press, 1961), p. 178. Cf. G. Quell, "The Old Testament Name for God" in *TWNT*, III, ed. G. Kittel, trans. by G. W. Bromiley (Grand Rapids, Michigan: Eerdmans, 1965), p. 1070, "The nature of God is . . . compressed in the name of God." See also H. H. Spoer, "The Origin and Interpretation of the Tetragrammaton," *AJSL*, XVIII (1901): 11.

[19]G. von Rad, *Old Testament Theology*, I, trans. by D. M. G. Stalker (London: Oliver and Boyd, 1962), p. 186, n. 26.

[20]*Ibid.*, p. 185.

[21]A. Murtonen, *A Philological and Literary Treatise on the Old Testament Divine Names* (Helsinki: 1952), p. 42, concludes that *ᵉlōhîm* is a plural of *ᵉlôah*. The singular meaning, "a god," appears at least as early as the Ras Shamra texts.

[22]F. Brown, S. R. Driver, and C. A. Briggs, *A Hebrew and English Lexicon of the Old Testament* (Oxford: Clarendon Press, 1906), p. 43a. In subsequent references this work will be referred to as BDB.

been the occasion for much speculation. Does the plural ending point to a primitive polytheism, long since lost as the concept of local deities gave place to the belief in one supreme divine Being? Or does the plural represent the abstract generic idea of deity? Grammarians have regarded Elohim as a plural of intensity or majesty, summing up the essential characteristics and intensifying the original idea, i.e., Godhead.[23] The plural ending retains a plural significance in those instances where the reference is clearly to the gods worshipped by non-Israelites, "other gods" (Exod.23:13; Deut.31:18), "foreign gods" (Judges 10:16; Jer.5:19), "gods of the nations" (2 Kings 18:33; Deut.29:18). Of particular interest is the use of Elohim in a double sense in Psalm 82:1. The first reference is clearly to the God of the Hebrews, whereas the second use of Elohim in this verse refers to the assembly of "the gods." Mitchell Dahood considers the Psalm to be very early, in view of the archaic language employed.[24] Artur Weiser regards the Psalm as designed to meet a problem of theodicy, "coming to terms with the deities of the pre-Israelite inhabitants of Canaan and with those of the neighbouring countries of Israel, whose originally polytheistic character was overcome by reducing them to the rank of servants of Yahweh who are subject to his judgment."[25] These Elohim, rulers and judges of the pagan nations, are stripped of their divinity (Ps.82:7). In other cases (e.g. Ps.138:1, Ps.8:5), the translation "angels," "divine beings," would not be inappropriate. An unusual occurrence is found when the medium at Endor, summoned by Saul to "bring up" Samuel, cries out, "I see a god ($^{e}l\bar{o}h\hat{i}m$) coming up out of the earth" (1 Sam.28:13).[26]

The plural sometimes refers to a single non-Israelite deity, such as Dagon (1 Sam.5:17), or Baal (1 Kings 18:24). In the majority of cases, however, Elohim is the generic term for God, plural in form but singular in meaning, and as such is often used appellatively as a synonym for YHWH (Ps.24:5; 38:21), i.e., the true God.

The Tetragrammaton, YHWH (i.e. YAHWEH), the proper name of the God revealed to Israel, occurs 6,823 times.[27] In addition, the Digrammaton, YH (i.e. YAH), occurs 50 times, if the phrase Hallelu-yah is included. As an element at the beginning or end of theophorous names, in various forms ($y\hat{o}$ or $y^{e}h\hat{o}$ at the

[23]GK, 124 (a) (g).

[24]M. Dahood, *Psalms II, 51-100* Anchor Bible N.Y.: Doubleday, 1958), p. 269.

[25]A. Weiser, *The Psalms: A Commentary*, trans. by Herbert Hartwell, OTL (London: S.C.M. Press Ltd., 1962), p. 557.

[26]The translators of *The Jerusalem Bible* (London: Darton, Longman & Todd, 1966) prefer to render $^{e}lohim$ as "a ghost" in this context. Perhaps "a god-like being" is intended.

[27]BDB, p. 217b. Raymond Abba, however, gives the number of occurrences as 5,321. Possibly, he has not taken into account those verses in which the Tetragrammaton occurs more than once, or in combination with $^{a}d\hat{o}n\bar{a}y$, $^{e}l\bar{o}h\hat{i}m$, or $s^{e}ba\hat{o}th$.

beginning, -yāh or -yāhû at the end), the divine name occurs about 150 times.[28]

The distinction of the names Elohim and YHWH in the Old Testament has been of special interest ever since Jean Astruc, in 1753, first used the occurrences in Genesis as the basis for distinguishing separate sources in the first book of the Bible.[29] The use of these names became one of the criteria for the delineation of Pentateuchal sources, with other literary and stylistic features providing additional evidence.[30] In 1912, Johannes Dahse published the results of his studies of the book of Genesis under the title, *Textkritische Materialen zur Hexateuchfrage*.[31] He claimed that the text of the LXX is a more reliable witness to the original text of the Hebrew than the MT. This view rests on an elaborate "Pericope-hypothesis," based on the Seder divisions of the Pentateuch in the lectionary of the synagogue, to account for the names in the Greek text, in which *kyrios* (YHWH) usually occurs at the beginning of a section, although *ho theos* (Elohim) may stand elsewhere. He contended that the editors of the MT, following the Parasha divisions of the Pentateuch, were influenced by this practice to make similar adaptations. John Skinner replied in a series of articles in the *Expositor* (April to September, 1913), later published under the title, *The Divine Names in Genesis* (1914). Skinner argued for the soundness of the Hebrew text, to which the Samaritan text bears convincing witness.[32] More recently, the discovery of the Qumran scrolls has added strength to Skinner's position.[33]

Many modern Old Testament scholars are less inclined to accept the occurrence of the divine names as a valid criterion for the identification of

[28]G. B. Gray, *Studies in Hebrew Proper Names* (London: Adam and Charles Black, 1896), p. 149.

[29]J. Astruc, *Conjectures sur les mémoires dont il paroit que Moyse s'est servi pour composer le livre de la Genèse* (1753).

[30]See Herbert F. Hahn, *The Old Testament in Modern Research*, rev. ed. (Philadelphia: Fortress Press, 1966), ch. 1. Note also the *caveat* of J. Skinner, *The Divine Names in Genesis* (London: Hodder and Stoughton, 1914), p. 7, "It is *true* to say that the use of the divine names was the critical fact first observed (by Astruc in 1753) which furnished a positive clue to the separation of documents in Genesis, and that it is still regarded as a valuable aid to the analysis. It is *untrue* to say that it is the sole criterion."

[31]J. Dahse, *Textkritische Materialen zur Hexateuchfrage* (I. Die Gottesnamen der Genesis; Jakob und Israel; P in Genesis 12-50), Giessen, 1912.

[32]See W. F. Albright, "Jethro, Hobab and Reuel in Early Hebrew Tradition," *CBQ*, XXV (1963): 2, "J. Skinner's demonstration that MT and Samaritan agree in the use of the names *Yahweh* and *Elohim* over 97% of the time, remains a convincing answer to those scholars who reject the Documentary Hypothesis *in toto*."

[33]P. W. Skehan, "The Qumran Manuscripts and Textual Criticism," *Supplements to Vetus Testamentum*, IV (Leiden: E. J. Brill, 1957), pp. 148-160. Referring to the Pentateuch, he writes (p. 149), "Qumran is not giving us, in these books, a multiplicity of unknown readings." Although sometimes readings from the LXX or Samaritan versions are upheld, confidence in MT is renewed.

different sources. Ivan Engnell claims that the alternation of divine names "is not due to an alternation of documents, but to an intentional stylistic use by those who handed down the tradition."[34] Rather than an indication of diverse sources, "the name *Yahweh* is used in contexts which distinguish Israel's national god from foreign gods, relate the history of the ancestors, etc., while the name *Elohim*, 'God', expresses a more theological, abstract, cosmic idea of God, and therefore is used in a broader, more comprehensive way."[35] However, D. B. Redford has stated cogently, "Scholars who have sought to invalidate the divine names as criteria for source analysis, have not replaced the hypothesis they hoped to have destroyed by any other plausible explanation."[36] In his study of the use of divine names in Egyptian literature, he comes to the conclusion that the question as to whether divine names and epithets may be used as criteria for source analysis is to be answered with a cautious affirmative.[37] A similar judgment may be made regarding the use of Yahweh and Elohim in the Pentateuch. The single criterion of the use of the divine name is insufficient for delineating Pentateuchal sources, especially after the revelation of the Tetragrammaton to Moses (Exod.3:15; 6:2). Yet if other criteria such as linguistic usage, stylistic features, and diversity of ideas are employed, the analysis into sources would seem to be a convincing explanation of these variations.[38]

The Yahwistic source (J)[39] regularly employs the Tetragrammaton (sometimes in combination with Elohim, as in chapters 2 and 3 of Genesis). The Elohistic (E) and Priestly (P) sources prefer Elohim, although P uses the divine name YHWH from Exod.6:2,3 on, a matter which will be referred to again in connection with the Kenite hypothesis of the origin of the divine name (see chapter two). YHWH occurs very frequently in the second division of the canon,

[34]I. Engnell, in an essay entitled "The Pentateuch" in *Critical Essays on the Old Testament*, trans. by John T. Willis (London: S.P.C.K., 1970), p. 55. Engnell finds support for his view in F. Baumgartel, *Elohim ausserhalb des Pentateuch* (Leipzig: J. C. Hinrichs, 1914), and U. Cassuto, *The Documentary Hypothesis and the Composition of the Pentateuch* (Jerusalem: Magnes Press, 1961). M. H. Segal has also argued against identifying literary sources through the change of divine names in *JQR*, XLVI (1955): 89ff.

[35]I. Engnell, *op. cit.*, p. 56.

[36]Donald B. Redford, *A Study of the Biblical Story of Joseph (Genesis 37-50)* (Leiden: E. J. Brill, 1970), p. 109. This is the position of M. Noth, *A History of Pentateuchal Traditions*, trans. by B. W. Anderson (Englewood Cliffs, N.J.: Prentice-Hall, Inc., 1972), p. 23.

[37]D. B. Redford, *op. cit.*, p. 128. However, Redford believes that the sources discernible in Genesis 37-50 are later than J and E.

[38]O. Eissfeldt, *The Old Testament: An Introduction*, trans. by P. R. Ackroyd (Oxford: Blackwell, 1965), pp. 182-188.

[39]For convenient summaries of the present position in source-analysis of the Pentateuch, see O. Eissfeldt, *op. cit.*, pp. 158-212; Sellin-Fohrer, *Introduction to the Old Testament*, trans. by David E. Green (N.Y.: Abingdon Press, 1968), pp. 103-195.

the historical books and the prophets. However, the Tetragrammaton is much less often found in the Wisdom writings and in other late writings among the Hagiographa. In the book of Job, the name YHWH occurs only in the prose Prologue and Epilogue, apart from the introduction to the Speeches of Yahweh (Job 38:1; 40:1), and one isolated reference (Job 12:9)[40] in the poetic Dialogue. The absence of the name YHWH and the use of such names as El, Elohim (without the definite article), Eloah and Shaddai in the poetic sections of the book are intended to provide the atmosphere of the patriarchal period, although the book of Job in its present form may be as late as the fifth century[41] or even later. The Chronicler often uses Elohim (with or without the definite article) even where his sources (e.g., Samuel and Kings) had employed the divine name YHWH.[42] Other late books, such as Ecclesiastes and Daniel, prefer Elohim (usually with the definite article) as the name for God. Daniel also frequently refers to God as the Most High (e.g., Dan.4:2,24; 7:18,22, etc.). The fact that the Tetragrammaton appears in the Book of Daniel only in Daniel's prayer (in Dan.9) perhaps indicates that this passage is an addition.[43] The divine name, YHWH, occurs regularly in the book of Ruth and is also found in Jonah. Nevertheless, in late books of the Hebrew bible, the Tetragrammaton has ceased to be used with the frequency which characterizes the earlier Old Testament literature.

The problem of the "Elohistic redaction" of the Psalter consists in the fact that Psalms 42-83 show a decided preference for the name Elohim rather than

---

[40]E. Dhorme, *A Commentary on the Book of Job*, first published 1926, trans. by Harold Knight (London: Thomas Nelson and Sons Ltd., 1967), p. 174, draws attention to Eloah in a few Hebrew MSS, and claims that the original text was changed to YHWH due to the reminiscence of Isa.41:20.

[41]See H. H. Rowley, *Job*, The Century Bible: New Series (London: Nelson, 1970), pp. 21-23. As to the use of the divine name, E. Dhorme, *op. cit.*, p. lxx, observes, "the entire book excludes the name Yahweh, accepts only very rarely and as if reluctantly that of Elohim, uses in the main only the three names, El, Eloah, Shaddai, and subjects its use of these names to certain laws, the most obvious of which is the parallelism of Shaddai with one or other of the two other names."

[42]M. H. Segal, "El, Elohim, and YHWH in the Bible," *op. cit.*, p. 100. Statistical evidence is also given for the occurrences of YHWH and Elohim in other books outside the Pentateuch.

[43]Cf. O. Eissfeldt, *op. cit.*, p. 529. See also N. W. Porteous, *Daniel: A Commentary*, OTL (London: S.C.M. Press, Ltd., 1965), pp. 135-139. J. A. Montgomery, *A Critical and Exegetical Commentary on the Book of Daniel*, ICC (Edinburgh: T. & T. Clark, 1927), p. 362, argues for the inclusion of the prayer: "The second-century author may well have himself inserted such a prayer in his book for the encouragement of the faithful, even as the calculation of the times was intended for their heartening." If this is correct, then the text has been revised, and the Tetragammaton substituted for ^{a}dônāy (p. 363). It would seem to me more likely that since the prayer consists largely of material adapted from liturgical prayers found elsewhere in the Old Testament (Montgomery, *op. cit.*, p. 361), the revision consists of substituting ^{a}dônāy, in reading, for the more original YHWH.

for YHWH, whereas Psalms 1-41 and 84-150 employ the Tetragrammaton much more frequently as the usual mode of address to God. G. F. Moore has suggested that the appellative Elohim in Psalms 42-83 was substituted by an editor who belonged to a circle in which there were now scruples about the use of the Tetragrammaton, for reverential reasons.[44] He claims that the Tetragrammaton appears almost exclusively in Psalms 90-150, since these collections are later still, reflecting a time when Adonai or Elohim would be substituted for the proper name in reading.[45] Robert Boling, however, has a very different explanation, arrived at by considering the patterns which emerge in poetic parallelism in the Psalms.[46] The use of the divine names follows a fixed traditional order. In Psalms 42-83, "the Tetragrammaton is frequently avoided in the first colon, perfectly acceptable in the second."[47] The stylistic preferences follow patterns which make a redaction theory improbable.

At some point in post-exilic times, $^{a}dôn\bar{a}y$ was pronounced in place of the Tetragrammaton, which had come to be regarded as too sacred for utterance. This is the practice in MT, where the Tetragrammaton is supplied with the vowels of the surrogate $^{a}dôn\bar{a}y$, which was to be read instead as a $Q^{e}r\hat{e}$ perpetuum, so as to avoid mention of the divine name.[48] This pointing eventually gave rise to the hybrid form, Jehovah, in an attempt to transliterate the consonants of the Tetragrammaton together with the vowels of $^{a}dôn\bar{a}y$.[49] The date when this change took place is debatable, as is also the precise reason for making such a change. G. F. Moore takes issue with those who claim that the pronunciation of the Tetragrammaton was prohibited on the basis of an erroneous inter-

[44]G. F. Moore, *Judaism*, I (Cambridge: Harvard Univ. Press, 1927), p. 424; III (Cambridge: Harvard Univ. Press, 1930), p. 127 (I, 424, n. 2). M. H. Segal, *op. cit.*, pp. 104-05, holds to a similar view. But why was the change of name so incomplete?

[45]G. F. Moore, *op. cit.*, III, p. 128.

[46]R. G. Boling, *JSS*, V (1960): 221-255.

[47]*Ibid.*, p. 250.

[48]R. Gordis, *The Biblical Text in the Making*, 1937 (repr. N.Y.: Ktav. Publising House, 1971), xvii, "The oldest *Kethibh-Qere* is in the Tetragrammaton, which was recognized in the Talmud as a *Qere perpetuum*: 'Not as I am written am I read: I am written *Yod He* and I am read *Aleph Daled* (i.e., *Adonai*) (B. Pesahim, 50a)." See also O. Eissfeldt, *op. cit.*, p. 686. A. Weiser, *Introduction to the Old Testament*, trans. by Dorothea M. Barton (London: Darton, Longman & Todd, 1961), p. 358, draws attention to the fact that Kittel's third edition of *Biblia Hebraica*, on the basis of old MSS, regularly supplies a $sh^{e}wa$ under the *yodh*, and a *qamets* under the *waw*, suggesting in place of reading the Tetragrammaton, either the substitution of the Aramaic $sh^{e}ma'$ (the equivalent to Hebrew *hashshēm*, "the Name"), or as an indication that $^{a}dôn\bar{a}y$ was to be read.

[49]Regarding "Jehovah," Hans H. Spoer, *op. cit.*, p. 30, writes, "The earliest appearance of this transliteration we find in two passages of the 'Pugio fidei.' 1278, though it is not improbable that this is due to a later copyist. We know for certain, however, that this misnomer was brought into prominence by Petrus Galatinus, confessor of Leo X."

pretation of Lev.24:16.[50] The passage in Leviticus declares that capital punishment will be meted out to the person who blasphemes the name of YHWH, and the context (Lev.24:10ff.) makes it clear that a foreigner may incur the penalty as well as a native; a test-case is cited. The law has to do with the deliberate cursing or vilifying of the Name. The rabbis did not appeal to this passage in support of prohibiting the pronunciation of the Name. However, fear of profanation of the divine Name seems to be the major motive for substituting $^{\prime a}d\hat{o}n\bar{a}y$ in popular usage.

Old Testament scholars have almost unanimously regarded Elohim as the generic term for God, or as a synonym for YHWH, the specifically Israelite name.[51] This view has now been challenged by Eliezer Berkovits, who maintains, on the contrary, that YHWH "is the biblical name for God in the universal sense, as the God of all creation, known as such by all nations,"[52] whereas Elohim is to be understood as God in his immanence, loving and caring for his people. On this understanding, YHWH represents the *revelatio generalis*; Elohim, the *revelatio specialis*. In support of his thesis, Rabbi Berkovits appeals to 1 Kings 18, the account of Elijah on Mount Carmel.[53] He claims that the usual translation of 1 Kings 18:21, "If the Lord (YHWH) is God ($H\bar{a}^{\prime\,e}l\bar{o}h\hat{\imath}m$), follow him," obscures the meaning of the passage, since the definite article before $^{e}l\bar{o}h\hat{\imath}m$ is ignored. The reference is to God in a specific sense as the one who may be followed, because he is near at hand. The usual translation suggests that the Israelites doubted whether YHWH was God or not. However, the issue is surely whether YHWH, the God of Israel, or Baal, whose worship the Phoenician Jezebel had introduced and forced upon Israel, can claim to be the true God. The Israelites have been like a bird hopping along a branch, unable to decide which fork of the branch to take (1 Kings 18:21a). The problem of syncretism, so acute for Israel in the ninth century, is reflected in the encounter on Mount Carmel. Israel must understand that YHWH is the God who admits no rivals. After YHWH has declared his power, the people cry out, "YHWH is the God" (1 Kings 18:39), i.e., YHWH is the true God (cf. Isa.45:18). Elijah's prayer (1 Kings 18:36) is instructive, for he identifies YHWH as the God of the patriarchs (cf. Exod.3:15) and prays, "let it be known this day that thou art God in Israel."[54]

---

[50]G. F. Moore, *op. cit.*, I, p. 427. In Lev.24:11, the phrase is "blasphemed the Name, and cursed"; in Lev.24: 16 this is interpreted to mean "Name of YHWH." At a later date, "the Name" became a synonym for God (e.g., Sirach 23:10; Wisdom of Solomon 14:21).

[51]E.g., W. Eichrodt, *op. cit.*, I, pp. 185-192; Th. C. Vriezen, *An Outline of Old Testament Theology*, Eng. ed., (Oxford: Basil Blackwell, 1962), pp. 194-198; P. van Imschoot, *Theology of the Old Testament*, I, *God*, trans. by Kathryn Sullivan and Fidelis Buck (N.Y.: Desclee Company, 1965), pp. 12-19; Edmond Jacob, *Theology of the Old Testament*, trans. by Arthur W. Heathcote and Philip J. Allcock (London: Hodder & Stoughton, 1958), pp. 43-54.

[52]Eliezer Berkovits, *Man and God* (Detroit: Wayne State Univ. Press, 1969), p. 63.

[53]*Ibid.*, pp. 22ff.

[54]The definite article is not used in the phrase "God in Israel" in 1 Kings 18:36.

The distinctions made by Berkovits between YHWH as always indicating transcendence and Elohim as expressing immanence seem artificial and do not reflect
the way in which the divine names are actually utilized. The Tetragrammaton
and Elohim are frequently synonyms, as for example in the Psalms, where stylistic considerations govern their use. Transcendence or immanence may be expressed by either name, depending on context (e.g., transcendence: Ps.29:10,
YHWH; Ps.77:13, Elohim; immanence: Ps.34:18, YHWH; Ps.14:5, Elohim).
YHWH was the characteristic name for God in the southern tradition, Elohim in
the northern tradition, still in use as an appellative after the Tetragrammaton had been accepted. The phrase, "YHWH, thy God (Elohim)," represents
the fusion of the two traditions.

Berkovits is on firmer ground in his treatment of the phrase, "the name of
YHWH."[55] In particular, he stresses the fact that "God's name is what God
does."[56] This phrase, "the name (shēm) of YHWH," would be tautological were
it not for the dynamism which gives content to it, based on the activity of
YHWH in the realm of history, expressed in his mighty deeds. The emphasis in
the Old Testament is on YHWH as the God who declares himself in his deeds and
actions.[57] This is the basis of his fame or reputation, as in Solomon's prayer for
the foreigner who comes to worship at the Temple in Jerusalem (1 Kings
8:41-43), in which YHWH's great name is equated with his mighty hand and
outstretched arm. It is also a revelation of his power to save or to judge (Psalm
54:1; Isa.30:27).

Oskar Grether, in his monumental study, *Name und Wort Gottes im Alten
Testament*,[58] has demonstrated the close connection between that which is
named and that which is known. Only that which is known can be given a name.
That which is completely hidden and unknown has no name. The self-revelation
of God is declared in the Tetragrammaton.[59] Although the Tetragrammaton is
the name of the *deus revelatus*, in the revelation the *deus absconditus* remains.
To know God is not to dispel the mystery which belongs to deity. God is
known, but not fully known.

Three passages in the Old Testament are especially instructive in connection
with the granting or withholding of the divine name: Gen.32:22-32, Judges

Anarthrous *eᵉlōhîm* appears to be interchangeable with *eᵉlōhîm* preceded by the definite
article, in this chapter.

[55] E. Berkovits, *op. cit.*, Ch. 3, pp. 85-140, "The Name of God." ·

[56] *Ibid.*, p. 87.

[57] Cf. G. E. Wright, *God Who Acts*, SBT (London: S.C.M. Press Ltd., 1952). Cf. also
Kornelis H. Miskotte, *When the Gods Are Silent* (London: Collins, 1967), p. 68, "The Name
is encountered, the Name is perceived, in the whole history in which he lives and reveals
himself; he is the 'quintessence of its meaning,' which becomes a reality solely in his concrete
presence."

[58] O. Grether, *Name und Wort Gottes im Alten Testament*, BZAW, LXIV (Giessen,
1934).

[59] *Ibid.*, p. 9.

13:2-25 and Exod.3:1-22. The account of the revelation of the divine name to Moses (Exod.3) will be analysed in detail in chapter four. The two other passages are of importance in that in each case a request is made regarding the revelation of a name. The passage which recounts Jacob's wrestling at the ford of the Jabbok (Gen.32:22-32), taken from the Yahwistic source, places heavy demands upon the exegete. We could apply to this narrative the warning which von Rad gives concerning the interpretation of Gen.22 (regarding Abraham and the command to sacrifice Isaac), "There are many levels of meaning, and whoever thinks he has discovered virgin soil must discover at once that there are many more layers below that."[60] There are traces of primitive ideas in the account of Jacob's struggle at Penuel, and yet the final impression is one of theological profundity. Jacob's assailant at first seems to be simply a human being (*'ish*, "a man," Gen.32:24). Yet, after receiving a blessing from his adversary, Jacob calls the name of the place Peniel, saying, "For I have seen God (Elohim) face to face, and yet my life is preserved" (Gen.32:30). Jacob had requested a blessing, but must first reveal his own name. In turn, Jacob asked the name of his adversary, but this was withheld. However, in answer to the first request, a blessing was bestowed. It is obvious that behind the narrative, in its condensed form, lies a long history. Hosea refers to this incident when he says of Jacob that "he strove with the angel and prevailed; he wept and sought his favor" (Hosea 12:4).[61] However the original physical encounter is to be understood, the Yahwist understands a deeper significance, Jacob's spiritual struggle with God. Primitive notions of exercising power over another by virtue of the knowledge of his name may lie back of this narrative.[62] Von Rad refers to the belief that to know the name of a *numen* carried with it the possibility of conjuring with the divine power of the name, yet in this context, the urgent question about the name gives an insight into the longing for God which characterizes Jacob.[63]

In Judges 13:2-25, the angel (*mal'ākh*) of YHWH, declares to Manoah's wife that she will bear a son who is to be a Nazirite, and on a second occasion renews the promise, after Manoah has been summoned. Manoah requests the name of the messenger, who replies, "Why do you ask my name, seeing it is wonderful?"

---

[60]G. von Rad, *Genesis* p. 238. In a recent form critical analysis of Gen.32:22-32, Gene M. Tucker describes this pericope as "a complicated and enigmatic passage"; *Form Criticism of the Old Testament* (Philadelphia: Fortress Press, 1971), p. 41.

[61]J. L. Mays, *Hosea: A Commentary*, OTL (London: S.C.M. Press, Ltd., 1969), pp. 163-64, claims that "angel" must be the intended subject of "he prevailed" (rather than "Jacob") and that the point of the reference is that "the Jacob whom Israel proudly claims as its representative ancestor was overcome by God and brought to tears and dependence."

[62]For notions regarding the magical power of names, especially the name of a god, see S. Cohon, "The Name of God, A Study in Rabbinic Theology," *HUCA*, XXIII, Pt. 1 (1951): 585; J. W. Wevers, "A Study in the Form Criticism of Individual Complaint Psalms," *VT*, VI (1956): 82-83.

[63]G. von Rad, *Genesis*, p. 317.

(Judges 13:18). There are textual difficulties[64] in connection with the final phrase in verse 18 and the participial form in the following verse. However, the reference to "him who works wonders" in verse 19 is intended to provide a connection with the enigmatic phrase "seeing it is wonderful" (verse 18), in the light of the ascension of the *mal'akh* of YHWH in the flame of the altar upon which the meal of hospitality has become a sacrificial offering. The adjectival form in verse 18, "wonderful," suggests the ineffable, that which cannot be communicated in its fulness. Both in the case of Jacob and of Manoah, the request for the name is turned aside. Yet these accounts were surely to be understood as containing traditions of a genuine encounter with deity. Manoah, like Jacob, says, "We shall surely die, for we have seen God" (Judges 13:22). The *deus absconditus* has become the *deus revelatus*, but has not ceased to be the *deus absconditus*. Raymond Abba aptly comments, "In the actual moment of visitation, God is hidden; only in retrospect does the *deus absconditus* become the *deus revelatus*."[65]

Prominent among the prohibitions of the Decalogue is the commandment, "You shall not take the name of YHWH your god in vain (*lashshāv'*)" (Exod.20:7 = Deut.5:11). This has a number of applications, not only in condemning the false swearing of oaths in which the divine name in invoked (Lev.19:12), but also in the control of the form of blessings (Numb.6:22ff.) and curses (Ps.118:10) and in proscribing sorcery. Martin Noth understands the phrase "in vain" (*lashshāv'*) as synonymous with the term "evil."[66] By employing the name of the divinity, the sorcerer gains a degree of power over him.[67] Every precaution, then, must be taken against the misuse of the name. If the use of the divine name implied some degree of possession or control of the deity, conversely, to be "called by his name" meant to be owned by him, and therefore, to be subject to his protection (e.g., Amos 9:12, Jer.15:16, Isa.43:7). Fear will be inspired in all the peoples of the earth when they see that Israel is "called by the name of YHWH" (Deut.28:10).

To call upon or invoke the name of YHWH meant to engage in prayer and in cultic worship (e.g., Gen.4:26; 12:8; 13:4; 21:33; 26:25; 1 Kings 18:24). Von Rad views *qārā b^e shem YHWH* as a cultic term which in other cults found a

---

[64]The adjectival form *pel'î* (*k^e thîbh*) is best taken in verse 18, and the definite article, rather than the conjunction, before the participle in verse 19. See G. F. Moore, *A Critical and Exegetical Commentary on Judges*, ICC (Edinburgh: T. & T. Clark, 2nd ed., 1898), pp. 322, 324; C. F. Burney, *The Book of Judges* (London: Rivingtons, 2nd ed., 1930), pp 349, 350; J. Gray, *Joshua, Judges and Ruth*, The Century Bible (London: Nelson, 1967), p. 345.

[65]R. Abba, "Name," *IDB*, III, p. 503.

[66]M. Noth, *Exodus: A Commentary*, OTL, trans. by J. S. Bowden (London: S.C.M. Press Ltd., 1962), p. 89.

[67]J. J. Stamm & M. E. Andrew, *The Ten Commandments in Recent Research*, SBT (London: S.C.M. Press Ltd., 1962), p. 89.

counterpart in the employment of the cultic image.[68] In order to safeguard the proper use of the name,[69] elaborate prescriptions and rituals of the cult were devised. There must have been a proper way in which Israelites made solemn oaths, swearing by the divine name (Deut.6:13; 10:20). The Aaronic blessing (Numb.6:24-26), used by the priests, with the threefold repetition of the divine name in successive pronouncements (vv. 24,25,26), was the means by which shālom (peace and prosperity) was conferred upon Israel. YHWH, in putting his name upon the people of Israel, blessed them (Numb.6:27).

Psalm 118:26 appears to reflect a liturgical occasion when the king is blessed by the priests, "Blessed be he who enters in the name of YHWH" (26a).[70] The priests then bless the festival congregation, "We bless you from the house of YHWH" (26b). J. W. Wevers has suggested another translation for 26a, "Blessed be the one coming with the name YHWH" for, "The one coming into the sanctuary is to be entrusted with the divine name which he may there cultically invoke."[71] The priests would normally be the persons so entrusted, although the king also could bless in the name of YHWH (2 Sam.6:18).

The name of YHWH is not only to be called upon in supplication, but is proclaimed in liturgical praise, extolling the greatness of YHWH, as for example in the Song of Moses (note especially Deut.32:3). The name of YHWH meant for Israel all that YHWH had made manifest concerning himself, his stability, his faithfulness, his justice (Deut.32:4), his character, his essential nature. Those who know the name of YHWH are those who put their trust in him (Ps.9:10), because of his deeds. When YHWH is implored to act for the sake of his name (e.g., Jer.14:7; Ps.25:11), the appeal is to act according to his character as this has been revealed in the past.

The memory or remembrance (zēkher) of YHWH is virtually synonymous with his name (Ps.135:13; cf. Exod.3:15). Eliezer Berkovits makes a distinction, however, on the ground that zēkher refers primarily to the revelation to past generations, whereas shēm applies to the present in which God makes himself known in contemporary experience.[72] In Psalm 74, which contains four references to "the name," God appears to be passive and inactive; he has withdrawn

---

[68]G. von Rad, Old Testament Theology, I, p. 183; P. Van Imschoot, Theology of the Old Testament, I, points out that the phrase means literally, "to cry by the name of Yahweh," i.e., "to call on Yahweh by pronouncing the divine name with a loud voice in an act of public worship."

[69]J. L. Mays, Amos: A Commentary, OTL (London: S.C.M. Press Ltd., 1969), p. 120, commenting on Amos 6:10 states, "The first speaker . . . fears lest another mention of the divine personal name renew the terrible curse which the Lord's appearing has brought."

[70]This is the interpretation of A. Weiser, The Psalms, A Commentary, OTL (trans. by Herbert Hartwell (London: S.C.M. Press, Ltd., 1962), p. 729; cf. M. Dahood, Psalms III, 101-150, The Anchor Bible (N.Y.: Doubleday, 1970), p. 160. Dahood suggests that 26b may refer to the king (plural of majesty) or to the king's troops.

[71]J. W. Wevers, op. cit., p. 86.

[72]E. Berkovits, op. cit., pp. 97ff., espec. p. 102.

his hand (verse 11). In this community lament, the worshippers plaintively deplore the fact that the enemy is now able to profane the name. Comfort is to be found in the memory of God's actions in the past (verses 12ff.); the Psalm ends with a plea to God for a new and contemporary manifestation of himself. Perhaps Berkovits makes the contrast too sharply, for every new manifestation of God brings vividly into the present all that God has made known concerning himself in the past, just as the *zikkārôn* of the Passover (Exod.12:14) becomes contemporary in each new celebration. "In the timeless moment NOW of the cultic celebration, the worshipper became a contemporary with all past and all future generations of Israel."[73] This *Vergegenwärtigung*, this actualization of the past in the present, gives both continuity and renewed meaning to every manifestation of YHWH to his people.

Grether traces the use of the phrase "the name of YHWH" in pre-Deuteronomic and in post-Deuteronomic times.[74] In the earlier period, "the name of YHWH" is used as a synonym for God (e.g., Amos 2:7; Micah 5:4; Isa.29:33). In two important passages (Exod.23:20,21; Isa.30:27f.), "the name" is equivalent to a direct manifestation of God. Exod.23:20,21 declares that "an angel" (*mal'ākh*)[75] will go before Israel, "to bring you to the place (*hammāqôm*) which I have prepared"; furthermore, "my name is in him (*bᵉqirbô*)." M. Noth comments, "The 'angel' is the ambassador of Yahweh (cf. 'my angel,' v.23) who represents Yahweh himself and in whom Yahweh himself is present; the latter is expressed in v.21 by saying that the 'name' of Yahweh is present in the 'angel' as the name represents the one who bears it."[76] U. Cassuto, drawing attention to the reference to the *mal'ākh* in Gen.24:7, interprets the passage in Exodus in similar figurative fashion, "the angel of God is simply God's action."[77] Isa.30:27,28 is a strongly anthropomorphic description of God, burning with anger, his lips full of indignation, his tongue like a devouring fire. The imagery is that of a thunderstorm.[78] "The name of the Lord" in Isa.30:27 is the equivalent of YHWH, displaying his power in a theophanic disclosure.

In the post-Deuteronomic period, "the name" is frequently used as a synonym for YHWH, especially in the Psalms (e.g., Isa.25:1; Mal.3:16; Ps.7:17; Ps.34:3; Ps.92:1; Ps.103:1). There are other passages where "the name" is virtually an hypostasis for YHWH (e.g., Prov.18:10; Mal.1:14; Zech.14:9). Eventually, *hashshēm* was used by the Rabbis as a usual periphrasis for God.

[73]James Plastaras, *The God of Exodus* (Milwaukee: The Bruce Publishing Company, 1966), p. 146.

[74]O. Grether, *op. cit.*, pp. 26-30; 35ff.

[75]Samar., LXX and Vulg. read "my angel" (cf. Exod. 20:23).

[76]M. Noth, *Exodus*, p. 193. Noth regards Exod.23:20-33 as secondary to 20:22-23:19 and as deuteronomic in style (pp. 173-74, 192).

[77]U. Cassuto, *A Commentary on the Book of Exodus*, p. 305.

[78]Cf. R. B. Y. Scott, "The Book of Isaiah, Chapters 1-39" in *IB*, V (N.Y.: Abingdon Press, 1956), p. 336.

Particular interest attaches to the "name-theology" of Deuteronomy. G. von Rad waxes almost ecstatic over the theological maturity of the book of Deuteronomy, comparable to the Fourth Gospel among the books of the New Testament.[79] Deuteronomy emphasizes the centralization of the cultus; the major themes are: one God, one people, one sanctuary. With minor variations, the phrase recurs, "the place which YHWH your God will choose to put his name there" (Deut.12:5,14,21; 16:2,6; 26:2, etc.). The actual place is not specifically named. The original reference may well have been to Shechem,[80] but certainly, at the time of the Deuteronomic reformation in the reign of Josiah, the temple at Jerusalem became the one legitimate central sanctuary of YHWH (cf. Isa.18:7). The close association of "the name" with one sanctuary replaces the concept in Exod.20:24, where a multiplicity of altars is entirely legitimate, erected "in every place where I cause my name to be remembered," with the promise, "I will come to you and bless you." Holy places were recognized wherever a theophany had taken place. But now, with the expressed intention of centralizing worship in Jerusalem, a new theology of "the name" must be put forward. G. von Rad admirably summarizes the situation, "The Deuteronomic theologoumenon of the name Jahweh clearly holds a polemic element, or, to put it better, is a theological corrective. It is not Jahweh himself who is present at the shrine, but only his name as the guarantee of his will to save; to it and it only Israel has to hold fast as the sufficient form in which Jahweh reveals himself. Deuteronomy is replacing the old crude idea of Jahweh's presence and dwelling at the shrine by a theologically sublimated idea."[81] The Deuteronomic theology is reflected in the magnificent prayer of dedication, in which the promise of the presence of YHWH ("my name shall be there") is not allowed to become a theology of localized presence, but must be understood in the light of the transcendence of God, who cannot be contained by "heaven and the highest heaven" (1 Kings 8:27-30). A progression may be traced from the earlier references to the name, such as those associated with the *mal'ākh*, which signify temporary manifestations of the deity, to the Deuteronomic view of the name as expressing the permanent presence of the transcendent God among his people, yet without being localized in an earthly dwelling place. An even more developed stage is reached when the name can be thought of as an hypostasis for God.

---

[79]G. von Rad, *Studies in Deuteronomy*, SBT, trans. by David Stalker (London: S.C.M. Press, Ltd., 1953), p. 37.

[80]*Ibid.*, p. 41. Note also the striking phrase in Jer.7:12, "Shiloh, where I made my name dwell at first," and G. von Rad's comments in *Deuteronomy: A Commentary*, OTL, trans. by Dorothea Barton (Philadelphia: The Westminster Press, 1966), p. 94, where Bethel is also mentioned in relation to the earlier use of the centralizing formula.

[81]G. von Rad, *Studies in Deuteronomy*, pp. 38, 39. Cf. E. W. Nicholson, *Deuteronomy and Tradition* (Philadelphia: Fortress Press, 1967), pp. 53-56; R. Clements, *God and Temple* (Oxford: Blackwell, 1965), Ch. VI. Note especially the statement of Clements, "For the first time . . . we have with the Deuteronomists a strictly theological endeavour to express the reality of Yahweh's presence with Israel, which did not throw in question his heavenly and transcendent nature" (*ibid.*, pp. 94, 95).

We have seen that the phrase "the name of YHWH" is theologically signifi-cant in Old Testament literature spanning several centuries. But we are still left with basic questions unanswered. What are the origins of Yahwism? What does the Tetragrammaton itself convey as a name with theological content? These are questions to which we shall seek answers in the following chapters.

II

THE TETRAGRAMMATON BEFORE MOSES

Various traditions in the Pentateuch reflect differing views of the origins of Yahwism which are not easily reconcilable. According to the Yahwistic tradition (J), the worship of Yahweh can be traced to remote antiquity: "To Seth also a son was born, and he called his name Enosh. At that time men began to call upon the name of the LORD [YHWH] " (Gen.4:26 - J).

The tradition of the Elohist, on the other hand, associates the revelation of the divine name with the experience of Moses at the burning bush, as contained in Exodus 3: "Then Moses said to God, 'If I come to the people of Israel and say to them, "The God of your fathers has sent me to you," and they ask me, "What is his name?" what shall I say to them?' God said to Moses, 'I AM WHO I AM.' And he said, 'Say this to the people of Israel, "I AM has sent me to you."' God also said to Moses, 'Say this to the people of Israel, "The LORD [YHWH] , the God of your fathers, the God of Abraham, the God of Isaac, and the God of Jacob, has sent me to you": this is my name for ever, and thus I am to be remembered throughout all generations" (Exod.3:13-15 - E).

The Priestly tradition confirms this understanding of a Mosaic background for the declaration of the divine name. Indeed, the patriarchs knew God not as YHWH but as El Shadday: "And God said to Moses, 'I am the LORD [YHWH] . I appeared to Abraham, to Isaac, and to Jacob, as God Almighty ['El Shadday], but by my name the LORD [YHWH] I did not make myself known to them'" (Exod.6:2-3 - P).

Pentateuchal source criticism has undergone modifications since the time of Graf, Kuenen and Wellhausen, yet in large measure scholars are agreed on the major sources.[1] According to Martin Noth's analysis,[2] Exod.6:2-7:7 contains the Priestly version of the call of Moses, which like the JE version in Exod.3:1ff. regards the divine name YHWH as a new revelation. In fact, the P strand in the Pentateuch now consistently uses the new title from this point on.[3] Clearly, the

---

[1]For important recent studies of J and P, see Peter F. Ellis, *The Yahwist* (Notre Dame, Indiana: Fides Publishers Inc., 1968); J. G. Vink, "The Date and Origin of the Priestly Code in the Old Testament," *OTS* XV (1969): 1-144; S. McEvenue, *The Narrative Style of the Priestly Writer*, Analecta Biblica No. 50 (Rome: Pont. Inst. Bibl., 1972). Since the work of P. Volz and W. Rudolph, *Der Elohist als Erzähler: ein Irrweg der Pentateuchkritik? BZAW*, LXIII (1933), the delineation of E has been less certain. See, however, Sellin-Fohrer, *Introduction to the Old Testament*, trans. by David E. Green (N.Y.: Abingdon Press, 1968), espec. pp. 152-158. Redaction of the J and E strata has complicated the task of analysis.

[2]M. Noth, *Exodus: A Commentary*, trans. by J. S. Bowden (London: S.C.M. Press, Ltd., 1962), pp. 56-62.

[3]See J. Skinner, *The Divine Names in Genesis* (London: Hodder & Stoughton, 1914), pp. 9, 14. A similar consistency is to be seen in the Priestly view that the sacrificial system

introduction of the new name YHWH is at variance with the J tradition in Gen.4:26, which states that the worship of YHWH had been engaged in from time immemorial. Umberto Cassuto, who denies that J, E, and P sources can be detected in the Pentateuch, on the grounds that the linguistic and literary differences are stylistic variations of a single author,[4] is left with the problem of how the statements in Exodus are to be interpreted. His approach is to assert that the Tetragrammaton was not unknown to the Patriarchs: rather, the *significance* of the name (i.e., "He is One who carries out His promises") was not understood prior to the revelation to Moses.[5] But when and how was the name revealed?

As we have seen, Gen.4:26 contains a tradition that the divine name was known in antiquity. Exod.3:13-15 and 6:2-3 make it clear that the revelation to Moses marks a new beginning in Israel's story. In the words of H. H. Rowley, "The J document of the Pentateuch ascribes the beginnings of Yahwism to the childhood of the human race, and knows no moment of its introduction to Israel by Moses, while the E document dates its introduction to Israel in the time of Moses."[6]

One approach to the problem would be to regard theological considerations as having superseded a strict historical viewpoint in the Yahwist narrative, in much the same way as the Fourth Gospel, compared with the Synoptic Gospels, has been viewed as theologically rather than historically oriented.[7] The Yahwist, one might argue, was concerned with the revelation of Israel's God as the Lord

---

in Israel originates with Moses. Cf. Curt Kuhl, *The Old Testament: Its Origins and Composition*, trans. by C.T.M. Herriott (London: Oliver & Boyd, 1961), p. 59, "In contrast with the other Pentateuchal sources, the Yahwist and the Elohist, no mention is made in P of any sacrificial offering or any place of worship in pre-Mosaic times."

[4]U. Cassuto, *A Commentary on the Book of Exodus*, trans. by Israel Abrahams (Jerusalem: The Magnes Press, the Hebrew University, 1967), p. 2. Cassuto maintains that the book of Exodus rests mainly on a heroic religious epic poem dealing with the liberation of the Israelites from Egyptian bondage, and their subsequent wilderness wanderings.

[5]*Ibid.*, pp. 77-79, where the interpretation of *lō nōdha^c tî* in Exod.6:3 (cf. *nōdha^c tî* in Ezek.20:9) is the decisive element in Cassuto's view. Cf. also M. Reisel, *Observations*, p. 28. Dr. Reisel translates Exod.6:2, "By Abraham, Isaac and Jacob I was seen as El Saddai, but as for my Y.H.W.H.-character I was not acknowledged by them." The translation would be more convincing if the *beth essentiae* (GK g 119i) were used in both clauses instead of with El Saddai only.

[6]H. H. Rowley, *From Joseph to Joshua:* The Schweich Lectures of the British Academy, 1948 (London: Oxford Univ. Press, 1950), p. 143. Cf. G. von Rad, *Old Testament Theology*, I (London: Oliver and Boyd, 1962), p. 180, n. 10.

[7]See W. F. Albright, *From the Stone Age to Christianity*, 2nd ed. (Baltimore: The John Hopkins Press, 1946), pp. 298-300. For a fuller treatment, see C. H. Dodd, *Interpretation of the Fourth Gospel* (Camb. Univ. Press, 1958), Appendix, "Some Considerations upon the historical aspect of the Fourth Gospel," pp. 444-453; *Historical Tradition in the Fourth Gospel* (Camb. Univ. Press, 1963); E. C. Hoskyns, *The Fourth Gospel*, ed. by F. N. Davey (London: Faber & Faber, 1940; 2nd rev. ed., 1947), espec. chs. 4, 7, & 8; A. J. B. Higgins, *The Historicity of the Fourth Gospel* (Toronto: Ryerson Press, 1960); M. F. Wiles,

of history, with benevolent designs embracing all mankind, in which Israel had a special mission. Accordingly, we are dealing with a theological insight, universal in its application, when we are told that at the time of the birth of Enosh (whose name could be interpreted as "man in his frailty," cf. Ps.8:4, H5), men began to invoke the name of the LORD (YHWH). The question of the relationship between historical trustworthiness and theological intention is not easily resolved. The complexity of this problem becomes apparent in any attempt to assess the merits of J and P as sources for historical reconstruction and theological understanding. Similarly, the relative contributions of the Fourth Gospel and of the Synoptics as historical and theological sources are not easily evaluated. Throughout the biblical narrative, theology and history combine and interpenetrate in ways that complicate the task of analysis. In general, J is the older and more reliable source, but the P tradition also contains very ancient material,[8] so that individual passages require careful scrutiny and analysis before conclusions can be reached.

There can be little doubt that E and P traditions give a special place to Moses in declaring the divine name to Israel. But does the name YHWH originate *de novo* with Moses?[9] In view of the J tradition, and the consistent use of the name YHWH in the J narrative, is there a pre-Mosaic history of the use of the Tetragrammaton?

In the light of these divergent traditions and in order to provide an explanation, the Kenite hypothesis was first put forward over a hundred years ago by F. W. Ghillany (under the pseudonym, R. von der Alm).[10] This hypothesis, admittedly speculative, finds a measure of probability on the basis of a cumulative argument. More recent proponents differ in details of presentation, but nevertheless agree on a number of propositions. Those who have held to some form of the Kenite hypothesis include B. Stade,[11] K. Budde,[12] H. Gressmann, [13]

The Spiritual Gospel (Camb. Univ. Press, 1960), Ch. 3, "Historicity and Symbolism"; Raymond Brown, *The Gospel According to John* (i-xii), The Anchor Bible (N.Y.: Doubleday, 1966), ch. III.

[8]See W. F. Albright's discussion, *op. cit.*, p. 192. Cf. also James Plastaras, *The God of Exodus* (Milwaukee: The Bruce Publishing Company, 1966), pp. 34-36, for a discussion of the way in which P interprets history theologically.

[9]This is the thesis of F. C. Burkitt; see "On the Name Yahweh," *JBL*, XLIV (1925): 355.

[10]R. von der Alm, *Theologische Briefe an den Gebilden der deutschen Nation*, I (1862), pp. 216, 480.

[11]B. Stade, *Geschichte des Volkes Israel*, I (Berlin: G. Grote, 1887), pp. 130f. Cf. also *ZAW*, XIV (1894): 250ff; *Biblische Theologie des Alten Testaments*, I (Tübingen: J. C. B. Mohr, 1905), pp. 42f.

[12]Karl Budde, *The Religion of Israel to the Exile* (N.Y.: G. P. Putnam, 1899), Ch. 1.

[13]Hugo Gressmann, *Mose und seine Zeit* (Göttingen: Vandenhoeck & Ruprecht, 1913), pp. 163ff., 432ff.

J. Morgenstern,[14] G. Beer,[15] and the most eloquent advocate of all, H. H. Rowley.[16] M. Noth[17] and J. Gray[18] also appear to be in general sympathy with the hypothesis, and even R. de Vaux, who rejects it, at least holds open the possibility that the divine name, YHWH, is pre-Israelite.[19]

The Kenite hypothesis may be summarized briefly as follows. Prior to the time of Moses, YHWH was already the God of the Kenites. When Moses fled from Egypt, he found sanctuary with Jethro, the priest of Midian, and married his daughter, Zipporah. Jethro, who belonged to a Kenite clan of the Midianites, introduced Moses to the god, YHWH, and later (Exod.18:11) rejoiced at the discovery that YHWH had delivered Moses and the Israelites in the Exodus from Egypt and the passage of the Sea of Reeds. This in no way detracts from the new understanding of YHWH gained by Moses as a result of the encounter at the burning bush (Exod.3:1-15). Various southern tribes, including Judah, which were not involved in the sojourn in Egypt, or in the Exodus under Moses, had penetrated Palestine from the south. Kenites had been associated with them in this northward movement from Kadesh-barnea. The worship of YHWH had been adopted by the southern tribes at a time much earlier than that of Moses, and indeed, according to Gen.4:26 and the J tradition, YHWH was acknowledged as having been worshipped from antiquity. The "Joseph" tribes, whom Moses led out of Egypt, did not worship God under the name YHWH, until Moses declared this name to them, after his return from Midian. This is the situation reflected in the E and P traditions, in which Moses is recognized as the prophetic figure who

[14]J. Morgenstern, "The Elohist Narrative in Exodus 3:1-15," *AJSL,* XXXVII (1920-21): 242-262 (espec. pp. 248-250). Later, in "The Oldest Document of the Hexateuch," *HUCA,* IV (1927): 1-138, Morgenstern maintained that sections of Exod.33 and 34, together with Num.10:29-33a and Exod.4:24-26 are part of an original document which he designates as the Kenite Document (K).

[15]G. Beer, *Exodus, mit einem Beitrag von Kurt Galling* (Tübingen: J.C.B. Mohr, 1939), p. 30.

[16]H. H. Rowley, *The Re-Discovery of the Old Testament* (London: James Clarke & Co., Ltd., 1945), pp. 79-87; *From Joseph to Joshua,* pp. 143-161; "Moses and Monotheism" in *From Moses to Qumran* (London: Lutterworth Press, 1963), pp. 35-63, espec. pp. 50-58 (first published in German in *ZAW* N.F. XXVIII [1957]: 1-21).

[17]E.g. M. Noth, *Genesis: A Commentary,* OTL (London: S.C.M. Press, Ltd., 1961), p. 104: "The Kenites were a difficult riddle to the Israelites. They too, like the Israelites, were worshippers of Yahweh, perhaps even before Israel."

[18]J. Gray, "The God YW in the Religion of Canaan," *JNES,* XII (1953): 278-283, espec. p. 280.

[19]R. de Vaux, "The Revelation of the Divine Name YHWH" in John I. Durham & J. R. Porter, eds. *Proclamation and Presence,* Old Testament Essays in Honour of Gwynne Henton Davies (London: S.C.M. Press Ltd., 1970), p. 56. De Vaux gives reasons for his rejection of the Kenite hypothesis in *W. F. Albright Festschrift,* ed. A. Malamat, *Eretz-Israel,* IX (1969), pp. 28-32, "Sur l'Origine Kénite ou Madianite du Yahvisme." Note espec., p. 32, "Nous ne savons pas quelle divinité les Madianites adoraient, nous ne savons rien de leur culte ni de leur sacerdoce."

introduced Yahwism to the tribes which he led out of Egypt. Later, Joshua led descendants of these same tribes into central Palestine. Yet another consideration we may wish to add to this very condensed summary of the Kenite hypothesis is that Josh.24 (the account of the covenant at Shechem) may be regarded as pointing to the occasion of the establishment of the twelve-tribe amphictyony in covenant with YHWH. Eventually, both northern and southern tribes incorporated into their traditions accounts of the mighty acts of YHWH in the events of the exodus and the revelation at the sacred mount in the giving of the law to Israel.[20]

Since the Kenite hypothesis has been rejected by a number of scholars, including E. König,[21] T. J. Meek,[22] P. Volz,[23] W. J. Phythian-Adams,[24] M. Buber,[25] and R. de Vaux,[26] the theory can hardly be regarded as established with any degree of certainty. Various aspects of the hypothesis deserve to be investigated in greater detail, in order to provide a basis for tentative conclusions.

[20]G. von Rad, *Das formgeschichtliche Problem des Hexateuchs* (Stuttgart, 1938), Eng. trans. by E. W. Trueman Dicken, *The Problem of the Hexateuch* (London: Oliver & Boyd, 1966), states his view that the Exodus tradition and the Sinai tradition were originally quite separate. Cf. M. Noth, *Überlieferungsgeschichtliche Studien, II: Überlieferungsgeschichte des Pentateuch* (Stuttgart, 1948); H.-J. Kraus, *Gottesdienst in Israel. Studien zur Geschichte des Laubhüttenfestes* (Munchen, 1954). W. Beyerlin, *Herkunft und Geschichte der altesten Sinaitraditionen* (Tübingen: J.C.B. Mohr, 1961), trans. by S. Rudman, *Origins and History of the Oldest Sinaitic Traditions* (Oxford: Blackwell, 1965), cogently argues that the two traditions belong together. In any case, the Pentateuchal sources combine a variety of traditions which were eventually regarded as an integral part of Israel's history, even although not all the tribes may have been involved in all situations.

[21]E. König, *Geschichte der alttestamentlichen Religion* (Gutersloh: C. Bertelsmann, 1912), p. 162ff.

[22]T. J. Meek, "Some Religious Origins of the Hebrews," *AJSL*, XXXVII (1920-21): 101-131 (espec. pp. 102-107); *Hebrew Origins*, 2nd ed. (Univ. of Toronto Press, 1950), pp. 93-98.

[23]P. Volz, *Mose und sein Werk*, 2nd. ed. (Tübingen: J.C.B. Mohr, 1932), p. 59.

[24]W. J. Phythian-Adams, *The Call of Israel* (London: Oxford Univ. Press, 1934), pp. 72-77.

[25]M. Buber, *Moses, The Revelation and the Covenant*, 1946 (N.Y.: Harper & Bros. repr. 1958), pp. 42, 94-100. Martin Buber offers a critique of the Kenite hypothesis in the Preface to the second Edition of *Königtum Gottes* (1936), Eng. trans. by Richard Scheimann, *Kingship of God* (London: George Allen and Unwin Ltd., 1967), p. 35, "The acceptable part of the Kenite hypothesis is that the Kenites worshipped the god of a mountain."

[26]See note 19. Among Roman Catholic scholars, Paul van Imschoot is also skeptical. See *Theology of the Old Testament, I: God*, trans. by Kathryn Sullivan and Fidelis Buck (N.Y.: Desclee Company, 1965), p. 18, "The claim for a Madianite (or Kenite) origin of the cult of Yahweh is far from being proved." On the other hand, James Plastaras, *The God of Exodus* (Milwaukee: The Bruce Publishing Company, 1966), pp. 47, 91-93, is favourably disposed towards the Kenite hypothesis.

The fact that the priest of Midian, Jethro, the father-in-law of Moses (Exod.3:1) is also named Reuel (Exod.2:18) and Hobab (Numb.10:29)[27] poses a problem. W. F. Albright has given a convincing explanation in his view that Reuel is a clan name,[28] and Hobab can then rightly be described in Numb.10:29 as "the son (i.e., descendant) of Reuel the Midianite."[29] However, Jethro and Hobab are not to be identified as one and the same person. Jethro is presumably an elderly man, the father of seven daughters (Exod.2:16), who can give counsel to Moses (Exod.18:19) in the light of long experience. Hobab, a younger man, is needed by Moses as a guide (Numb.10:31) through unfamiliar territory in the wilderness. J. Morgenstern has argued that *hôtēn* in Numb.10:29 should be translated "brother-in-law," rather than "father-in-law."[30] Albright changes the vocalization to *hătăn*, "son-in-law,"[31] Furthermore, the descendants of Hobab are definitely designated as Kenites in Judges 4:11. Moses' father-in-law is called "the Kenite" in Judges 1:16, in which verse some Greek MSS add the name Hobab. If the conjecture is correct that Jethro and Hobab are interrelated and that both are descendants of Reuel, there is every justification for considering them to have neen members of a Kenite clan of the Midianites.

The role of Jethro, the priest of Midian, in relation to Moses, especially in the events recorded in Exod.18, is not easily established. Exegetes have been anything but unanimous in their interpretation of this chapter. Jethro, accompanied by his daughter Zipporah, Moses' wife, and her two sons, comes to meet Moses in the wilderness at the mountain of God (18:5), rejoices over the deliverance of Israel from Egypt by YHWH, offers a burnt offering and sacrifices to God (Elohim) and partakes of a sacrificial meal. An additional pericope (18:13-27) relates that on the morrow, before returning to his own country, Jethro counselled Moses to appoint able Israelites to assist him in judging the people, since the burden of the administration of justice was proving to be too heavy for him.

M. Noth has drawn attention to the fact that both 18:1-12 and 18:13-27 are derived from the Elohistic tradition, since the generic word "God" (Elohim) is frequently used, especially in the pericope, verses 13-27. The use of the divine name YHWH in verses 1b, 8 and 9-11 indicates expansion of the E material.[32]

[27]Unless with M. Noth, *Numbers: A Commentary*, OTL, trans. by J. D. Martin (London: S.C.M. Press, 1966), p. 77, the words *hôtēn mōshĕh* are taken as in apposition to Reuel rather than Hobab. But see Judges 4:11.

[28]W. F. Albright, "Jethro, Hobab and Reuel in Early Hebrew Tradition," *CBQ* XXV (1963): 1-11; *Yahweh and the Gods of Canaan* (London: The Athlone Press, 1968), pp. 33-37.

[29]Cf. G. B. Gray, *A Critical and Exegetical Commentary on Numbers*, ICC (Edinburgh: T.&T. Clark, 1903), p. 93.

[30]J. Morgenstern, "The Oldest Document of the Hexateuch," *HUCA*, IV (1927): 40.

[31]W. F. Albright, *CBQ* XXV (1963): 7.

[32]M. Noth, *Exodus: A Commentary*, OTL, trans. by J. S. Bowden (London: S.C.M. Press Ltd., 1962), p. 146.

The verses in which YHWH is used, however, emphasize the fact that it is YHWH who has delivered Israel.

According to the Kenite hypothesis, Exod.18:1-12 records Jethro's glad acceptance of the fact that YHWH, the deity whom he worships, has proved to be the deliverer of Israel from the bondage of Egypt. His appreciation of the greatness of YHWH is therefore considerably enhanced. Martin Buber, on the other hand, regards the event as the occasion when Jethro acknowledges the greatness of Moses' god, and just as Abraham had identified his god with the *'El 'Elyon* of Melchizedek (Gen.14:22), makes a similar identification between his god and YHWH, the god of Moses.[33] Much depends on the interpretation of the phrase *^cattah yādha^ctî* in Exod.18:11. A parallel may be made with the "Now I know" of Gen.22:12, where Abraham's response to the testing command to sacrifice Isaac, confirms the fact that he indeed fears God. Likewise, the "Now I know" of Jethro in Exod.18:11 indicates that he has received confirming evidence that his god is in fact the greatest of all.

C. H. W. Brekelmans has understood Exod.18 in a different way.[34] He draws attention to the phrase, " priest (*kōhēn*) of Midian." Since Midian is a place name rather than the name of a deity, he concludes that this is a title meaning "chieftain" rather than "priest" in the narrow sense of one who performs cultic functions. In this he may be correct, although it does not necessarily follow that the purpose of Jethro's meeting with Moses was political, with a view to the making of a covenant-alliance with Israel. To offer sacrifice[35] to YHWH and participate in a sacred meal would seem to be an altogether appropriate priestly action on the part of Jethro, whose seniority as one who has worshipped YHWH for many years makes him the proper person to act as priest. Although Aaron's role as priest belongs to the P tradition (Exod.28:1; Lev.8:5-12), it is perhaps not without significance that in Exod.18:12, Aaron is specifically mentioned as participating in the sacred meal with Jethro. It is at this point, also, that the pericope Exod.18:13-27 should be seen as concerned with another priestly function, for in judging the people, Moses was engaged

---

[33]M. Buber, *Kingship of God*, 3rd. ed., trans. by Richard Scheimann (London: George Allen and Unwin Ltd., 1967), pp. 29-36; *Moses* (N.Y.: Harper & Brothers, 1958), pp. 94-100. W. J. Phythian-Adams goes a stage farther in claiming that Jethro in the act of sacrifice to YHWH is declaring his new allegiance to the God of Israel. See *The Call of Israel* (London: Oxford Univ. Press, 1934), pp. 73-74. But as H. H. Rowley has rightly observed, "it is unusual for a novice to preside at his own initiation"; see "Moses and Monotheism," *From Moses to Qumran* (London: Lutterworth Press, 1963), p. 52.

[34]Chr. H. W. Brekelmans, "Exodus XVIII and the Origins of Yahwism in Israel," *OTS*, X (Leiden: E. J. Brill, 1954), pp. 215-224; Cf. C. F. Whitley, *The Genius of Ancient Israel* (Amsterdam: Philo Press, 1969), pp. 20-21.

[35]The verb *lāqah* is frequently used in a cultic sense (e.g., Gen.8:20; Lev.12:8). As M. Noth observes, "the mountain of God" was a proper Midianite sanctuary, where one might expect the priest of Midian to offer sacrifices; see *Exodus*, p. 148.

principally in a religious activity, the dispensing of *tôrôth*. The whole passage is best understood as aetiological and should be read in the light of the function of the judges and kings who were later regarded as interpreters of the divine law, and mediators of the covenant.[36] Once again, it is appropriate that Jethro should counsel Moses in such matters.[37]

A debatable but nevertheless plausible additional support for the Kenite hypothesis is to be found in the view that Moses received from Jethro the so-called "ritual decalogue" of Exod.34:10-26 - J. This decalogue, according to H. H. Rowley,[38] is the precursor of the decalogue of Exod.20:1-17 - E. The great achievement of Moses was the ethicizing of the original ritual decalogue (or dodecalogue). The relative dates of the various law codes in the Pentateuch are not readily determined; it is not surprising that there is considerable divergence in viewpoint on the part of Old Testament scholars.[39] In particular, the precise relationship between Exod.34:10-26, Exod.20:1-17, Deut.5:6-21 and parts of the Code of the Covenant (e.g., Exod.20:23-26; 22:28-29; 23:10-19),[40] is far from clear. These codes are almost entirely apodeictic rather than casuistic in character. Deut.5:6-21 is closely parallel to Exod.20:1-17; both versions of the decalogue contain additions such as Exod.20:11, which relates Sabbath observances to the priestly Creation narrative (Gen.1), and Deut.5:15, which supplies humanitarian motives for keeping the Sabbath. So far as Exod.34:10-26 is concerned, H. H. Rowley contends that "the whole flavour of this table is primitive and its ritual interest does not carry the stamp of P."[41] The ritual decalogue presupposes a settled, agricultural people, but this does not preclude a pre-Mosaic date, if indeed the southern tribes had already adopted YHWH as their God from the Kenites, together with the ritual laws which the Kenites observed.

[36]Cf. 1 Sam.7:15-17; 2 Sam.15:2 and M. Noth's interpretation of the role of the "minor judges," *The History of Israel*, trans. by Stanley Godman (London: Adam & Charles Black, 1958), pp. 101-102.

[37]H. H. Rowley's response to Brekelmans carries weight, "it can hardly be supposed that it was customary for the suppliant for a treaty to give instructions as to how justice should be administered," "Moses and Monotheism," *From Moses to Qumran*, p. 53.

[38]H. H. Rowley, "Moses and the Decalogue," *BJRL*, XXXIV (1951-52): 81-118, repr. in *Men of God* (London: Thomas Nelson and Sons, Ltd., 1963), pp. 1-36.

[39]H. H. Rowley, *op. cit.*, provides very adequate bibliographies. See also J. J. Stamm and M. E. Andrew, *The Ten Commandments in Recent Research*, SBT, Second Series, 2 (London: S.C.M. Press Ltd., 1967): Eduard Nielsen, *The Ten Commandments in New Perspective*, SBT, Second Series, 7 (London: S.C.M. Press Ltd., 1968).

[40]S. Mowinckel, *Le Décalogue* (Paris, 1927) regards these sections of the Code of the Covenant as containing the work of the Elohist. Exod.20:1-17 is regarded as a later interpolation.

[41]H. H. Rowley, *Men of God*, p. 11. See also R. H. Pfeiffer, "The Oldest Decalogue," *JBL*, XLIII (1924): 294-310; H. Kosmala, "The So-called Ritual Decalogue," *ASTI*, I (1962): 31-61.

Julian Morgenstern claims that the original law code in Exod.34 contained eight laws, reflecting an environment partly agricultural, partly pastoral.[42] The code in its present form has been revised, but nevertheless must be traced back in origin to the Kenites.

Since each of the codes under discussion has been expanded to meet later conditions, date and origin cannot be easily decided.[43] Certain basic laws prohibiting the worship of any god other than YHWH, or the making of images, and commanding cessation from work on the Sabbath, could very well have been taken over from the ritual decalogue to serve as the nucleus of the ethical decalogue of Exod.20:1-17. The course of development proposed by Rowley is eminently reasonable and cannot be lightly dismissed as an improbable theory.

An objection to the Kenite hypothesis has been raised by T. J. Meek,[44] on the basis that Jochebed, the name of Moses' mother, is a theophorous name containing as a prefix the element *yô*, implying that the family of Moses were Yahweh worshippers. The name occurs in two passages only, Exod.6:20 and Numb.26:59, both of which are ascribed to P. The name is not given in Exod.2:1, where one might have expected to find it. Although M. Noth has questioned the view that Jochebed is a theophorous name,[45] Murtonen readily accepts the meaning, "YHWH is powerful."[46] G. B. Gray understood the name to be theophorous, although he doubts whether this was so understood by the priestly writer, who in keeping with his belief that names compounded with the divine name YHWH could occur only after the revelation of the name to Moses, asserts that even the theophorous name "Joshua" was originally "Hoshea" (Numb.13:8,16).[47] The name Jochebed need not carry the implication that

---

[42] J. Morgenstern, "The Oldest Document of the Hexateuch," *HUCA*, IV (1927): 1-138, espec. pp. 54-98.

[43] M. Noth, *Exodus*, p. 265, finds no evidence of mutual literary dependence of the law codes in Exodus. The temporal relationship between the decalogue of Exod.34 and that of Exod.20 remains enigmatic. Exod.34 contains the tradition inherited by J as to the foundation of the Sinai covenant. However, the loose relationship of Exod.20:2-17 to the context suggests that the passage has been inserted, although this in itself "implies nothing about its age and provenance" (p. 154).

[44] T. J. Meek, *Hebrew Origins*, 2nd ed., (Univ. of Toronto Press, 1950), p. 97.

[45] M. Noth, *Die israelitischen Personennamen* (Stuttgart: 1928), p. 111. Geo. Widengren, "What do we know about Moses?" in *Proclamation and Presence*, ed. by John I. Durham and J. R. Porter (London: S.C.M. Press Ltd., 1969), p. 35, accepts the name as theophorous, but casts doubt on the historical value of the genealogies in Exod.6:14-25 and Numb.26:57-62.

[46] A. Murtonen, *A Philological and Literary Treatise on the Divine Names* (Helsinki, 1952), p. 46. Cf. P. van Imschoot, *op. cit.*, p. 17, "Yahweh is glory, or Yahweh is powerful."

[47] G. B. Gray, *Studies in Hebrew Proper Names* (London: Adam and Charles Black, 1896), pp. 156, 257. Cf. also M. Noth, *Numbers: A Commentary*, OTL (London: S.C.M. Press, Ltd., 1968), p. 103. The opposite process is at work when Joseph is spelled $Y^e h \hat{o} s \bar{e} p h$ in Ps.81:5 (H 6), to make this a theophorous name.

YHWH was already worshipped by the family of Moses prior to the revelation at the burning bush. H. H. Rowley offers a different explanation: the name occurs as the result of intermarriage between a Levite and a Kenite woman, thereby introducing a Kenite name, compounded with the divine name, into the line from which Moses descended, in fact the name by which his mother was known.[48] This also provides a reason for Moses to find sanctuary with Jethro, after killing an Egyptian taskmaster, in order to live among the Kenites, since he himself was partly of Kenite descent. H. H. Rowley draws attention to a similar situation at a much later period (in the fifth century, B.C.), when Egyptian names were introduced by intermarriage among the Jews in Elephantine.[49] However, another matter to consider is the extent to which family names recur at this earlier time. Naming a child after a kinsman had become a common practice by the first century of the Christian era (e.g., Luke 1:59-61), yet there is little support for such a practice in early Israel.[50] Nevertheless, an *argumentum e silentio* is not conclusive; an interesting exception in the period of the early monarchy is to be found in the case of Absalom's mother and daughter, each named Maacah (2 Sam.3:3; 1 Kings 15:2), David having married a foreign wife.

Historical reconstruction of the events surrounding the sojourn in Egypt, the exodus from Egypt (perhaps more than one), and the settlement in Palestine, is a complicated task. The results are far from conclusive.[51] The early history and movements of the various tribes cannot be traced with exactitude because of the complexity and insufficiency of the evidence. Considerable interest attaches to the Levite ancestry of Moses (Exod.2:1; 6:16-20; Numb.26:59). The "blessing" of Jacob in Gen.49:5-7 indicates clearly that Levi was originally a secular tribe.[52] These verses reflect the incident recorded in Gen.34:25-31, in which Simeon and Levi took revenge on the Shechemites for the ravaging of Dinah. The tribe of Levi must have occupied the central hill country in Palestine at one time. The "Leah" tribes, of which Levi was one, and among which Judah emerged as the most powerful (Gen.49:8-12), belonged to the wave of Israelites

---

[48]H. H. Rowley, "Moses and Monotheism," in *From Moses to Qumran* p. 56.

[49]H. H. Rowley, *op. cit.*, p. 56, n. 2. Cf. B. Porten, *Archives from Elephantine* (Univ. of California Press, 1968), pp. 250, 251.

[50]G. B. Gray, *op. cit.*, pp. 4-6.

[51]For various views regarding these events, see H. H. Rowley, *From Joseph to Joshua*, Schweich Lectures, 1948 (London: Oxford Univ. Press, 1950); M. Noth, *Das System der zwölf Stämme Israels* (Stuttgart, 1930); *Überlieferungsgeschichte des Pentateuch* (Stuttgart: W. Kohlhammer, 1948); M. Weippert, *The Settlement of the Israelite Tribes in Palestine*, SBT Second Series No. 21, trans. by James D. Martin (London: S.C.M. Press, Ltd., 1971).

[52]T. J. Meek, *Hebrew Origins*, 1nd ed., (Univ. of Toronto Press, 1950), pp. 121-22. H. Schmökel, "Jahweh und die Keniter," *JBL*, LII (1933), on the contrary, claims that the tribe of Simeon was led on by fanatical Levite-priests.

which occupied Palestine prior to the time of Moses.[53] H. H. Rowley maintains that the tribe of Levi was connected also with a wave of immigration into Egypt.[54] The tribe of Levi provides a link with both groups, those who were resident in Egypt and those tribes who penetrated Palestine in the Amarna age. The status of the tribe of Levi as fulfilling a priestly function (cf. Deut.33:8-11; Judges 17:7-13; Exod.32:25-29; Numb.1:47-54) does not necessarily arise from the sacralization of the secular tribe. Rather, the equation of the Levitical priesthood with the tribe of an earlier period may be a later development, after the secular tribe had ceased to exist.[55]

The allocation of cities as Levitical settlements (Josh.21; cf. Numb.35:1-8; I Chron.6:54-81), took place probably in the reign of David.[56] The tradition connecting Moses' ancestry with the house of Levi (Exod.2:1) was valued by later generations because this made him a priestly figure, the promulgator of the priestly laws recorded in the Pentateuch. If we are able to assert that the tradition stems originally from a connection with the secular tribe of Levi, and if this tribe had historical associations both with the "Leah" tribes and the "Rachel" tribes, Moses could be claimed as a kinsman by both groups. In course of time, a tribal amphictyony would emerge, in which the God of Moses was acknowledged as Israel's God.

Moses fled from Pharaoh's court into the land of Midian and lived among the Midianites, of which the Kenites were a clan (e.g. Judges 4:11). In the biblical records, the Kenites are usually associated with the southern tribes and with locations in the south.[57] For instance, Numb.10:29-31 indicates that Hobab knew the southern trade routes to the north. According to Judges 1:16, the Kenites came to Palestine with "the people of Judah" and settled in the Negeb. Josh.15 lists Kain (Josh.15:57) among the cities assigned to Judah, in the southern hill country, west of the Jordan. Heber the Kenite is mentioned in

[53]K. Elliger, article "Simeon," *IDB*, IV (N.Y.: Abingdon Press, 1962), p. 356. Cf. M. Noth, *The History of Israel* (London: Adam & Charles Black, 1958), pp. 70-71, 77; *Das System der zwölf Stämme Israels* (Stuttgart: W. Kohlhammer, 1930); M. Weippert, *op. cit.*, p. 146.

[54]H. H. Rowley, *From Joseph to Joshua*, Schweich Lectures, 1948 (London: Oxford Univ. Press, 1950), pp. 140ff.

[55]See M. Weippert, *op. cit.*, p.p. 43, n. 139; R. de Vaux, *Ancient Israel*, trans. by John McHugh (Darton, Longman & Todd Ltd., 1961), pp. 360-61; cf. Aelred Cody, *A History of Old Testament Priesthood* (Rome: Pontifical Biblical Institute, 1969), pp. 33-38, in which the view is put forward that there may indeed be a direct historical connection between the secular tribe and the later priestly Levites. The occurrence of Egyptian names in the tribe of Levi, such as Hophni and Phinehas, supports this view.

[56]G. Henton Davies, article "Levitical Cities," *IDB*, III (N.Y.: Abingdon Press, 1962), pp. 116-117. Cf. J. Gray, *Joshua, Judges and Ruth*, The Century Bible (London: Nelson, 1967), pp. 174f.

[57]Cf. Hartmut Schmökel, "Jahwe und die Keniter," *JBL*, LII (1933), pp. 212-229.

Judges 4:11 as one who had migrated to the north, away from the main group of Kenites. His wife, Jael, receives high praise in the Song of Deborah for slaying Sisera (Judges 5:24ff.). Saul, concerned to protect the Kenites, warned them to depart from among the Amalekites, so as not to be put to the sword by his troops. The reason given is that the Kenites "showed kindness to all the people of Israel when they came up out of Egypt" (1 Sam.15:6).[58] David deceived Achish by claiming that he had been campaigning against Israel rather than against the Amalekites; his claim that he had made raids against "the Negeb of the Kenites" (1 Sam.27:10) is a clear indication that the Kenites were allies of Judah and of the Jerahmeelites, mentioned in the same context. The Rechabites, whose fidelity to their vows is held up as an example to Israel by Jeremiah (Jer.35), are included among the Kenites by the Chronicler (I Chron.2:55). Jonadab, the son of Rechab, gave full support to Jehu in his zeal for YHWH and in his destruction of the worshippers of Baal (2 Kings 10:15-28).

The genealogy of the Kenites is given in Gen.4:17-24. Cain is regarded as the eponymous ancestor. The clan apparently consisted of smiths and metal-workers (cf. Gen.4:22, "Tubal-cain . . . was the forger of all instruments of iron").[59] Yet, Cain himself is described as "a tiller of the ground" (Gen.4:2), and as a city-builder (Gen.4:17), which suggests that the Kenites were not exclusively nomadic smiths.[60] According to the J tradition, Cain, after murdering his brother Abel, though condemned to be a fugitive and wanderer, received the protective mark of YHWH, "lest any who came upon him should kill him" (Gen.4:15).[61]

The many references in the Old Testament to the Kenites indicate that they were closely allied to Israel, especially to the southern tribes, and that they were

---

[58]The oracle against the Kenites (Numb.24:21, 22), attributed to Balaam, following an oracle against the Amalekites, is a late oracle, according to M. Noth, *Numbers*, p. 193, since Assyria is specifically mentioned. The paronomasia is striking ($qayin$ = Cain; $q\bar{e}n$ = nest). The location of the Kenites would seem to be in the Judaean hill-country. W. F. Albright, "The Oracles of Balaam," *JBL*, LXIII (1944), p. 227, argues for an early date for the oracle, on the grounds that the Kenites were eventually scattered among the Israelites.

[59]Hebrew $qayin$ has affinities with Arabic $qain$ and Aramaic $qain\^ay\^a$. See W. F. Albright, *From the Stone Age to Christianity*, 2nd ed. (Baltimore: The John Hopkins Press, 1946, p. 196. The connection of $qayin$ with the verb $q\bar{a}n\bar{a}h$ (Gen.4:1) is an example of paronomasia rather than an etymological derivation; cf. S. R. Driver, *The Book of Genesis*, 8th rev. ed. (London: Methuen & Co. Ltd., 1911), p. 63.

[60]Cf. M. Noth, *The History of Israel* (London: Adam and Charles Black, 1956), p. 57, n. 4, where the claim is made that "the Kenites who had settled were certainly farmers like the other inhabitants."

[61]According to Rashi, a letter of the divine name was inscribed on the forehead of Cain; see *Pentateuch with Rashi's Commentary, Genesis*, ed. A. M. Silberman (London: Shapiro, Valentine & Co., 1929), p. 19. M. Noth, *Genesis*, p. 104, suggests, "A tribal sign, a kind of tatoo, externally recognizable" by which the Kenites indicated their relationship to Yahweh.

known to be worshippers of YHWH. May there not be justification for postulating that their worship of YHWH goes back to pre-Mosaic times? The question of origins is not resolved by such an hypothesis, since nothing is known of the circumstances under which the Kenites first came to worship YHWH. At least this view gives support to the contention of the Yahwist that the worship of YHWH existed long before the time of Moses.

The Yahwist tradition seeks to establish that YHWH was first worshipped in the days of Seth, son of Enosh. Gen.4 concludes (verse 26) with a statement regarding the line of Seth, to whom a son, Enosh, was born: "At that time men began to call upon the name of the LORD (YHWH)." The fact that Enosh is of little significance in the Genesis narrative has led I. Lewy to postulate different sources for 4:25, 26a and 4:26b.[62] According to Lewy, 4:26b originally followed 4:16. Sigmund Mowinckel, on the other hand, believes that the name Enosh ("Man") originally indicated the first living man.[63] Samuel Sandmel, in a careful historical study of the text and interpretation of 4:26b,[64] refers to the difficulty of deciding the exact implication of the statement. The LXX offered an interpretation, rather than a translation: "He (Enosh) hoped to call on the name of the LORD (*kyriou tou theou*)." This suggests that the verb *yāḥal*, "to hope," was understood rather than *ḥālal (hiph^{c}il)*, "to begin." Although some modern scholars such as H. Gunkel and J. Skinner emend the text by reading the *hiph^{c}il* of *ḥalal* rather than the *hoph^{c}al*, the MT can be sustained. An additional reason to those advanced by Sandmel may be found in the assonance which exists between the passive *yullad* in verse 26a and the indefinite passive form *hûhal* in verse 26b. The repetition of the verb *qārā'* and the noun *shēm*, also militates against Lewy's view of the dislocation of the second half of the verse.

Gen.4:26b cannot be fully harmonized with Exod.3:15 and 6:2. The J tradition would appear to reflect a genuinely historical reminiscence of the fact that the divine name, YHWH, goes back to pre-Mosaic times. The Kenite hypothesis offers a possible explanation of the process by which the Tetragrammaton eventually became the name by which Israel as a people knew God. However, important questions still remain to be considered. What extra-biblical evidence, if any, supports the contention that the Tetragrammaton is earlier than the time of Moses? Even if an early date can be established, a further question remains unanswered: What did the divine name mean to the Kenites? Many attempts have been made to determine the origin and primary meaning of the Tetragrammaton. Some of these will be examined subsequently. In this area, dogmatic

---

[62]Immanuel Lewy, "The Beginning of the Worship of Yahweh: Conflicting Biblical Views," *VT* VI (1956): 430.

[63]S. Mowinckel, "The Name of the God of Moses," *HUCA*, XXXII (1961): 121. Cf. T. J. Meek, *Hebrew Origins* 2nd ed., (Univ. of Toronto Press, 1950), p. 93, and p. 118, n. 93, where he quotes from G. H. Skipwith, *JQR*, Old Series, XI (1899): 50 in support of this view.

[64]S. Sandmel, "Genesis 4:26b," *HUCA*, XXXII (1961): 19-29.

views are unconvincing. The path of wisdom would seem to lie in the direction of dispensing with claims to assured results. All theories are highly speculative.

In the following chapter an attempt will be made to assess the beliefs held in patriarchal times, prior to the full acceptance of the name YHWH among the Israelites. Advocacy of the Kenite hypothesis carries with it only the recognition that the name was known in a limited way by some tribes before the thirteenth century, B.C. Whatever meaning the name had already acquired was to give way to an incomparably richer understanding in the light of the revelation to Moses and in the events which are so dramatically set forth in the book of Exodus.

III

THE GOD OF THE FATHERS

A landmark in the study of the religion of the patriarchs was reached in 1929, when Albrecht Alt published *Der Gott der Väter*.[1] The historical background of the patriarchal period can be reconstructed only in a tentative way. Alt contends that solid ground is attained in the historical reconstruction of Israel's past at the time when the tribes united in their allegiance to YHWH. "If we are in any way justified . . . in arguing back from the later history of the Israelite nation to its origins, we can only conclude that the event on which all further development was based took place when the tribes united in the worship of Yahweh."[2] Although Alt has reservations about the precise historical value of the sagas which come down from the patriarchal period, he draws on these sagas to establish the nature of the religion of the Israelite tribes before the decisive event of the adoption of Yahwism.

The Elohistic narrative in Exodus 3 serves the double function of emphasizing the radical nature of the new allegiance to Yahweh, while recognizing at the same time a measure of continuity with the religion of the patriarchs. The God who reveals himself as YHWH is indeed the God of the fathers, "the God of Abraham, the God of Isaac, and the God of Jacob" (Exod.3:6, 15). Alt maintains that the harmonizing purpose of the Elohist tends to obscure the fact that there is a much greater divergence between YHWH and the God of the fathers than the Elohist narrative suggests. Likewise, the Priestly tradition in Exod.6:2 gives the impression that God was known to Abraham, Isaac, and Jacob only as *El Shaddai*. In actual fact, in addition to the God of Abraham, specific mention is made of the *Pahad Yitshaq* (Gen. 31:42) and the *ᵃbîr Yaᶜkôbh* (Gen.49:24). According to Alt, three entirely distinct *numina*, special patron deities, are represented by these divine titles. "The God of Abraham" refers to the God worshipped by Abraham; the Fear (*Pahad*) of Isaac is "the numen whose appearance terrified Isaac and thereby bound him to himself for ever";[3] the Mighty One

---

[1] A. Alt, "Der Gott der Väter," *BWANT*, II:12 (Stuttgart: W. Kohlhammer; 1929), trans. by R. A. Wilson, in *Essays on Old Testament and Religion* (Oxford: Blackwell, 1966), pp. 1-77.

[2] *Ibid.*, Eng. trans., p. 3.

[3] *Ibid.*, p. 26. W. F. Albright translates the title, "Kinsman of Isaac," pointing to Palmyrene *pahdâ*, meaning "family, clan, tribe," see *From the Stone Age to Christianity*, 2nd ed. (Baltimore: The John Hopkins Press, 1946), p. 189 and p. 327, n. 71. However, the phrase *pahad ᵉlōhim* in Ps.36:1 - H2 corroborates the translation, "Fear." Delbert Hillers, in a critical note entitled "Paḥad Yiṣhaq," *JBL*, XCI (1972):90-92 also disagrees with Albright's translation and advances arguments for the usual translation. Otto Eissfeldt, "Jahwe, der Gott der Väter," *Kleine Schriften*, IV (Tübingen: J.C.B. Mohr, 1968), p. 85, accepts the possibility of either translation. H. J. Franken, *The Mystical Communion with*

($^{a}b\hat{\imath}r$)[4] of Jacob is an entirely distinct *numen*. The fact that the three patriarchs have different sites and districts associated with them reinforces Alt's contention that these gods were not originally connected with one another, although the worship in each cult represented the same general type of religion. From a later perspective, these *numina* merged into one, the God of the fathers. By a telescoping of history, the patriarchs were regarded as direct descendants in a single genealogical line. The worship of the tribes at the sanctuary of Shiloh was a later development, at a time when YHWH was worshipped by the nation as a whole. This marks the end of a process in which the earlier *numina* were absorbed into the one transcendent deity, YHWH. The gods of the fathers paved the way for a new stage in religious development, the union of all the tribes under YHWH, who replaced the earlier *numina*.

In order to propose a theory regarding the nature of patriarchal religion, one must have some appreciation of the historical background of the second millenium. If, indeed, "Abraham stands as the ultimate ancestor of Israel's faith,"[5] an attempt must be made to understand the history and religious norms of patriarchal times. So far as methodology is concerned, Martin Noth reminds us that "the Old Testament contains popular historical traditions especially concerning the early history of Israel, which were transmitted by word of mouth to begin with and not written down until later";[6] consequently, "what is important is . . . to grasp as precisely as possible the historical assumptions behind these traditions and then to assess as objectively as possible what they can contribute to our knowledge of the outward course of the history of Israel, and what they cannot contribute."[7] For example, the account of the birth of the tribal ancestors of the Moabites and Ammonites (Gen.19:30-38), although based on popular beliefs, does indicate some kinship between Israel and these peoples, in spite of enmity between them.[8] Gunkel's study, "The Legends of Genesis"[9] was a pioneer work in which he sought to establish the narrative literary types employed

JHWH in the Book of Psalms (Leiden: E. J. Brill, 1954), p. 88, comments, "The *paḥad* is the 'numinous' element in religious life."

[4]Cf. Ps. 132:2,5; Isa.49:26; 60:16; the description "the Mighty One of Israel" is used in Isa.1:24. Paul van Imschoot, *Theology of the Old Testament*, I, Eng. trans. (N.Y.: Desclee Company, 1965), p. 26, drawa attention to the theological scruple which accounts for the pointing *'abîr*, when the adjective applies to God, as over against *'abbîr*, when men or bulls are described.

[5]John Bright, *A History of Israel* (Philadelphia: The Westminster Press, 1959), p. 87.

[6]M. Noth, *The History of Israel*, trans. by Stanley Godman (London: Adam & Charles Black, 1958), p. 44.

[7]*Ibid.*, p. 45.

[8]Cf. A. H. van Zyl, *The Moabites* (Leiden: E. J. Brill, 1960), p. 109.

[9]H. Gunkel's study, first published in 1901, as the introduction to his *Commentary on Genesis*, has been reissued in a Schocken paperback edition (N.Y., 1964), under the title, *The Legends of Genesis: The Biblical Saga and History*, trans. by W. H. Carruth.

and to make judgments regarding their historical value. John M. Holt defends the value of legend when he writes, "Because of its historical background legend lies on the boundary of fact, of documentary source."[10] Archaeological research has helped immeasurably in illuminating the biblical patriarchal narratives,[11] yet because of the incompleteness of the evidence, "we will never be able to write a historical biography of Abraham, of Isaac, of Jacob, of Joseph or even a real history of the patriarchal period."[12] W. F. Albright comes to the conclusion that "the Patriarchs were indeed human beings who were the heroes of stories handed down from the Patriarchal Age. It is, however, quite true that there is a good deal of ethnic tradition intermingled with the Patriarchal narratives of Genesis."[13]

The problem which faces the historian and the exegete in the study of the book of Genesis arises from the fact that the patriarchal period is viewed from the perspective of later times. Even although Alt based his theory of distinct deities of the patriarchs on late analogies in Nabataean and Palmyrene inscriptions, he was seeking to penetrate beyond the theological views of later authors and redactors, in order to discover the nature of patriarchal religious faith. Doubtless, in the long process of oral and literary transmission, and in the work of editorial redaction, patriarchal religion has been made to appear closely in harmony with later Yahwism. Indeed, the Yahwist consistently understands the call of Abraham and the movements of the patriarchs as initiated by YHWH. That there is a real continuity, one would not deny. At the same time, the Yahwism that emerged when the tribes were consolidated as one nation, represented a new level of religious awareness and understanding.

Faithfulness to the sources and traditions which they inherited, has led authors and editors to preserve references to the names given to deity in the patriarchal age. These names hold a special interest for those who attempt a reconstruction of religious beliefs in the patriarchal period. There are specific epithets which consist of the element 'ēl followed by a second determinative term, such as shadday, ʿôlām, or ʿelyôn. 'Ēl with the definite article appears in

---

[10]John M. Holt, *The Patriarchs of Israel* (Nashville: Vanderbilt Univ. Press, 1964), p. 33.

[11]For example, E. A. Speiser, *Genesis*, The Anchor Bible (N.Y.: Doubleday, 1964), draws on the customs of the Hurrians to illuminate the wife-sister motif of Gen.12:10-20; 20:1-18; 26:6-11; and the significance of the possession of the household gods (Gen.31:10-35), in the light of the Nuzi documents.

[12]Ignatius Hunt, *The World of the Patriarchs* (Englewood Cliffs, N.J.: Prentice-Hall, Inc., 1967), p. 158. John M. Holt, *op. cit.*, p. 82, reminds us that "there is not one extra-biblical reference to any person mentioned in Genesis." W. F. Albright, however, refers to the appearance of the name "Jacob" as a placename in the Tuthmosis list (fifteenth century B.C.), and in the early eighteenth century tablets from Chagar Bazar, *From the Stone Age to Christianity*, 2nd ed. (Baltimore: The John Hopkins Press, 1946), p. 180, and p. 325, n. 51.

[13]W. F. Albright, *Yahweh and the Gods of Canaan* (London: The Athlone Press, 1968), p. 56.

isolation in a number of passages, including Gen.35:1 (probably referring to the somewhat enigmatic *hā'ēl beth-'ēl* of Gen.31:13); Gen.46:3, "I am *hā'ēl*, the God of your father" (the declaration made to Jacob at Beersheba); Ps.68:20,21 - H; Deut.10:17 ("the great, the mighty, the terrible God"; cf. Jer.32:18). The identification with YHWH is clearly made in Deut.10:17; Ps.68:20 - 21H); Ps.29:3[14] ("the God of glory," *'ēl hakkābôdh*). Without the definite article, *'ēl* occurs numerous times both in the book of Job and the Psalms as a proper name, rather than as an appellative. The appellative use is to be seen in such passages as Exod.20:5 (*'ēl qannā'*); Deut.4:24; Josh.24:19. With the exception of the Ethiopians, *'ēl* is used as the generic name for God among all the Semitic peoples.[15] The plural, *'ēlîm*, occurs in biblical passages differing widely in date (e.g., Exod.15:11; Dan.11:36; *'ēl 'ēlîm*, "the God of gods"). Various derivations of the word *'ēl* have been proposed.[16] Tentatively, one may point to a root meaning, "to be strong," for which support can be found in such expressions as "mighty cedars" (Ps.80:10 - 11H), literally, "cedars of El," and in the striking phrase, "the *'ēl* of my hand," usually taken to mean "the power of my hand" (Gen.31:29; cf. Prov.3:27; Micah 2:1; Deut. 28:32; Neh.5:5). Nevertheless, the derivation remains uncertain.

El appears as the principal deity among North-Western Semites in the second millenium. In particular, the Ugaritic literature clearly indicates that El stands at the head of the Canaanite pantheon, even although his place was eventually usurped by Baal.[17] H. G. May has no hesitation in asserting, "The patriarchs in Canaan worshipped the West-Semitic deity El, the head of a pantheon."[18] W. F. Albright believes that YHWH replaced Baal in Yahwistic poems, whereas El names, long dominant on the edge of the desert, were eventually

[14]M. Dahood, *Psalms I*, The Anchor Bible (N.Y.: Doubleday, 1966), p. 175, accepts the view that Psalm 29 is "a Yahwistic adaptation of an older Canaanite hymn to the storm-god Baal." However, he agrees (*contra* Gunkel) that the clause *'ēl hakkābôd hīr^cîm* is genuine, for "thunder was predicated of El as well as of Baal," p. 176.

[15]Paul van Imschoot, *Theology of the Old Testament*, I, trans. by Kathryn Sullivan and Fidelis Buck (N.Y.: Desclee & Co., 1965), p. 7; R. W. Gleason, *Yahweh the God of the Old Testament* (New Jersey: Prentice-Hall, Inc., 1964), p. 113.

[16]Various derivations are discussed by W. Eichrodt, *Theology of the Old Testament*, I, trans. by J. A. Baker (Philadelphia: The Westminster Press, 1961), p. 179. See also Marvin H. Pope, *El in the Ugaritic Texts* (Leiden: E. J. Brill, 1955), pp. 16-21, and especially p. 19, "The bottom of the etymological barrel has been thoroughly scraped and the etymology remains obscure."

[17]For a fuller treatment, see Otto Eissfeldt, *El im ugaritischen Pantheon: Berichte über die Verhandlungen der Sächsischen Akademie der Wissenschaften zu Leipzig*, Phil.-hist. Klasse, Band XCVIII, Heft 4, 1951; Marvin H. Pope, *op. cit.*; John Gray, *The Legacy of Canaan*, 1957, 2nd ed. (Leiden: E. J. Brill, 1965).

[18]H. G. May, "The Patriarchal Idea of God," *JBL*, LX (1941): 114. In Exod.34:6, *rahum* and *hannun* may be traits of El assimilated to YHWH; see Marvin H. Pope, *op. cit.*, p. 25.

replaced by Elohim.[19] W. Eichrodt, discussing the place of El as the supreme God in the Ras Shamra documents and the way in which Baal overshadows El, understands the relationship in this way, "The figure of El, the divine Father, embodies the link with the civilized world at large, whereas it is the particularistic development of religion in Canaan that is reflected in Baal."[20] In similar fashion, the particularistic development of religion in Israel, associated with the divine name YHWH, accounts for the fact that El names became subordinate and receded into the background as synonyms, infrequently used.

This view of the development of patriarchal religion finds confirmation in the biblical traditions coming down from the patriarchal period, in which wide use is made of theophorous names with '$\bar{e}l$ as an element.[21] W. F. Albright claims that many personal names in their present form are abbreviated, but originally included the name of a deity, usually El; for example, "$Ya^c qobh$ is an abbreviation of $Ya^c qobh$-$\bar{e}l$, 'May El Protect,' which actually appears as a personal name in northwestern Mesopotamia (18th century) and as a Palestinian placename in an Egyptian list of the 15th century B.C.; $Yishaq$ stands for $Yishaq$-'el, 'May El Smile (favorably upon me in my distress).'"[22] M. Dahood theorizes that the original form of the Tetragrammaton was $yhwh$ 'el, in which a verbal form is followed by the name of the deity, El, meaning "El brings into being."[23] This interesting viewpoint will be discussed in the following chapter.

Exod.6:3 gives priority to El Shadday as the paternal god of the patriarchs. The full title occurs in the Pentateuch in Gen.17:1, 28:3, 35:11, 43:14, 48:3,

---

[19]W. F. Albright, *Yahweh and the Gods of Canaan* (London: The Athlone Press, 1968), p. 29.

[20]W. Eichrodt, *Theology of the Old Testament*, I, trans. by J. A. Baker (Philadelphia: The Westminster Press, 1961), p. 180, n. 1.

[21]M. Noth, *Die israelistischen Personennamen im Rahmen der gemeinsemitischen Namengebung* (Stuttgart: W. Kohlhammer, 1928), pp. 82-101. Cf. also M. Segal, "El, Elohim, and Yhwh in the Bible," *JQR*, XLVI (1955): 113. For extra-biblical evidence of proper names compounded with '$\bar{e}l$, see A. Murtonen, *A Philological and Literary Treatise on the Old Testament Divine Names* (Helsinki, 1952), Appendix, pp. 93-103; for Ugaritic personal names containing *il*, see M. Pope, *El in the Ugaritic Texts*, Supplements to Vetus Testamentum (Leiden: E. J. Brill, 1955), pp. 22-24; the word Elohim, however, does not appear in proper names; see H. P. Smith, "Theophorous Names in the Old Testament," *AJSL*, XXIV (1907): 38.

[22]W. F. Albright, *From the Stone Age to Christianity*, 2nd ed. (Baltimore: The John Hopkins Press, 1946), p. 186.

[23]M. Dahood, *Psalms I (1-50)*, The Anchor Bible (N.Y.: Doubleday, 1966), pp. 64, 177.

[24]In Balaam's oracles, Numb.24:3-9 and 24:15-19, Shadday parallels 'El in verse 4, ^{c}Elyon in verse 16. M. Noth, *Numbers: A Commentary*, OTL, trans. by James D. Martin (London: S.C.M. Press, 1968), p. 190, understands these designations of God as subjective genitives; i.e., the words of 'El which Balaam hears in an auditory revelation, the knowledge

49:25, while Shadday alone is found in Numb.24:4,16.[24] Thirty-one references to Shadday are also found in the book of Job, where the name is a conscious archaism; in addition, the title occurs in Ps.68:14 - H15; Ps.91:1 (parallel to ᶜElyon); Ruth 1:20, 21; Isa.13:6 and Ezek.1:24. In Ezek.10:5 the full title is found. The name also appears as a theophorous element in such personal names as Zurishaddai ("Shadday is a rock," Numb.1:6), and Ammishaddai ("Shadday is kinsman," Numb.1:12). Shadday is uncertain in derivation. From LXX, *pantokratōr*, and Vulgate, *omnipotens*, English translators have understood the title to mean "Almighty." The Rabbinical derivation (*shĕ*, relative particle, with *day*, "sufficient") is reflected in the *hikanos* of the second century Greek revisions of Aquila, Theodotion and Symmachus. However, the "Almighty," or the "One Who is Sufficient" are late derivations. W. F. Albright has reviewed the major etymologies which have been proposed, concluding that a North-Mesopotamian designation, *šaddâyŭ*, provides the clue to the derivation, and that the title should be understood as meaning originally, "the one of the mountain(s)."[25] The fact that El Shadday was regarded as a mountain-god provides a valuable link with the revelation to Moses which took place on "the west side of the wilderness" at "Horeb, the mountain of God" (Exod.3:1), and the further revelation when YHWH called to Moses from "the mountain," i.e. Mount Sinai (Exod.19:3)[26] That a mountain-god, El Shadday, should later be subsumed under the name of YHWH, also closely associated with a mountain, seems entirely in keeping with the Priestly tradition of Exod.6:2,3.[27] During the course of the ninth century Syrian wars with Israel, the servants of Benhadad, king of Syria, explained their defeat at the hands of the Israelites on the grounds that "Their gods are gods of the hills" (1 Kings 20:23; cf. verse 28, "YHWH is a god of the hills").[28] Elijah himself fled to "Horeb the mount of God" (1 Kings 19:8), returning to the place of revelation in order to seek YHWH.

At Beersheba, Abraham planted a tamarisk tree, and "called there on the name of YHWH, 'Ēl ᶜŌlām" (Gen.21:33). As F. M. Cross has pointed out, "the

which ᶜElyon gives, and the vision which Shadday provides (cf. the appearance of El Shadday to Abram in Gen.17:1).

[25]W. F. Albright, "The Names *Shaddai* and *Abram*," *JBL*, LIV (1935): 173-204. F. M. Cross, Jr., "Yahweh and the God of the Patriarchs," *HTR*, LV (1962): 249, writes, "it is abundantly clear that 'El is associated with the cosmic mountain, the seat of the divine council, and that an appellation, 'the One of the (cosmic) mountain,' would not be inappropriate."

[26]Although "Horeb" is the usual Elohistic and Deuteronomic designation, in the Yahwist and Priestly strata reference is made to "Mount Sinai." In all likelihood these names are synonyms. For the theories regarding the location of the mountain, see G. E. Wright, *IDB*, IV (N.Y.: Abingdon Press, 1962), pp. 376-378.

[27]Cf. H. G. May, "The Patriarchal Idea of God," *JBL*, LX (1941): 123, "The later identification of Yahweh with Shaddai is more easily understood in the light of the mountain associations of both."

[28]See E. Dhorme, "Le Nom Du Dieu d'Israel," *RHR*, CXLI (1952): 7.

formula *'ēl* *ʿôlām* is ambiguous, capable of being read 'the god *ʿôlām'* or *''El* the ancient one.'"[29] Alternatively, the title may be translated "God of the world."[30] *ʿÔlām* has the general sense of "long duration," "antiquity," and is used not in the sense of timelessness, but rather of time extending backward and forward indefinitely. In all likelihood, the reference is to a local god, worshipped by the Canaanites in Beersheba, and later identified with YHWH. Such passages as Jer.10:10, *melekh* *ʿôlām*, "the everlasting king": Isa.40:28, *ʾelōhē* *ʿôlām*, "the everlasting God" (cf. ' *ʾelōhē qedem* in Deut.33:27) and Ps.90:1-2, indicate how this idea of duration was applied to YHWH.

Similar observations may be made regarding the names *El Rᵒ ʾî* (Gen.16:13) and *El Bethel* (Gen.31:13; cf.35:7). *El Rᵒ ʾî*, "God of Seeing," is the name given by Hagar to the deity at the spring Beer-lahai-roi, possibly intended as a *double entendre* ("see" and "provide"), as in the case of the place named by Abraham, *"YHWH yireh"* (Gen.22:14). Once again, the Yahwist firmly makes the identification with YHWH in Gen.16:13a. In the MT of Gen.31:13, the definite article appears, *ha'ēl bethel*, which would require the translation, "the God, Bethel," rather than "the God of Bethel." The LXX reads, "I am the god who appeared to you in the place of God." The definite article does not appear in Gen.35:7, and the LXX, Vulgate and Syriac versions omit the word *'ēl* in this passage. Bethel as the name of a deity is referred to in the Ras Shamra texts and in the Elephantine papyri, and could be so interpreted in Amos 5:5, although in this latter case the context suggests a place name rather than the name of a deity. It is not impossible that an original reference to a God, Bethel, a god in the Canaanite pantheon, is preserved here, but as Speiser indicates, the text is uncertain and missing words supplied by the versions permit a reconstruction of the text.[31]

The name *'El-ʾelōhē-yisrāēl* occurs in Gen.33:20 in connection with the altar erected by Jacob at Shechem. This name, preserved in the Elohistic stratum, doubtless reflects the covenant tradition associated with Shechem. The Canaanite background of Shechem is to be seen in the reference to Baal-berith, "Baal of the Covenant" (Judges 8:33,9:4), which becomes El-b̊ rith in Judges 9:4b. In the light of Josh.24, the account of the covenant at Shechem, and Josh.8:30, we can discern the stages by which YHWH became the God of the covenant *par excellence*, the God of Israel, replacing all other deities.[32]

[29]F. M. Cross, Jr., *op. cit.,* p. 235. See also F. M. Cross, *Canaanite Myth and Hebrew Epic* (Cambridge, Mass: Harvard University Press, 1973), pp. 47-49.

[30]E. Dhorme, *op. cit.,* p. 6. F. M. Cross, however, denies that the proper name El is in construct relationship to the noun *'ôlām, Canaanite Myth and Hebrew Epic* (Cambridge, Mass.: Harvard University Press, 1973), p. 49.

[31]E. A. Speiser, *Genesis,* The Anchor Bible (N.Y.: Doubleday, 1964), p. 244.

[32]Cf. G. E. Wright, *Shechem* (N.Y.: McGraw-Hill Book Company, 1965), ch. 8, espec., p. 136. For a somewhat similar interpretation, see also E. Nielsen, *Shechem: A Traditio-Historical Investigation* (Copenhagen: G.E.C. Gad, 1959), espec. pp. 133-134.

In some respects, the most interesting of the El epithets in the book of Genesis is El ^{c}Elyon (Gen.14:18, 19, 20, 22). Whereas El ^{c}Olam is associated with Beersheba, El Bethel with Bethel, and El 'Elohe-Yisrael with Shechem, El ^{c}Elyon is associated with Jerusalem. The full name El ^{c}Elyon occurs also in Ps.78:35: YHWH ^{c}Elyon is found in Ps.7:17 - H18 and in Ps.47:3 Elohim ^{c}Elyon occurs in Ps.57:2 - H3 and in Ps.78:56. ^{c}Elyon alone as a name for God ("Most High") occurs in several poetic passages, such as Deut.32:8, Numb.24:16, 2 Sam.22:14, clearly as a synonym for YHWH. In the late post-exilic period, the name came into prominence again, especially in the book of Daniel (e.g., Dan.3:26, Aram. ^{ʾe}lāhā illīyaʾ, cf. 3:32A, 4:21A, 5:18A, etc.) and in the apocrypha (e.g. 50 times in Ben Sira) and Pseudepigrapha, *hypsistos* (1 Esdras 2:3, 6:31, 8:19, etc.).

Gen.14 does not correspond to any of the usual Pentateuchal-sources, yet contains very ancient material.[33] The aetiological narrative in which Abram receives a blessing from Melchizedek, king of Salem, after defeating Chedor-laomer and his allies (Gen.14:17-24) contains four references to El ^{c}Elyon (verses 18, 19, 20, 22).[34] Melchizedek is designated as the priest of El ^{c}Elyon. The Canaanite background is of special interest. G. Levi Della Vida claims that El ^{c}Elyon corresponds to no actual deity in the Canaanite pantheon, but has been artificially set up through the combination of El, the Lord of Earth, with ^{c}Elyon, the Lord of Heaven, and is, therefore, "the result of theological specula-tion."[35] The two names are associated in the eighth century Aramaic Sefire inscription.[36] F. M. Cross regards El as exclusively the Creator God of the Canaanites, to whom the epithet ^{c}Elyon has been conjoined; the two names may be regarded either as a double name of a single god, or, alternatively, ^{c}Elyon may be taken as an early epithet of El, "split apart in a separate cult and hence taken as an independent deity."[37] In Gen.14:19, El ^{c}Elyon is described as "maker (*qōnēh*) of heaven and earth." Although G. Della Vida understands the

---

[33] G. von Rad, *Genesis: A Commentary*, OTL, trans. by John H. Marks (London: S.C.M. Press Ltd., 1961), pp. 170-176. For recent important contributions to the study of Gen.14, see J. A. Emerton, "Some False Clues in the Study of Genesis XIV," *VT*, XXI (1971): 24-47; "The Riddle of Genesis XIV," *VT*, (1971): 403-439; J. G. Gammie, "Loci of the Melchizedek Tradition of Genesis 14: 18-20," *JBL*, XC (1971): 386-396; Werner Schatz, *Genesis 14:Eine Untersuchung* (Bern: Herbert Lang, 1972).

[34] The names El and ^{c}Elyon are also found in parallelism in Balaam's oracle, Numb.24:16.

[35] G. Levi Della Vida, "El ^{c}Elyon in Genesis 14:18-20," *JBL*, LXIII (1944): 9. M. H. Pope considers El ^{c}Elyon to represent a fusion of the gods of earth and of heaven, *op. cit.*, p. 15, n. 84; and p. 27, "El's abode, as described in the Ugaritic texts, is clearly subter-ranean."

[36] G. Levi Della Vida, *op. cit.*, p. 3. See J. A. Fitzmyer, *The Aramaic Inscriptions of Sefire* (Rome: The Pontifical Biblical Institute, 1967).

[37] F. M. Cross, *Canaanite Myth and Hebrew Epic* (Cambridge, Mass.: Harvard University Press, 1973), p. 51.

participle, *qōnēh*, as expressing the idea of lordship rather than creation (i.e., the original sense of the root *qānāh* is "to purchase," then, "to possess"), Loren Fisher has made a careful examination of the passage and has come to the conclusion that the idea "create," "beget," is implicit in the verb, and that El *c*Elyon is to be understood as the parent of all the gods of heaven and earth.[38]

The MT of Gen.14:22, which contains Abram's oath, identifies YHWH with El *c*Elyon. The LXX and Syriac versions and 1Q Gen. Apocryphon omit the Tetragrammaton, possibly, as G. von Rad suggests,[39] because such a tolerant attitude towards a Canaanite cult seemed offensive from a later perspective. Yet, it may well be that H. H. Rowley is on the right track in interpreting the passage in the light of developments at the time that David captured Jerusalem, the Jebusite stronghold, and made this city his political and religious capital.[40] The Jebusites were not put to the sword or expelled from the city (2 Sam. 24:18-25). This suggests that some accommodation between the Israelites and the Canaanites was made. If this involved Jebusite acceptance of YHWH, and if indeed, as Rowley believes, Zadok was the priest of Jerusalem in pre-Davidic days, he was then given a place of priestly leadership, serving jointly with Abiathar.[41] The aetiological narrative in Gen.14:17-24, in which Abram is blessed by Melchizedek, priest of El *c*Elyon, and pays tithes to him, provides a recognition of the existing Jebusite priesthood in Jerusalem prior to David's time, and legitimates that priesthood, together with its contemporary representative, Zadok. The dangers of syncretism were doubtless inherent in the bold action of David, especially since Zadok, in his support of Solomon, later became the leading priestly figure, when Abiathar was banished to Anathoth (1 Kings 2:26, 27, 35). Canaanite features in Solomon's temple,[42] indicate that some

[38]G. Levi Della Vida, *op. cit.*, p. 1; L. Fisher, "Abraham and His Priest-King," *JBL*, LXXXI (1962): 264-270, espec. pp. 266-267. Cf. P. Humbert, "Qânâ en hébreu biblique" in *Festschrift Alfred Bertholet* (Tübingen: J.C.B. Mohr, 1950), pp. 259-266; Frank Moore Cross, Jr., "Yahweh and the God of the Patriarchs," *HTR*, LV (1962): 241, 244; M. H. Pope, *op. cit.*, pp. 51-54; R. B. Y. Scott, *Proverbs, Ecclesiastes*, The Anchor Bible (N.Y.: Doubleday, 1965), p. 71.

[39]G. von Rad, *Genesis: A Commentary*, p. 175.

[40]H. H. Rowley, "Melchizedek and Zadok (Gen. 14 and Ps. 110)," in *Festschrift Alfred Bertholet*, ed. W. Baumgartner, O. Eissfeldt, K. Elliger, and L. Rost (Tübingen: J.C.B. Mohr, 1950), pp. 461-472.

[41]*Ibid.*, p. 466. For a discussion of various views regarding Zadok's origins, see Aelred Cody, *A History of the Old Testament Priesthood*, Analecta Biblica No. 35 (Rome: Pontifical Biblical Institute, 1969), pp. 88-93, in which Rowley's view is sympathetically regarded. The Chronicler gives Zadok a Levitical pedigree (1 Chron.6:1-8). In all probability, this is based on 2 Sam.8:17, a verse which seems to be in disorder; see R. de Vaux, *Ancient Israel*, trans. by John McHugh (London: Darton, Longman & Todd, 1961), p. 373.

[42]W. F. Albright, *Archaeology and the Religion of Israel*, 2nd ed. (Baltimore: The John Hopkins Press, 1946), pp. 147, 152; R. E. Clements, *God and Temple* (Oxford: Blackwell, 1965), ch. 5; H. H. Rowley, *Worship in Ancient Israel* (London: S.P.C.K., 1967), pp. 79ff.

measure of syncretism did indeed take place. However, what is significant for the purpose of this study is the fact that the original Canaanite El epithets were subsumed under the name of Israel's deity, YHWH,[43] although traces of the earlier background (e.g., such a liturgical formula as *qōnē shāmayim wāʾārets*; Gen.14:19, 22) remain in the patriarchal narratives.

Albrecht Alt, in *Der Gott der Väter*, postulates three distinct *numina*, the God of Abraham, the Fear of Isaac and the Mighty One of Jacob, but claims that these eventually became fused into one figure, the God of the Fathers.[44] The God of the Fathers is identified with YHWH in Exod.3:15, "YHWH, the God of your fathers, the God of Abraham, the God of Isaac, and the God of Jacob." According to F. M. Cross, Jr., "The gods of the Fathers were *paidagōgoi* to the great god Yahweh who later took their place."[45] Alt claims that the genitive phrase, "the God of X" means "the God worshipped by X"; in fact, an even more precise original meaning attaches to the phrase, i.e., "the God first worshipped by X," the founder of the particular cult.[46] In Alt's view, the important difference between this concept of the patriarchal deities and the *ʾelīm*, who are associated with particular shrines, is that the gods of the Fathers are patrons of a social group, the clan. Yet even those Canaanite *ʾelīm* who were associated with a specific geographical location were often cosmic deities in the Canaanite pantheon, and El, in particular, was worshipped at shrines such as Beersheba, Shechem, and Jerusalem, where tradition recalled a local manifestation.

H. G. May finds a basic confusion here, and seeks to resolve the problem by pointing out that the formula, "the God of your (their) fathers" is rare in early sources (such as Exod.3:13,15,16; 4,5), although it is frequently found in Deuteronomic passages (Deut.1:11, 21; 6:3; 12:1; 26:7; 27:3; Judg.2:12; 2 Kings 21:22, etc.) and is even more common in the work of the Chronicler (e.g., 1 Chron. 12:17; 2 Chron.11:16; 13:18; 17:4; Ezra 7:27; 8:28; 10:11, etc.).[47] The phrase is to be regarded as secondary in character. This is to be seen in view of the fact that in thirty-four of the forty-one occurrences, "the God of your (their, etc.) fathers," the name YHWH is included at the beginning of the formula.[48] The more original formula is "the God of your (my) father" (Gen. 26:24; 31:5,29,42; 32:9; 43:23; 46:1,3; 49:25; 50:17; Exod. 3:6; 15:2; 18:4).

---

[43]Note the statement of M. Pope, *op. cit.*, p. 104. "The El of the patriarchs was the god at the height of his power and prestige and this was the god with whom YHWH was identified."

[44]A. Alt, *Essays on Old Testament History and Religion*, trans. by R. A. Wilson (Oxford: Blackwell, 1966), pp. 54, 55.

[45]F. M. Cross, Jr., *op. cit.*, p. 228.

[46]A. Alt, *op. cit.*, p. 41.

[47]H. G. May, *op. cit., JBL*, LX (1941): 124, n. 32.

[48]H. G. May, "The God of My Fathers—A Study of Patriarchal Religion," *JBR*, IX (1941): 155.

The name YHWH does not precede this formula. The conclusion which H. G. May draws from this evidence is that the formula in the singular points not at all to an ancestral or clan deity, but rather to the god worshipped by the immediate parent of the patriarch or person mentioned in the narrative.

J. P. Hyatt has studied the formula as used in the book of Exodus, and has come to the conclusion that the title "ought to be taken seriously as part of the living vocabulary of Moses' religion as well as of patriarchal religion."[49] There can be little doubt that the MT of Exod.3:6 is correct in reading the formula in the singular.[50] The Samaritan text reads the plural, "fathers," but this would appear to be under the influence of Exod.3:15. The phrase in the singular also occurs in Exod.15:2, in the Song of Moses after the crossing of the Sea of Reeds. This, too, Hyatt regards as a genuine reminiscence of the Mosaic age.[51] The third reference is found in Exod.18:4, in connection with the name of Moses' second child, Eliezer. Hyatt suggests that the original name of this son may have been "El-abi-ezer" (hence, "the God of my father was my help"), later abbreviated to Eliezer, but containing a genuine recollection of the formula, "the god of my father."[52] According to this view, the very specific reference to the god of Moses' father points to an ancestor of Moses himself.[53] Exodus 3 is to be understood in the light of this background. YHWH, who had revealed himself to Moses' ancestor, revealed himself anew to Moses at the burning bush, and since his fellow Hebrews were already acquainted with the name of the deity venerated by Moses' own clan, they were ready to follow his leadership. As indicated in the previous chapter, the Kenite hypothesis offers an alternative view, although this by no means precludes the possibility that the name YHWH was known to some of the Israelites in Egypt.[54]

[49] J. Philip Hyatt, "Yahweh as 'The God of My Father.'" *VT*, V (1955): 133.

[50] Julian Morgenstern's view, "The Elohist Narrative in Exodus 3:1-15," *AJSL*, XXXVII (1920-21): 248, that the text read originally, "your father-in-law" (referring to Jethro) arises from his conviction regarding the Kenite hypothesis, but overlooks the formulaic nature of the phrase as it stands in MT.

[51] J. P. Hyatt, *op. cit.*, p. 134.

[52] *Ibid.*, p. 135.

[53] As against Hyatt's literal understanding of the phrase, "the god of my father," H. G. May, *JBR*, IX (1941): 157, asserts, "the formula is an archaism, and not to be taken literally, but is interpreted with much the same meaning which was later to characterize the exilic and post-exilic formula."

[54] H. H. Rowley, *From Joseph to Joshua*, Schweich Lectures, 1948 (London: Oxford Univ. Press, 1950), p. 149, "So far as the tribes that were led by Moses are concerned, it is scarcely to be doubted that he introduced them to the worship of Yahweh as their God. It is true that by syncretism he identified Yahweh with the God their fathers had worshipped, but in so doing he made it clear that Yahweh was a new name by which they were to worship their God. This does not mean that it was a brand-new name for God, first heard on the lips of Moses. The name may not even have been an unknown name to the Israelites in Egypt, though it was not the name they had used hitherto for their own God."

Once again, we must face the problem of the antiquity of the Tetragrammaton. The earliest extra-biblical attestation to the full form of the Tetragrammaton is found in the ninth century Moabite stone, line 18, in which Mesha, king of Moab, boasts that in carrying out the rite of ḥerem against Nebo, "I took from there the vessels of YHWH and dragged them before Chemosh," the Moabite deity.[55] The Tetragrammaton also appears twelve times in the Lachish ostraca, ca. 589 B.C.[56] The extra-biblical evidence from the 9th to the 2nd century B.C. has been summarized by G. R. Driver.[57] Is it possible to go back to an earlier period for evidence of a component of the Tetragrammaton in theophorous names? Roland de Vaux has reviewed the claims that have been made regarding Babylon, Ugaritic, Amorite and Egyptian names, but finds no direct evidence of the use of the divine name, YHWH.[58] In his view, "it is possible—it is even likely, given its archaic form—that the divine name *Yhwh* existed outside Israel before Moses, but we have as yet no conclusive proof of this."[59] *Yaum* in the ancient Babylonian name *Yaum-ilum* is not to be regarded as a reference to YHWH, but is an Akkadian first person possessive pronoun, so that the name means, "Mine is god," i.e., "I have a [protecting] deity."[60] Although Virolleaud and Dussaud have claimed that *yw* in the Ras Shamra tablets is to be identified with YHWH, John Gray and others have found the claim unconvincing.[61] Amorite personal names, in which *ya-ah-wi* (or the orthographic variant, *ya-wi*) appears as an

[55]E. Ullendorf, "The Moabite Stone," in *Documents From Old Testament Times*, ed. D. Winton Thomas (London: Thomas Nelson and Sons Ltd., 1958), pp. 195-198; see also W. F. Albright, "The Moabite Stone" in *Ancient Near Eastern Texts*, ed. James B. Pritchard (Princeton, N.J.: Princeton Univ. Press, 2nd ed., 1955), p. 320.

[56]Lachish, 2:2, 2:5, 3:3, 3:9, 4:1, 5:1, 5:7, 6:1, 6:12, 8:1, 9:1, 21:3. See D. Winton Thomas, "Letters from Lachish" in *Documents From Old Testament Times*, ed. D. W. Thomas (London: Nelson, 1958), pp. 212-217, espec. the bibliography on p. 217. D. W. Thomas states, p. 214, "The free use of the Tetragrammaton in a military correspondence is highly noteworthy."

[57]G. R. Driver, "The original form of the name, 'Yahweh': evidence and conclusions," *ZAW*, XLVI (1928): 7-25.

[58]R. de Vaux, "The Revelation of the Divine Name YHWH" in *Proclamation and Presence*, ed. by John I. Durham and J. Roy Porter (London: S.C.M. Press, Ltd., 1970), pp. 48-75.

[59]*Ibid.*, p. 56. Cf. C. F. Whitley, *The Genius of Ancient Israel* (Amsterdam: Philo Press, 1969), p. 18.

[60]See R. de Vaux, *op. cit.*, p. 52; W. F. Albright, "The Name Yahweh," *JBL*, XLII (1924): 370; *From the Stone Age to Christianity*, 2nd ed. (Baltimore: The Johns Hopkins Press, 1946), p. 198.

[61]See Anat X.IV. J. Gray, "The God YW in the Religion pf Canaan," *JNES*, XII (1953): 278-283; H. H. Rowley, *From Joseph to Joshua*, Schweich Lectures, 1948 (London: Oxford Univ. Press, 1950), p. 148. R. de Vaux, "Les textes de Ras Shamra et l'ancien Testament," *RB*, XLVI (1937): 553, states that the evidence is insufficient to establish the presence of a God *Yaw* in the pantheon of Ugarit. W. F. Albright, *From the Stone Age to Christianity*, p. 197, prefers to read *yr*, "offspring," rather than *yw*, as more suitable to the context, but

element, followed by a divine name, could point to the root *hwy*, "to live," or
hwy, "to oe."[62] The reference cannot be to YHWH,[63] although the verbal form
may offer some support for the claim that the Tetragrammaton is also a verbal
form, in this case a causative (*hiph*[c]*il*) imperfect of the verb "to be," a view that
will be examined subsequently in the following chapter. An Egyptian list of
South-Palestinian place-names, *ca.* 1300 B.C., contains a name of a region or a
place (or ethnic group?) which is very similar, and possibly identical, to the
Tetragrammaton.[64]

The extra-biblical evidence has so far yielded no assured results with regard
to the early (pre-Mosaic) use of the Tetragrammaton. The biblical evidence,
especially the appearance of the name in early poems, such as the Song of
Miriam (Exod.15:21) and the Song of Moses (Exod.15:1-18), nevertheless leads
W. F. Albright to an important conclusion, "The preservation of the name as the
indicative verbal element in ancient liturgical formulas is so archaic and was so
little understood in later times, that it must go back to extremely early
times."[65] G. Quell argues from Hosea 12:9 ("I am YHWH your God from the
land of Egypt," cf. 13:4) and the P tradition in Exod. 6:3, that no serious
question can be raised concerning the tradition that Moses founded the Yahweh
religion, but from Gen.4:26 and the Yahwist tradition he sees an indication,
"that the name of God was already present and had some location in primitive

see the critique offered by T. J. Meek, *Hebrew Origins*, 2nd ed. (Univ. of Toronto Press,
1950), p. 105, n. 60. A. Murtonen, "The Appearance of the name YHWH outside Israel,"
Studia Orientalia, XVI:3 (Helsinki: 1951), p. 6, also argues against Albright's reluctance to
read *yw*, and indeed concludes that a deity by this name was included in the Ugaritic
pantheon.

[62]H. B. Huffmon, *Amorite Personal Names in the Mari Texts: A Structural and Lexical
Study* (Baltimore: The Johns Hopkins Press, 1965), p. 72.

[63]R. de Vaux, "The Revelation of the Divine Name YHWH," in *Proclamation and
Presence*, ed. by John I. Durham and J. Roy Porter (London: S.C.M. Press Ltd., 1970), pp.
48-75. W. F. Albright, *Yahweh and the Gods of Canaan* (London: The Athlone Press, 1968),
pp. 148-49, finds in the 'Amorite' personal name *Yahwī-il an indication that "the appellation is pre-Mosaic."* Note, however, the *caveat* of Frank Moore Cross, that Amorite *yahwi*
and *yahū* must not be regarded as divine epithets, *Canaanite Myth and Hebrew Epic* (Cambridge, Mass.: Harvard Univ. Press, 1973), p. 62, n. 64.

[64]B. Grdseloff, "Edom, d'après les sources égyptiennes," *Bulletin des études his-
toriques juives*, No. 1 (1946): 69-99. See H. H. Rowley, *op. cit.*, p. 153; R. de Vaux, *op.
cit.*, pp. 55-56. An Egyptian counterpart to Exod. 3:14 has also been recognized by A. Alt,
"Ein Ägyptisches Gegenstück zu Ex.3:14," *ZAW* LVIII (1940): pp. 159-160, in the instructions of Pharaoh Achthoes to his son Merikare (third millenium B.C.). No dependence is
suggested, but the idiom in each case implies that "being" (*Wesen*) denotes "power" (*Kraft*).
Raphael Giveon, "Toponymes Ouest-Asiatiques à Soleb," *VT*, XIV (1964): 245, has identified *yh* as a toponym in column IV of the Temple of Amon at Soleb, in a 14th cent.
inscription.

[65]W. F. Albright, *Yahweh and the Gods of Canaan* (London: The Athlone Press, 1968),
p. 149.

history before Moses introduced it to the children of Israel."[66] This, indeed, has been one of the considerations which lie behind the Kenite hypothesis.

On the question of origins, how is the formula, "the god of my (your) father," to be understood? In the context of both the patriarchal narratives and the book of Exodus, the formula serves as a means of expressing continuity with the past and indeed becomes an almost stereotyped formula for the god of the covenant.[67] The clue to the nature of patriarchal religion is to be found in the references to El Shadday, El ᶜOlam and El ᶜElyon, in which El is worshipped in various manifestations. The Deuteronomist and the Chronicler use the formula, "the god of your (their) fathers" as a comprehensive term, and unite very closely the religion of the patriarchs with that of Moses and later times by using as a preface, YHWH, in order to establish the fact that, according to their understanding, the revelation to Moses was a fuller revelation of the God who had been directing Israel's history from patriarchal times. Exod.3:15 provides the essential connecting link. For an appreciation of the unique features which characterize the fuller revelation to which Exodus 3 bears witness, we turn in the following chapter to undertake a careful analysis of this key passage.

---

[66]G. Quell, "Der alttestamentliche Gottesname," in article on *kyrios, TWNT,* III, ed. G. Kittel (Stuttgart, W. Kohlhammer, 1938), p. 1062. See Eng. trans. by G. W. Bromiley, *Theological Dictionary of the New Testament,* III (Grand Rapids, Michigan: Wm. B. Eerdmans Publishing Company, 1965), p. 1064.

[67]J. C. Rylaarsdam, "The Book of Exodus," *IB,* I, (N.Y.: Abingdon Press, 1952), p. 872, "This formula draws together the ethnic and religious past of the Hebrews and their existence as the Israel of the exodus covenant." Cf. also W. F. Albright, *Yahweh and the Gods of Canaan* (London: The Athlone Press, 1968), p. 146, "Belief in the Covenant and the God of the Fathers are undoubtedly the two most important elements taken by Moses from Patriarchal tradition."

IV

THE GOD OF MOSES

Half a century ago, Julian Morgenstern undertook an analysis of Exodus 3, in which he first of all compared the views of ten biblical scholars regarding the composition of the chapter.[1] He claims that the Elohist narrative consists of verses 1,4b,6,9-15, in which a Yahwist insertion has been made by the redactor, consisting of verses 2-4a, 7-8, 16-22. Indications of Elohistic authorship are to be found in the use of the name Elohim (equated with YHWH in verse 15, where the Tetragrammaton is for the first time introduced to the E source), the use of the names Jethro and Horeb, as well as the repetition of the name Moses in verse 4b (cf. "Abraham, Abraham!" Gen. 22:11; "Jacob, Jacob," Gen. 46:2; both E passages). The Yahwist uses the characteristic phrase *mal'akh YHWH* in verse 2, which, together with verse 8, "I have come down to deliver them," implies a particular theophany involving a descent from his heavenly abode. On the other hand, the Elohist regards God as dwelling permanently in the bush (Exod. 3:4; cf. Deut. 33:16, "the dweller in the bush"). In these distinctions, a theology of transcendence and a theology of immanence are brought together.

Morgenstern's analysis has not found universal acceptance,[2] but in essentials represents a position held by subsequent scholars.[3] The problem area is to be found in Exod. 3:13-15, where Moses asks (verse 13), "If I come to the people of Israel and say to them, 'The God of your fathers has sent me to you,' and they ask me, 'What is his name?' what shall I say to them?" In verses 14a, 14b and 15 no less than three answers are given. The repetition of the phrase, "Say this to the people of Israel" (14b, 15) was regarded by Elias Auerbach as evi-

---

[1]Julian Morgenstern, "The Elohist Narrative in Exodus 3:1-15," *AJSL*, XXXVII (1920-21): 242-262.

[2]E.g., M. Buber, *Moses*, Harper Torchbook ed. (N.Y.: Harper, 1958), p. 39, "All that is needed is to remove a few additions, and there appears before us a homogeneous picture," Cf. also S. Mowinckel, "The Name of the God of Moses," *HUCA*, XXXII (1961): 122, "As I no longer believe in the theory of a coherent literary 'source' E, I neither see any cogent or convincing reasons for a source analysis of the pericope Exod.3-4. In all essentials it belongs tto J, containing, however, secondary elements."

[3]E.g., E. Auerbach, *Moses* (Amsterdam: G. J. A. Ruys, 1953), pp. 31-33; Immanuel Lewy, "The Beginnings of the Worship of Yahweh: Conflicting Biblical Views," *VT*, VI (1956): 432-33; M. Noth, *Exodus: A Commentary*, OTL, trans. by J. S. Bowden (London: S.C.M. Press Ltd., 1962), p. 34; G. Henton Davies, *Exodus*, Torch Bible Commentaries (London: S.C.M. Press, Ltd., 1967), p. 68; J. Kenneth Kuntz, *The Self-Revelation of God* (Philadelphia: The Westminster Press, 1967), p. 139, n.10, states, "The disentanglement of J and E cannot be accomplished with complete confidence. It is widely held, however, that most of the initial phrases of the theophany belong to the Yahwist."

dence for different sources.[4] The point of view which to me seems most convincing is to regard verse 15 as the original answer to the question, containing the Tetragrammaton, although the association with the God of the fathers may well be secondary. The phrase *'ehyeh ʾᵃsher 'ehyeh* in 3:14 is not so much the revelation of a name as a subsequent attempt to explain the meaning of the name, through an etymological explanation. This runs counter to the view of M. Noth, who maintains[5] that verse 14a contains the giving of the name *'ehyeh ʾᵃsher 'ehyeh*, verse 14b uses the verbal form *'ehyeh* alone as a catchword, and verse 15 uses the Tetragrammaton, making the transition to the third person, for which the use of the first person had already supplied an unmistakable hint to the Israelite ear. The opposite view seems more probable, namely that verse 15a provides the Elohist with the opportunity to introduce the Tetragrammaton as the divine name given to Moses, with the added statement (verse 15b), 'this is my name for ever, and thus I am to be remembered throughout all generations." The Tetragrammaton, YHWH, is enigmatic, however. Verse 14a is intended to give an interpretation of the name; verse 14b supplies a connecting link with verse 15.[6]

Numerous attempts have been made to find a satisfactory etymological origin for the Tetragrammaton, usually from roots not found in Hebrew at all.[7] From the outset, an etymological approach has limitations. T. J. Meek makes the cautionary observation that, "etymology alone is rarely a safe guide to the meaning of a word and must always be checked by its usage."[8] Likewise, W. F. Albright has issued a warning, "Words change their meaning through use to such

---

[4]E. Auerbach, *op. cit.*, p. 37.

[5]M. Noth, *op. cit.*, p. 43.

[6]Some support for this view is found in Oskar Grether's contention that the influence of Exod.3:14 on other passages in the Old Testament is not readily discernible. See *Name und Wort Gottes im Alten Testament*, BZAW, LXIV (Giessen, 1934): 8-10, in which he argues against J. Hehn, *Die biblische und babylonische Gottesidee* (1913), who had sought to demonstrate otherwise. Note also that W. R. Arnold in "The Divine Name in Exodus iii 14," *JBL*, XXIV (1905): 107-165, claimed that verse 14 is much later than verse 15, with 14a interpolated as a gloss on 14b. Arnold is emphatic, p. 109, that, "Exodus 3:14 affords no data for the scientific determination of the name Jahweh." B. S. Childs, however, cautions against a literary solution in isolation from the history of the ttradition of the text, *The Book of Exodus*, OTL (Philadelphia: The Westminster Press, 1974), p. 62. He regards Exod.3:14 as supplying an explanation of the significance of the name, rather than the name itself. This Elohist tradition has been influenced by the later question of the true and false prophet, yet early in Israel's history, prophesying in the name YHWH was the test for being a true messenger. In moving from the oral to the literary level, verse 14a is a parallel to verse 15, while verse 15b provides a literary bridge back to verse 13 (*ibid.*, pp. 68-70).

[7]A. Murtonen, *A Philological and Literary Treatise on the Old Testament Divine Names* (Helsinki, 1952), pp. 61-67, reviews many of the suggested etymologies and exposes their weaknesses.

[8]T. J. Meek, *op. cit.*, p. 150, n. 7.

an extent that the etymological method of fixing significance is only employed as a last resort, where other evidence is inadequate."[9]

Several derivations from Arabic roots have been proposed. Julius Wellhausen sought to derive the Tetragrammaton from the root *hwy*, "to blow," claiming that YHWH was originally a storm-god.[10] H. Holzinger postulated a derivation from the root *hww*, "to fall," in a causative sense; i.e., "the one who destroys."[11] H. Torczyner looked to a reduplicated root, *whwh*, "to roar"; YHWH is "the one who roars," (i.e., in the thunder).[12] J. A. Montgomery takes the root to be *hwh*, "to befall"; YHWH is "The Incident One," who appears how and when he will.[13] G. A. Barton suggested a causative from another Arabic root, *hwy*, "he who causes to love passionately."[14] This derivation has been taken up by S. D. Goitein, who regards the form as *qal* rather than *hiph^c il* and views the divine name as meaning, "The Passionate."[15] Goitein's arguments are buttressed

---

[9]W. F. Albright, *From the Stone Age to Christianity* 2nd ed. (Baltimore: The Johns Hopkins Press, 1946), p. 18. The values and limitations of etymological study are set forth by J. Barr, *Comparative Philology and the Text of the Old Testament* (Oxford: Clarendon Press, 1968); see espec. ch. XII.

[10]J. Wellhausen, *Israelitische und judische Geschichte*. 3rd ed. (Berlin: 1897), p. 25, n. 1. T. J. Meek, *Hebrew Origins*, 2nd ed. (University of Toronto Press, 1950), p. 99, states that the derivation is uncertain, but that numerous references in the Old Testament point to the fact that originally YHWH was a storm-god, and draws attention, p. 101, to Ps.68:1; Isa. 19:1, where YHWH is known as "The Rider on the Clouds" (cf. the storm-god Baal in the Ras Shamra texts). See also W. H. Ward, "The Origin of the Worship of Yahwe," *AJSL*, XXV (1925): 175-187, espec. p. 183; J. Hempel, 'Gott und Mensch im Alten Testament," *BWANT*, III: 2 (Stuttgart: 1926, 2nd ed., 1936), pp. 27f and 38f.

[11]H. Holzinger, *Einleitung in den Hexateuch* (Leipzig: 1893), p. 204, perhaps following W. Robertson Smith, *The Old Testament in the Jewish Church* (N.Y.: D. Appleton and Company, 1881), p. 423, who understands that a storm-god is indicated, one who causes rain or lightning to fall.

[12]H. Torczyner, *Die Bundeslade und die Anfänge der Religion Israels* (Berlin: 1922), pp. 73ff. W. F. Albright, "The Name Yahweh," *JBL*, XLII (1924): 370, criticizes this view ·on the grounds that Torczyner has not explained the absence of a *mappiq* in the final *He*.

[13]J. A. Montgomery, "Some Hebrew Etymologies," *JQR*, XXV (1934-35): 268-69. Montgomery draws attention to Exod. 4:24, in which the first word *way^e hi* is itself a play upon the divine name, and comments, p. 269, "This conception of the 'casual,' demonic deity, which in one line of development might have resulted in a god like the Greek Pan, lies at the basis of the higher theology of the God of absolute will and self-determination. What is chance to man, *incidit, accidit* is revelation of the holy, mysterious purpose of the deity." See also his *Arabia and the Bible* (Philadelphia: Univ. of Pennsylvania Press, 1934), p. 169. Montgomery later abandoned this view, postulating that the divine name is based on the pronoun *hû*', "verbalized with the invention of a verbal root, *hwy*; see "The Hebrew Divine Name and the Personal Pronoun Hu," *JBL*, LXIII (1944): 161-163.

[14]G. A. Barton, *Semitic and Hamitic Origins, Social and Religious* (Philadelphia: Univ. of Pennsylvania Press, 1934), p. 338. W. R. W. Gardner, "The Name 'Yahweh,'" *Expository Times,* XX (1908-0): 91-92, had proposed a similar derivation.

[15]S. D. Goitein, "YHWH the Passionate: The Monotheistic Meaning and Origin of the Name YHWH," *VT*, VI (1956): 1-9.

by appeal to the Qoran (e.g., iv 135, xxv 43), where the verb *hwy* is used in the sense of passionate love. He appeals also to the Hebrew noun *hawwāh* (e.g., Micah 7:3, Prov. 10:3), where, however, the sense is pejorative. The attempts to derive the Tetragrammaton from an Arabic root or some other root have been singularly unsuccessful. We appear to be moving in a realm of conjecture and speculation.

Norman Walker has proposed an Egyptian origin for the Tetragrammaton, suggesting that the first half of the divine name, YH, comes from the Egyptian, *I-Ḥ*, "Moon," and the second half, WH, from the Egyptian epithet, "one" (cf. Ikhnaten's naming of the sun-disc "the God-One").[16] Walker surmised that "whether through Semitic or Egyptian, the Kenite '*Yah*' became 'Yah-weh' meaning 'Yah-One,' with tacit monotheistic implication."[17] Walker's view corresponds in some respects to the Kenite hypothesis. He believes that the Midianite Jethro introduced his son-in-law, Moses, to a primitive monotheism of the Moon-god, under the name *YAH-WEH*. This name was a modification of the original Egyptian *YAH-WE*, "Moon-One," the meaning of which was transformed by Moses by a new association with the Hebrew verb, "to be." One difficulty with this thesis is the transition from an original Heth to He as the second letter of the Tetragrammaton.

Friedrich Delitzsch made the proposal that the divine name (*Yah*) was borrowed from Babylonia, derived from the Akkadian *ia-u*, meaning "exalted," "noble."[18] John Allegro has recently sought a Sumerian background in his claim that YHWH is derived from *IA-U*, meaning "juice of fertility," "seed of life," "spermatozoa"; the same linguistic background lies behind the name of the Greek God Zeus.[19] Enno Littmann has also proposed that there is a connection

[16]N. Walker, "Yahwism and the Divine Name 'Yhwh,'" *ZAW* LXX (1958): 262-265; *The Tetragrammaton* (West Ewell, England, 1948), espec. pp. 10-14. A critique of this view is offered by J. Vergote, "Une théorie sur l'origine égyptienne du nom de Yahweh," *Ephemerides Theologicae Lovanienses*, XXXIX (1963): 447-452.

[17]N. Walker, *op. cit.*, p. 264. For a general critique of theories of Egyptian origin, see H. H. Spoer, "The Origin and Interpretation of the Tetragrammaton," *AJSL*, XVIII (1901): 12-13. Sigmund Freud, in *Moses and Monotheism*, trans. by Katherine Jones (N.Y.: Vintage Books, 1939) regarded Moses himself as an Egyptian, representative of a monotheistic episode in Egyptian history. There was, however, a Midianite Moses, who took over the worship of a volcano-god, YHWH, from a tribe of Midianites. In Freud's view, p. 49, "the Egyptian Moses never was in Qades and had never heard the name of Jahve, whereas the Midianite Moses never set foot in Egypt and knew nothing of Aton." The evidence hardly calls for so complicated an explanation.

[18]F. Delitzsch, *Babel und Bibel* (Leipzig: J. C. Hinrichs, 1921), pp. 79-80.9-80.79-80.

[19]J. M. Allegro, *The Sacred Mushroom and the Cross* (London: Hodder and Stoughton, 1970), pp. xvi, 20, 130, 215, n. 1. For a general critique of Allegro's book, see John H. Jacques, *The Mushroom and the Bride* (Derby: The Citadel Press, 1970); John C. King, *A Christian View of the Mushroom Myth* (London: Hodder and Stoughton, 1970). Edgar Krenz, *The Lutheran Quarterly*, XXIII (1971): 403-4, dismisses Allegro's arguments as "folk etymology based on similarity of sound," p. 404.

between the name YHWH and Zeus, although he makes the derivation from *Dyeus*, Indo-European in origin.[20]

Raymond Bowman has drawn from Ugaritic literature, from the root *hwy*, "to speak" (the noun *hwt* means "word," "command"; cf. Akkadian, *awātu*), in maintaining that the original meaning of the Tetragrammaton is "The Speaker."[21] He appeals to the revelations received by Moses at the tent of meeting and specifically to the statement, "Thus YHWH used to speak to Moses face to face, as a man speaks to his friend" (Exod.33:11). Certainly, YHWH appears in the role of speaker, but the root *dbr* is used in this context. A. Murtonen has followed Bowman's suggestion regarding the root *hwy*, but regards the divine name as a kind of *nomen agentis,* a noun formed by means of the *y*-prefix. On this basis, he claims that "we have good grounds for supposing that the name *Yhwh* is an ordinary *y*-prefixed noun from the root *hwy*, with the original meaning 'the Commander,' a meaning which is included in the later meaning, 'the Lord.'"[22]

Otto Procksch sought to discover the divine name in the first element in the name of the tribe, Judah (*Yᵉhûdâh*).[23] T. J. Meek, following the etymology in Gen.29:35, has also claimed that the divine name appears with a form of the verb, *yādāh*, and that, "Yahweh was originally the tribal God of Judah and only gradually became the god of the other Hebrew tribes as the influence of Judah came to dominate them."[24] But Gen.29:35 provides the folk etymology, and the supposition that each tribe had its own tribal god[25] requires to be demonstrated. W. F. Albright comes to the conclusion that *Yᵉhûdâh* is a passive verbal form, the *hophᶜal* or *yādāh* (causative = "to praise"), and was originally followed by *'ēl*, i.e., "Let El be praised"; the name is very ancient and is probably a

[20]See W. F. Albright, *From the Stone Age to Christianity*, 2nd ed. (Baltimore: The Johns Hopkins Press, 1946), p. 328, n. 84.

[21]Raymond A. Bowman, "Yahweh the Speaker," *JNES* III (1944): 1-8. Bowman refers to A. Guillaume's study of *hōwāh* in Isa.47:11 in "Magical Terms in the Old Testament," *Journal of the Royal Asiatic Society,* Part II (1942): 111-131, where the term has the sense of "incantation," "curse" (RSV "disaster"). C. R. North, however, associates *hōwāh* with the root "to fall." *Hōwāh* occurs elsewhere in the Old Testament only in Ezek.6:26; see *The Second Isaiah* (Oxford: Clarendon Press, 1964), p. 172.

[22]A. Murtonen, *op. cit.*, p. 90, states, "The fact that the etymology is not based upon Hebrew must not be viewed suspiciously, for *Yhwh* was worshipped by the Israelites even before they entered the land of Canaan and appropriated the Hebrew dialect while, on the other hand, the appearance of the name (originally) only among the North-Western Semites prevents us from seeking its origin and etymology elsewhere."

[23]O. Procksch, *Die Genesis*, 3rd ed. (Leipzig: A. Deichert, 1924), p. 178. But see W. F. Albright, "The Names 'Israel' and 'Judah' with an excursus on the Etymology of Todah and Torah," *JBL*, XLVI (1927): 151-185.

[24]T. J. Meek, "Some Religious Origins of the Hebrews," *AJSL*, XXXVII (1920-21): 110, 101..

[25]T. J. Meek, *Hebrew Origins*, 2nd ed. (Univ. of Toronto Press, 1950), p. 110.

pre-Mosaic tribal name.[26] If this is the case, the Tetragrammaton is not part of the name of the tribe Judah.

The view adopted in this study is as follows. The *'ehyeh *[a]*sher 'ehyeh* clause in Exod. 3:14 is a relatively late attempt to explain the divine name by appeal to the root *hayah*, the verb "to be." The use of the verb in the first person *qal* ("I am" or "I shall be") is demanded by the context, since God is the speaker. The use of *aleph* as the preformative in *'ehyeh* obscures the fact that the divine name begins with a *yodh*. This is another indication that the explanation of the name in Exod.3:14 is late. The Tetragrammaton contains the original four letters *yodh, he, waw, he*, for which an explanation is being offered in verse 14. A more detailed examination of the passage in its context will demonstrate that a particular theological understanding of the Tetragrammaton was being put forward at a time when the original meaning had been lost. One of the primary tasks for the exegete is to seek to determine what is being said theologically in the declaration *'ehyeh *[a]*sher 'ehyeh*. The attempt must then be made to penetrate behind this later explanation to a more original meaning. Here we are engaged in a somewhat speculative enterprise, with no assured results. The more primitive background of the divine name may well indicate the use of a causative form of the verb "to be." This hypothesis will be examined subsequently in this chapter.

Exod.3:14 brings into focus the importance of the verb "to be" in providing an explanation for the divine name. R. de Vaux remainds us that, "Almost all recent authors derive the name *Yhwh* from the north-western Semitic root *hwy*, 'to be.'"[27] M. Noth, for example, is of the opinion that, "the name Yahweh is in fact probably to be derived from the stem *hwh*, frequent in the Aramaic and Arabic dialects, which corresponds to the Hebrew root *hyh*, 'be.'"[28] This statement is not at variance with that of de Vaux, as the final *he* would represent a more original *yodh*, and the medial *waw* is more original than the medial *yodh*.

We must now investigate the enigmatic formula, *'ehyeh *[a]*sher 'ehyeh*, in order to establish the meaning of the phrase and to draw out some of the theological implications.[29] Attention must first be given to the grammar and syntax of the passage. W. A. Irwin regards the ' *[a]sher* clause as the predicate of a nominal sentence, as in Isa.41:24, which he translates, "An abomination (is)

[26]W. F. Albright, "The Names 'Israel' and 'Judah' with an Excursus on the Etymology of Todah and Torah," *JBL*, XLVI (1927): 151-185; espec. pp. 168-178.

[27]R. de Vaux, *op. cit.*, p. 59.

[28]M. Noth, *Exodus: A Commentary*, OTL, trans. by J. S. Bowden (London: S.C.M. Press, Ltd., 1962), p. 44. He suggests in a footnote that *yahweh* was perhaps originally "a noun derived from the root *hwh* and formed by the prefix *ya* being added = 'the being one.'"

[29]M. Noth, *Exodus: A Commentary*, p. 44, points out that, "v. 14a (b) however old it is is of great significance as the only explanation of the Old Testament name for God which has actually been handed down in the Old Testament."

who-chooses-them." *'Ehyeh *^asher 'ehyeh* would then be rendered, "I-AM is who I am."[30] But this as it stands is simply tautological. E. Schild would also regard the relative clause as the predicate. On the basis of G.K. 138 (d) and on the analogy of 1 Chron.21:17, he translates, "I am the one who is."[31] A similar point of view has been advanced by J. Lindblom, who also appeals to 1 Chron.21:17.[32] Schild makes a distinction between two connotations of the verb "to be"; one of which expresses "identity," the other, "existence." The formula is not then tautological, for in the translation, "I am the one who is," "am" expresses identity, and "is" expresses existence. The formula expresses the reality of the existence of the God who reveals himself. Bertil Albrektson has subjected the views of Schild and Lindblom to a searching analysis.[33] He questions whether the two passages (1 Chron.21:17 and Exod.3:14) are really parallel, since, "in 1 Chron.21:17 there is an *^anî* which the relative clause refers back to and which decides the form of the verb, whereas in Exod. 3:14 no such pronoun is found, only the verbal form *'ehyeh*."[34] In fact, "the main clause in 1 Chron.21:17 is a nominal clause, whereas in Exod.3:14 it is a verbal clause."[35] Since neither Schild nor Lindblom has presented arguments against the usual syntactical understanding of the formula, Albrektson accepts the translation, "I am who I am," or "I shall be who I shall be."

Th. C. Vriezen has drawn attention to the "paronomastic" aspect of the formula, *'ehyeh *^asher 'ehyeh*, a stylistic method of expressing either something undetermined, *idem per idem*, i.e., that which cannot be fully defined, or the idea of totality or intensity.[36] In particular, he refers to Exod.33:19 and Ezek.12:25. In response to Moses' plea to see the divine glory, the reply is given,

---

[30]W. A. Irwin, "Critical Note: Exodus 3:14," *AJSL*, LVI (1939): 297-98.

[31]E. Schild. "On Exodus iii 14 - 'I AM THAT I AM,'" *VT*, IV (1954): 296-302. GK §138 (d) reads, "If the governing substantive forms part of a statement made in the first or second person, the retrospective pronoun (or the subject of the appositional clause) is in the same person." Schild claims that Edouard Reuss, *La Bible* (Paris, 1879) had anticipated this point of view.

[32]J. Lindblom, "Noch einmal die Deutung des Jahwe-Namens in Ex.3,14," *ASTI*, III (1964): 4-15.

[33]B. Albrektson, "On the Syntax of *'Ehyeh *^asher 'ehyeh* in Exodus 3:14," in *Words and Meanings*, ed. P. R. Ackroyd and Barnabas Lindars (Cambridge University Press, 1968), pp. 15-28.

[34]B. Albrektson, *op. cit.*, p. 23.

[35]*Ibid.*, p. 23.

[36]Th. C. Vriezen, "'ehje *^aser 'ehje*" in *Festschrift Alfred Bertholet*, ed. W. Baumgartner *et al.* (Tübingen: J.C.B. Mohr, 1950), pp. 498-512. So far as the paronomastic aspect is concerned, E. A. Speiser, *Genesis*, The Anchor Bible (N.Y.: Doubleday, 1964), p. 38, has expressed his view that Exod. 3:14 presents us with "sound symbolism" rather than with a technical etymology. Cf. B. D. Eerdmans, "The Name Jahu," *OS*, V (1948): 15, "the full tetragrammaton is an onomatopoeia."

"I will make my goodness pass before you and will proclaim before you my name, YHWH; and I will be gracious to whom I will be gracious, and will show mercy on whom I will show mercy" (Exod.33:19); i.e., "I am altogether gracious and merciful."[37] Ezek.12:25 states that, "I YHWH will speak the word which I will speak, and it will be performed"; i.e., "When I speak, my words come to fulfilment." In addition to the intensive meaning which is conveyed by this literary device, another observation might well be considered, that in both these passages as well as in Exod.3:14, YHWH is unconditioned, sovereign in his actions, which express his true nature and being.

It is possible to be more precise about the meaning of the formula, "I am who I am"? The translators of the LXX rendered the formula in Greek as *egō eimi ho ōn*, literally, "I am THE BEING," "I am the One Who Is,"[38] "I am the Existing One," a translation which enabled later theologians to interpret the text in a highly metaphysical manner, and to find the notion of pure being paramount.[39] This leads us to raise questions about the significance of the verb "to be," in the original context. Carl H. Ratschow has made a careful study of the verb *hāyāh* in the Old Testament,[40] in which he finds three interrelated meanings, "to become," "to be," and "to effect," with the third sense providing a bridge between "becoming" and "being." Thorlief Boman, following Ratschow, maintains that the *hayah* of God is understood in the Old Testament in dynamic terms.[41] "The *hayah* of God is to act as God, to deal as God, and to carry into effect as God."[42] The name YHWH may indeed be older than the time of

---

[37] According to J. Morgenstern, "The Oldest Document of the Hexateuch," *HUCA*, IV (1927): 31, this passage derives from the Kenite narrative (K). He claims, p. 32, that "the K account of the revelation of the divine name is more natural and logical, and presumably therefore also more original, than either the E or P account." But Exod.33:19 and 34:6,7 appear to draw out the significance of the name given to Moses in Exod.3, by adumbrating the nature and character of YHWH.

[38] Cf. C. H. Dodd, *The Bible and the Greeks* (London: Hodder & Stoughton, 1935), p. 4, "The meaning of this is that God has no individual name: he is simply 'the Self-existent.'"

[39] Philo, by using *ho ōn*, and also the neuter, *to on*, was able to identify God with the Absolute of philosophy; C. H. Dodd, *op. cit.*, p. 4. Cf. also Charles Bigg, *The Christian Platonists of Alexandria* (Oxford: Clarendon Press, 1913), p. 195, who in summarizing Origen's views of God states, "Being incorporeal God is independent of the Laws of Space and Time, omniscient, omnipresent, unchanging, incomprehensible. . . . He has in a sense no titles, and His fittest name is He that Is."

[40] C. H. Ratschow, *Werden und Wirken. Eine Untersuchung des Wortes hajah als Beitrag zur Wirklichkeitserfassung des alten Testaments*, BZAW No. 70 (Berlin: A. Topelmann, 1941). Exod.3:14 is discussed on pp. 81-84. A recent article by G. S. Ogden is concerned with the understanding of "tense"; see "Time, and the verb *hayah* in O.T. Prose," *VT*, XXI (1971): 451-469. No specific application to Exod.3:14 is made, however.

[41] Thorlief Boman, *Hebrew Thought Compared with Greek*, trans. by Jules L. Moreau (London: S.C.M. Press Ltd., 1960).

[42] T. Boman, *op. cit.*, p. 47.

Moses, but Exod.3:14 provides a clarification of the name by ascribing to
YHWH an unalterable *hayah*; a dynamic, energetic, effective, personal being. The
"One Who Is," then, is the eternally effective YHWH, the creator.[43] James Barr,
however, offers a vigorous critique of Boman, in that Boman's view of the
dynamic aspect of Hebrew thought overstates the case.[44] Boman's thesis is "a
grotesque attempt to overload *hayah* with the associations of the incidents and
situations in which it is used, with the intention of maximizing the sense of
'effect' rather than that of 'be,' since the former is supposed to fit the presup-
posed picture of the Hebrew mind and its dynamism.[45] A study of the Hebrew
word *yesh* demonstrates the fact that the idea of being did not always convey a
dynamic sense.[46] M. Reisel also engages in a discussion of the static and dynamic interpretations of the verb "to be" in Hebrew, and comes to the conclusion
that the dynamic orientation of *hayah* is more original, but that a static meaning
has developed from the dynamic one.[47] In general, it is the static interpretation
which is reflected in the versions, especially in the LXX (*ego eimi ho ōn*) and in
the Vulgate (*ego sum qui sum*). Reisel seeks to bring both points of view together by stating, "I am convinced that the formula '*EHYEH aser EHYEH*'
should be explained *both* statically and dynamically. On the one hand the Revelation of the absolute and external Existence of God must be considered the
conditio-sine-qua-non of the Revelation of His continuous Readiness to fulfill
His Promises."[48] Static and dynamic interpretations may be combined, so long
as R. de Vaux's *caveat* is kept in mind, "One must take care not to introduce . . .
the metaphysical notion of Being in itself, of aseity, as elaborated by Greek
philosophy"; "'to be' is first and foremost 'to exist' in the terms of existentialist
philosophy, a *Dasein.*'[49]

In Exod.3:14, by use of the imperfect *qal*, first person, of the verb (meaning
both "I am" and "I shall be"), YHWH is understood to be expressing the reality
of his unconditioned existence and sovereignty over the future. But in terms of

---

[43]*Ibid.*, p. 49. A similar point of view is expressed by S. Mowinckel, "The Name of the
God of Moses," *HUCA*, XXXII (1961): 127, "this 'being' is not the abstract Greek *einai*, the
mere existence *per se*. To the Hebrew 'to be' does not just mean to exist—as all other beings
and things do as well—but to be active, to express oneself in active being, 'The God who
acts,' 'I am what in creative activity I always and everywhere turn out to be,' or 'I am (the
God) that really acts.'"

[44]J. Barr, *The Semantics of Biblical Language* (Oxford Univ. Press, 1961), espec. pp.
58-72. Barr has renewed his attack against the view that the Greek mind and the Hebrew
mind are fundamentally different in *Old and New in Interpretation* (London: S.C.M. Press
Ltd., 1966), espec. ch. 2.

[45]J. Barr, *Semantics*, p. 70.

[46]*Ibid.*, pp. 59-61.

[47]M. Reisel, *Observations*, p. 12.

[48]*Ibid.*, p. 18.

[49]R. de Vaux, *op. cit.*, p. 70.

the theophany to Moses, the emphasis is placed upon the reality of his continuing presence with Moses and with his people. This is the view which has been put forward so strongly by Martin Buber; the twofold *'ehyeh* means, "I am and remain present," "I will always be present"; in the words of Exod.3:12, *'ehyeh* *cimmakh*, "I will be with you."[50] Kenneth Kuntz has analysed the formal elements of the theophanic *Gattung* in the Old Testament.[51] Within a framework of introductory and concluding description, there are included a divine self-asseveration, the quelling of human fear evoked by the theophany, and a *hieros logos* addressed to a particular situation. It will be seen that these elements are present in the theophanic disclosure of Exod.3. In the initial verses, 1-6, YHWH declares to Moses that he is the God of the patriarchs (this is to be repeated in verse 15). Moses is fearful, and hides his face from God (verse 6). In 3:7-12, YHWH declares that he has come to deliver his afflicted people from the Egyptians and to bring them into a land flowing with milk and honey. Over Moses' protests of unworthiness to act as the divine messenger, he is given the assurance, "I will be with you" (verse 12). The further explanation of the divine name in 3:14 is secondary,[52] but nevertheless comes out of a keen appreciation of the fact of the divine presence with Moses and with Israel in the very events which the book of Exodus describes.

There is yet another dimension in the *'ehyeh 'asher 'ehyeh* of Exod.3:14. The answer to Moses' question regarding the identity of God is not intended to be evasive, contrary to the claim of B. D. Eerdmans.[53] But the element of the numinous and the mysterious is present. YHWH is not subject to precise and limiting definition.[54] There is a hiddenness, an inscrutability, in the deity who

[50]M. Buber, *Moses*, Harper Torchbooks (N.Y.: Harper & Brothers, 1958), p. 52. Cf. U. Cassuto, *A Commentary on the Book of Exodus*, trans. by Israel Abrahams (Jerusalem: The Magnes Press, The Hebrew University, 1967), p. 38. G. von Rad, *Old Testament Theology*, I (London: Oliver and Boyd, 1962), p. 180, writes, "It has always been emphasized, and rightly so, that in this passage at any rate, the *hayah* is to be understood in the sense of 'being present,' 'being there,' and therefore precisely not in the sense of absolute, but of relative and efficacious, being—I will be there (for you)." Cf. W. Eichrodt, *Theology of the Old Testament*, I, trans. by J. A. Baker (Philadelphia: The Westminster Press, 1961), pp. 189-190; Th. C. Vriezen, *An Outline of the Old Testament Theology* (Oxford: Blackwell, 1962), pp. 235-36.

[51]K. Kuntz, *The Self-Revelation of God* (Philadelphia: The Westminster Press, 1967), espec. ch. 2. For a somewhat different treatment, see Jörg Jeremias, *Theophanie; die Geschichte einen alttestamentlichen Gattung* (Neukirchen-Vluyn: Neukirchener Verlag des Erziehungsvereins, 1965).

[52]Cf. G. Quell, "The Old Testament Name for God" in *Theological Dictionary of the New Testament*, III, ed. G. W. Bromiley (Grand Rapids, Michigan: William B. Eerdmans Publishing Co., 1965), p. 1073.

[53]B. D. Eerdmans, "The Name Jahu," *OS*, V (1948): 12.

[54]Cf. A. M. Dubarle, "La Signification du Nom de Yahweh," *Revue des Sciences Philosophiques et Théologiques*, XXXV (1951): 20.

addresses Moses. G. Henton Davies declares that, "I will be what I will be" brings out the sense of indefiniteness and mystery, and has the practical meaning, "I AM who and what, and where and when, and how and even why you will discover I AM. I am what you will discover me to be."[55] He is the God with whom the initiative always resides, independent and in control of the future.[56]

The use of the *qal* imperfect of *hayah*, "to be," in Exod.3:14, is intended to convey to the reader the theological possibilities implicit in the divine name. If one is correct in understanding this as a late development, the question must be raised, what was the original background and meaning of the Tetragrammaton? In Rudolf Otto's view, we are dealing essentially with a numinous sound, such as the dervishes might cry out ecstatically.[57] Sigmund Mowinckel had been in correspondence with Otto, and had suggested that *ya* was to be understood as an interjection (as in Arabic), and that this was followed by the personal pronoun, *hû'*.[58] However, for Mowinckel, *hû'* was more than a numinous sound without any special rational meaning, but rather, "'He' with whom we have to do in cult and devotion; 'He' whose mystical forces we feel and experience; 'He' whose inmost essence and being we cannot see and understand, *'das ganz Andere';* 'He' on whom our whole existence is dependent; 'He' whom we cannot meet without fear and awe, and yet again and again cannot help seeking."[59] It is this explanation which makes Isa.43:10 ("that you may know and believe me and understand that I am He"' luminous with meaning for Mowinckel, expressing as it does the activity and creativity of God in nature and in history. Indeed, Mowinckel claims, "It can scarcely be denied that *hû'* is here very close to a sort of divine 'name"';[60] furthermore, Ps.102:27 - H28, "but thou art the same" (*wᵉ 'attā-hû'*, literally, "thou art He") leads to a similar conclusion. G. R. Driver has long maintained that the divine name was ejaculatory in origin, a primitive cry using the universal Semitic exclamation, *yā.*[61]. E. C. B. MacLaurin believes that the

[55] G. H. Davies, *Exodus*, Torch Bible Commentaries (London: S.C.M. Press, Ltd., 1967), p. 72. Cf. W. R. Arnold, "The Divine Name in Exodus iii 14," *JBL*, XXIV (1905): 128, who translates, "I will be whatever I choose." B. S. Childs draws attention to the paradoxical element in Exod.3:14, for the formula is both an answer and a refusal of an answer. "God announces that his intentions will be revealed in his future acts, which he now refuses to explain," *The Book of Exodus* (Philadelphia: The Westminster Press, 1974), p. 76.

[56] According to Yehezkel Kaufmann, EHYEH aser EHYEH means "I am independent," "The initiative will remain mine," *Tôlᵉdôth ha'emûnâh hayyisr'elit* (Tel Aviv: Bialik Institute Dvir, 1937), Part I, p. 481; cf. G. von Rad, *Old Testament Theology*, I (London: Oliver and Boyd, 1962), p. 181, "in the words 'I will be what I will be' there also lies censure of Moses' question. At all events, in giving the information which he does, Jahweh reserves his freedom to himself."

[57] R. Otto, *The Idea of the Holy*, trans. by John W. Harvey (London: Oxford Univ. Press, rev. ed., 1946), Appendix III, "Original Numinous Sounds," p. 198, n. 1.

[58] S. Mowinckel, "The Name of the God of Moses," *HUCA*, XXXII (1961): 131.

[59] *Ibid.*, p. 132.

[60] *Ibid.*, p. 128.

[61] G. R. Driver, "The original form of the name 'Yahweh': evidence and conclusions," *ZAW*, XLVI (1928): 24.

second syllable of YHWH in all likelihood "represents an early stage in the development of the personal pronoun, probably currently in use when the great events at Mount Sinai took place and which with true religious conservatism was 'frozen' at this stage."[62] M. Reisel refers to the third Surah of the Qoran, *La ilaha illa Huwa*, "No God exists but He." Surah III:5, *wamā ya^c lamu ta-wīlahu*, is interpreted by Moslem modernists as "No one knows the interpretation of *Hū*." Reisel concludes, "these views lead to the assumption that practically the same primitive sounds are at the root of both the liturgical exclamation *Yā Huwa* and of the Tetragrammaton."[63]

These proposals raise acutely the problem of the relative antiquity of *Yāh* and *YHWH* and the relationship between them. G. R. Driver, in reviewing the extra-biblical evidence, finds that *YW*- and *YH*- as an initial element in proper names occurred in the 9th and 7th centuries B.C.; *YHW*- and *YHH*- in the 6th and 5th centuries B.C.[64] Buchanan Gray's summary of the biblical evidence points to the early use of *YW*- and -*YH* (final element) in theophorous names in pre-Davidic times and in the early monarchy, with the increasing use of -*YH* in the late monarchy and the post-exilic period.[65] Driver concluded that the Tetragrammaton arose from a prolonging of the primitive ejaculation to *ya(h)wá(h), ya(h) wá(h)y*, or the like.[66] In this case, *YH* is the more primitive form. W. F. Albright has argued frequently and consistently, that YHWH is the more original form, verbal in origin, and that other forms are reductions or abbreviations.[67] This is also the view of A. Murtonen, arguing from the verbal form in Exod.3:14 and the Greek transliterations; he concludes that, "all the attempts to derive tht tetragram from a shorter form are unsuccessful."[68] W. Eichrodt conjectures that although both the full form and shorter forms of the Tetragrammaton go back

---

[62]E. C. B. MacLaurin, "YHWH: The Origin of the Tetragrammaton," *VT* XII (1962): 459.

[63]M. Reisel, *Observations*, p. 48.

[64]G. R. Driver, *op. cit.*, tabulation, p. 19; E. C. B. MacLaurin, *op. cit.*, p. 446.

[65]See E. C. B. MacLaurin, *op. cit.*, pp. 444-446, for a brief summary of G. B. Gray's tables.

[66]G. R. Driver, *op. cit.*, p. 24. See also E. Auerbach, *Moses* (Amsterdam: G. J. A. Ruys, 1953), pp. 44-47.

[67]W. F. Albright, "The Name Yahweh," *JBL*, XLII (1924): 370ff.; *From the Stone Age to Christianity*, 2nd ed. (Baltimore: The Johns Hopkins Press, 1946), pp. 197-198; cf. W. O. E. Oesterley, *The Psalms* (London: S.P.C.K., 1939, p. 323.

[68]A. Murtonen, *op. cit.*, p. 61. Cf. R. de Vaux, "The Revelation of the Divine Name" in *Proclamation and Presence*, ed. John I. Durham and J. Roy Porter (London: S.C.M. Press Ltd., 1970), pp. 50-51. De Vaux, p. 51, claims that "a contraction of the long form is more readily explained philologically than the lengthening of a short one." See also G. Quell, "The Old Testament Name for God," art. *Kyrios, TWNT*. III (Stuttgart: W. Kohlhammer, 1938), p. 1067; Eng. trans. by G. W. Bromiley (Grand Rapids, Mich.: Wm. B. Eerdmans, 1965), p. 1069.

to the earliest period and existed side by side, the shorter form may have been expanded at the time of Moses.[69] Although the problem has obviously not yet been resolved, *Yah* is probably best regarded as a hypocoristicon (term of endearment), a shortened form, resulting from apocopation of the final syllable.

The view that the Tetragrammaton consisted originally of an interjection, *ya*, followed by the personal pronoun, *hû*, receives some support from the use of the phrase *ʿanî hû* in Deutero-Isaiah. This phrase will be examined more carefully in chapter five, where the conclusion is reached that *ʿanî hû* is not a clue to the origin of the divine name, but rather a liturgical formula, a self-predication of the deity, which in the sublime monotheism of Deutero-Isaiah, negates every claim of Near Eastern deities, couched in similar language. Certainly *ʿanî hû* is a substitute for *ʿanî YHWH*, but *hû* is not necessarily an indication of part of the original form of the Tetragrammaton.

J. Obermann has argued that the Tetragrammaton in form must be understood as a causative participle, "a *nomen agentis*, in the form of a participle."[70] The difficulty of regarding *yhwh* as a verbal form arises from the use of the formula *ʿanî yhwh* (Exod.6:2, Lev.19:14, etc.), which presents us with "the enigma of a third person imperfect having as its subject or agent a first person pronoun."[71] Obermann adduces further evidence from Phoenician inscriptions at Karatepe, where a similar pattern occurs.[72] The formula, ' *ʿanî yhwh* then means, "I am he who sustains, maintains, establishes! viz. strength or weakness, victory or defeat, life or death; and, accordingly, the primary meaning of YHWH, as an epithet of the God of Israel, would have been 'Sustainer, Maintainer, Establisher.'"[73] G. R. Driver, however, disputes Obermann's interpretation of the Karatepe inscriptions, and his view that YHWH is a participial form.[74] Furthermore, one may argue that the formula ' *ʿanî yhwh* represents a liturgical form in which the Tetragrammaton is now a proper name, divested of its more original verbal significance.

The most influential advocate of the view that *yhwh* is a causative form of the verb "to be" in origin is undoubtedly W. F. Albright.[75] The Greek transcrip-

---

[69]W. Eichrodt, *Theology of the Old Testament,* I trans. by J. A. Baker (Philadelphia: The Westminster Press, 1961), pp. 188-189. See also E. Auerbach, *Moses* (Amsterdam: G. J. A. Ruys, 1953), p. 47, where he argues that the addition of an emphatic *He* at the time of Moses served to emphasize the new concept of God which he brought to his people.

[70]J. Obermann, "The Divine Name YHWH in the Light of Recent Discoveries," *JBL,* LXVIII (1949): 312.

[71]J. Obermann, *op. cit.,* p. 302.

[72]*Ibid.,* pp. 303, 308.

[73]*Ibid.,* p. 308.

[74]G. R. Driver, "The Interpretation of YHWH as a Participial Form from a Causative Theme of the Verb," *JBL* LXXII (1954): 125-131. See also the critique of A. Murtonen, *op. cit.,* p. 61.

[75]W. F. Albright, "The Name Yahweh," *JBL,* XLIII (1924): 370-378, espec. pp.

tions uniformly employ an *a* vowel in the first syllable. Albright argues from the *a* vowel that the form must be causative. He writes, "If we . . . regard Yahweh as an imperfect verb, it is most naturally to be derived from *hwy* (as still in Aramaic), later *hayah*, 'to come into existence, become, be.' The preservation of an archaic form with *waw* in proper names is illustrated also by *Hawwah*, 'Eve,' as is well known."[76] The causative (*hiph^c il*) sense of the verb means, "He Causes to Come into Existence," and the early jussive means, "Let Him Bring into Existence." Albright has been closely followed in this interpretation by D. N. Freedman,[77] and by Frank Moore Cross, Jr.[78] Albright mentions that the view that the divine name is derived from a causative form of the verb "to be," goes back at least to the time of Le Clerc, who in 1700 suggested the meaning *creator et effector rerum.*[79] In all probability, the verbal form was part of a longer expression, used liturgically, from which the verbal form emerged in abbreviated fashion, as the Tetragrammaton, the name of God. M. Dahood maintains that the original form was *"yhwh-'el,"* "El brings into being,"[80] a view which has the virtue of providing a close association between the Tetragrammaton and the worship of El in the patriarchal period.

At least three difficulties have been found with Albright's proposal. H. Bauer has pointed out that in Hebrew the verb *hyh* is never used in the causative form.[81] But, on the other hand, Aramaic and Syriac do use the causative form of the verb "to be" and the participial form *m^e hawweh* occurs in Late

374-75; cf. his review of B. N. Wambacq, *L'épithète divine, Jahvé S^e ba'òt; Étude philologique, historique et exégétique* (Desclée, De Brouwer, 1947) in *JBL*, LXVII (1948): 377-381, espec. 380.

[76]W. F. Albright, "The Name Yahweh," *op. cit.*, p. 374.

[77]D. N. Freedman, "The Name of the God of Moses," *JBL*, LXXIX (1960): 151-156, espec. p. 152.

[78]F. M. Cross, Jr., "Yahweh and the God of the Patriarchs," *HTR*, LV (1962): 225-259, espec. pp. 251-253. See also *Canaanite Myth and Hebrew Epic* (Cambridge, Mass.: Harvard University Press, 1973), p. 65 and n. 78.

[79]W. F. Albright, "The Name Yahweh," *op. cit.*, p. 375. Paul Haupt, "Der Name Jahwe," *Orientalistische Literaturzeitung*, XII (1909), col. 211-214, claimed a causative sense, *Insdaseinrufer*, i.e., *Macher*.

[80]M. Dahood, *Psalms I (1-50)*, The Anchor Bible (N.Y.: Doubleday, 1966), pp. 64, 177. Cf. I. Engnell, *Gamla Testamentet*, I (Upsala, 1945), p. 262f. Dahood defends the text of Ps.10:12, which he translates "Arise, O Yahweh God, lift up your hand!" As early as 1901, H. H. Spoer, "The Origin and Interpretation of the Tetragrammaton," *AJSL*, XVIII (1901): 35, claimed that the full name of the deity was *yahweh ēl ^c immānu*, "He will be God with us."

[81]H. Bauer, "Die Gottheiten von Ras Schamra," *ZAW*, LI (1933): 93, n. 7. Cf. G. Quell, "The Old Testament Name for God," art. *Kyrios*, trans. by G. W. Bromiley, *Theological Dictionary of the New Testament*, III (Grand Rapids, Mich.: Wm. B. Eerdmans Publishing Company, 1965), p. 1068, n. 151, "all attempts at a causative meaning seem to be artificial, and thus break down."

Hebrew,[82] facts which make this argument less cogent.

A second objection is raised by S. Mowinckel, who thinks that the idea, "He who causes to be, who brings into existence," is much too philosophical and abstract for the pre-Mosaic age; in fact, "That the conception of the divinity among the seminomads should have had its main interest in the idea of world creation seems to me very improbable."[83] Admittedly, the Ugaritic texts contain no creation story or clear indication of El's cosmic creativity.[84] On the other hand, the reference to El Elyon in Gen.14:19 as *qōnēh shāmayim wāʾarets* cannot lightly be dismissed, especially since the participle is understood in the sense of "create" in the LXX, Syriac and Vulgate versions.[85]

Another possibility should be considered. The causative idea "to bring into being" could refer to the creation of Israel as a people, rather than to cosmic creative activity. If Dahood is correct in his theory that the Tetragrammaton was originally a causative verbal form with El as subject, "El brings into existence . . . ," the question to decide is what will be the most suitable noun in the accusative as object to complete the sentence. An object such as "Israel" or "his people" would be entirely appropriate. There are strong grounds for asserting that the Exodus narrative is the basic narrative in the traditions of Israel, to which patriarchal narratives have first been added, and finally the creation narratives of Genesis.[86] God is first and foremost the creator of a people and is only later recognized as creator of the cosmos. The Song of Moses contains the significant statement, "Is not he your father, who created (*qānāh*) you, who made you and established you?" (Deut.32:6). Deutero-Isaiah also speaks of YHWH as the creator of his people, "But now thus says YHWH, he who created (*bārāʾ*) you, O Jacob, he who formed you, O Israel . . ." (Isa.43:1; cf. Isa.43:15). The enduring value of the account of Moses' meeting with YHWH at the burning bush is that here we have the record of an initial stage in the creation of a people with a sense of destiny, a people who stand in a special relationship to God. M. Buber has drawn attention to the importance of the word *ʿammi*, "my people," in Exod.3:7 and 3:10, and has stated eloquently, "With this repeated 'my people' at the commencement and close of the passage, YHVH recognizes Israel in a fashion more powerful and unequivocal than would

---

[82]R. de Vaux, *op. cit.*, p. 63.

[83]S. Mowinckel, "The Name of the God of Moses," *HUCA*, XXXII (1961): 128.

[84]M. H. Pope, *El in the Ugaritic Texts*, Supplements to Vetus Testamentum, II (Leiden: E. J. Brill, 1955), p. 49.

[85]See also Paul Humbert, "'Qânâ' en Hebreu Biblique," in *Festschrift Alfred Bertholet*, ed. W. Baumgartner *et al.* (Tübingen: J. C. B. Mohr, 1950), pp. 259-266; cf. Norman C. Habel, "'Yahweh, Maker of Heaven and Earth': A Study in Tradition Criticism," *JBL*, XCI (1972): 321-337.

[86]B. W. Anderson, *Understanding the Old Testament*, 2nd ed. (N.J.: Prentice-Hall, Inc., 1966), Chs. 1 and 6; following Gerhard von Rad, *The Problem of the Hexateuch*, trans. by E. W. Trueman Dicken (London: Oliver Boyd, 1966), p. 53ff.

have been possible by any other verbal means."[87] Psalm 100 becomes an extended commentary on this theme. Verse 2 - H3 is particularly powerful, "Know that YHWH is Elohim! It is he that made us, and we are his; we are his people." Indeed, there is much to be said in support of Dahood's translation, "he himself made us when we, his people and the flock of his pasture, were nothing."[88] In other words, the initial meaning of the divine name had to do with what God brings into being in history, his mighty deeds, and specifically his creating of a people, with whom he stands in a covenant relationship. But since this theme involves Israel's election and mission to the nations, in course of time, YHWH was seen to be the one and only true god, lord of history, and indeed creator of the universe. YHWH brings into being a people by the act of redeeming them from the bondage in Egypt, leading them through the wilderness and establishing them as his covenant people in the land which he had promised. As the P stratum in the Pentateuch makes clear, these mighty deeds of YHWH were seen within a perspective of cosmic creation. G. von Rad summarizes the situation in an excellent statement, "Faith in creation is neither the position nor the goal of the declarations in Gen., chs. 1 and 2. Rather, the position of both the Yahwist and the Priestly document is basically faith in salvation and election. They undergird this faith by the testimony that this Yahweh, who made a covenant with Abraham and at Sinai, is also the creator of the world."[89]

A third objection to Albright's understanding of the meaning of the Tetragrammaton is that it necessitates changes in the MT of Exod.3:14.[90] Albright follows Haupt in treating the initial verb in the formula as causative, and in changing the preformative from *aleph* to *yodh* in the case of the second verb; i.e., reading, *'ehyeh* *ᵃsher yihyeh*, "I cause to be what comes into existence."[91] Is it not preferable to retain the Hebrew text as it stands, and to find in verse 14 an explanation of the name, which in verse 15 remains unexplained? A new content is given to the name by moving from the *hiph^cil* to the *qal*. The name is now no longer looked upon as causative, but the verb "to be" is still the basis of the etymological explanation which the formula, *'ehyeh* *ᵃsher 'ehyeh*, seeks to give. By retaining MT, elaborate reconstructions of the text are rendered unnec-

[87]M. Buber, *Moses,* Harper Torchbook edition (N.Y.: Harper & Brothers, 1958), p. 45.

[88]M. Dahood, *Psalms II (51-100),* The Anchor Bible (N.Y.: Doubleday, 1968), p. 371. Dahood sees no reason to abandon the *k^ethîbh, w^elō',* in this context.

[89]G. von Rad, *Genesis: A Commentary,* OTL, trans. by John H. Marks (London: S.C.M. Press, Ltd., 1961), p. 44.

[90]This objection is decisive for R. de Vaux, *op. cit.,* p. 63. Cf. also C. F. Whitley, *The Genius of Ancient Israel* (Amsterdam: Philo Press, 1969), p. 22.

[91]W. F. Albright, "The Name Yahweh," *JBL,* XLII (1924): pp. 376-77; *From the Stone Age to Christianity,* 2nd ed. (Baltimore: The Johns Hopkins Press, 1946), pp. 198-99 Immanuel Lewy, "The Beginnings of Worship of Yahweh:Conflicting Biblical Views," *VT,* VI (1956): 433, claims that the *hiph^cil* occurred twice in the original text, *'ahyeh* *ᵃsher 'ahyeh,* "I shall cause things to be which I want."

essary. The causative sense does not appear in Exod.3:13-15, for the passage is dominated by the use of the *qal*. A good case can be made for the view that the divine name rests originally on a causative use of the verb "to be." But the *hiph^{c}il* has been superseded by the *qal* in the etymological explanation given in Exod.3:14, with a consequent shift in emphasis from the deeds of God to the continuing presence of God among his people in his freedom and sovereignty.

V

THE TETRAGRAMMATON IN THE OLD TESTAMENT

The use of the Tetragrammaton in the Old Testament carries with it a variety of theological implications. The Yahwist was interested in the cultic significance of the divine name in his insistence that the worship of YHWH goes back to remote antiquity (Gen. 4:26). The Yahwist[1] was also concerned with the mystery of election, God's power over history, and the freedom which has been given to man. In the primeval history, he opens up in masterly fashion areas of psychological and theological concern regarding the nature of man and his relationship to God (e.g., Gen. 3). In spite of an anthropomorphic representation of God, there is a theological profundity and maturity in the presentation of his narrative. The love and righteousness of YHWH are strongly proclaimed in a key statement (Exod.34:6,7): "The LORD [YHWH] passed before him [Moses], and proclaimed, 'The LORD [YHWH], the LORD [YHWH], a God [El] merciful and gracious, slow to anger, and abounding in steadfast love and faithfulness, keeping steadfast love for thousands [i.e. to the thousandth generation], forgiving iniquity and transgression and sin, but who will by no means clear the guilty, visiting the iniquity of the fathers upon the children and the children's children, to the third and the fourth generation." This is the character of the covenant God of Israel. The narrative of the Elohist[2] begins with the patriarchal period. The sense of the immediacy of God is lacking in the patriarchal narratives, although in Exod.3, against his reluctance to assume leadership, Moses is assured that God is immanent and available to his people (Exod.3:12). The Deuteronomist, in introducing a "name-theology," is able to overcome any restrictive view of a localized presence of God and to retain the notion of transcendence by asserting that although his "name" is present in the central sanctuary (Deut.12:5)[3] even the heaven and the highest heaven cannot contain him (1 Kings 8:27-29). In the

---

[1]For the Yahwist's theology, see P. Ellis, *The Yahwist* (Notre Dame, Indiana: Fides Publishers, Inc. 1968), ch. 6; G. von Rad, *Old Testament Theology*, I (London: Oliver & Boyd, 1962), Ch. B; C. Kuhl, *The Old Testament* (London: Oliver & Boyd, 1961), pp. 64-72; H. W. Wolff, "The Kerygma of the Yahwist," *Interpretation*, XX (1966): 131-158.

[2]For distinctions between the Yahwist and Elohist view of God, see G. von Rad, *Genesis: A Commentary*, OTL (London:S.C.M. Press, Ltd., 1961), pp. 24-26; M. Newman, *The People of the Covenant* (N.Y.: Abingdon Press, 1962), pp. 46-71.

[3]Ezekiel may reflect this viewpoint in his vision of the reconstituted Temple of the future, when the city of Jerusalem is to be renamed *YHWH shammāh*, "Yahweh is there" (Ezek. 48:35). For Eichrodt, *Ezekiel: A Commentary*, OTL (London: S.C.M. Press Ltd., 1970), p. 593, the new name of the city "points to the nearness of Yahweh, who has not taken up residence in the city in the same way as before, but in still greater closeness." For the priestly Ezekiel, the theocratic community is the ideal.

Sh^ema^c (Deut.6:4,5), the Deuteronomist declares that YHWH is unique ('$ehad$),[4] commanding the unreserved loyalty and obedience of his prople.

In the previous chapter, the explanation of the meaning of the divine name in Exod.3:14 was investigated, together with an attempt to discover a more original meaning of the Tetragrammaton. In this chapter, attention will focus on the cultic phrase "YHWH of hosts," and the liturgical expression, "I am YHWH" and "I am He." In the latter phrase, "I am He" ($h\hat{u}$'), the personal pronoun becomes almost a surrogate for the divine name, important because of its implications for New Testament interpretation and Christology, especially in the Fourth Gospel, where Jesus makes known to men the name of God (Jno.17:6,26). The revelatory significance of the divine name in the New Testament is recognized by Walther Eichrodt, when he states that "it is in the person of Jesus that the function of the Name of Yahweh as a form of the divine self-manifestation finds its fulfilment."[5]

A descriptive title, used frequently in the prophets, is $YHWH \, s^eb\bar{a}'\hat{o}th$, usually translated, "the Lord of hosts." On grammatical grounds, the validity of this translation may be questioned: nevertheless the longer (and later) phrase, $YHWH \, 'El\hat{o}h\hat{e} \, s^eb\bar{a}'\hat{o}th$ treats $s^eb\bar{a}'\hat{o}th$ as a genitive rather than as an attributive or as a proper name.[6] This latter form occurs 18 times in all, whereas the shorter title is found 267 times. B. N. Wambacq, in an important monograph, argued that the shorter form is primary.[7]

The precise significance of this title has been much debated, especially since $s\bar{a}b\bar{a}$ has such a variety of connotations in the Old Testament. The title appears to have undergone a process of evolution in meaning from an original "YHWH of armies," i.e., Israel's fighting forces, to "YHWH of hosts," where YHWH's lord-

----

[4]The difficulties in translation of Deut.6:4 are well-known; cf. G. von Rad, *Deuteronomy: A Commentary*, OTL (Phila: The Westminster Press, 1966), p. 63. Perhaps both the unity and uniqueness of God are conveyed by the use of '$ehad$, as is suggested by S. R. Driver, *A Critical and Exegetical Commentary on Deuteronomy*, ICC, 2nd ed. (Edinburgh: T. & T. Clark, 1896), pp. 89-90.

[5]W. Eichrodt, *Theology of the Old Testament*, II, trans. by J. A. Baker (Philadelphia: The Westminster Press, 1967), p. 45.

[6]In keeping with his view that YHWH is a verbal form, W. F. Albright has argued that $s^eb\bar{a}'\hat{o}th$ is the object in a phrase meaning, "He who brings armies into existence." See *JBL*, LXVII (1948):380, where Albright claims, "In later centuries, after the verbal force of $yahw\grave{e}$ had been completely forgotten, $Yahw\hat{e} \, S^eb\bar{a}'\hat{o}t$ came to mean 'Lord of Hosts,' and the alternative expression, $Yahw\grave{e} \, ^e l\hat{o}h\hat{e} \, Seb\bar{a}'\hat{o}t$, 'Yahweh, God of Hosts,' arose to explain its enigmatic grammatical construction." Frank Moore Cross also regards the insertion of $^e l\hat{o}h\hat{e}$ as a way of easing the ungrammatical phrase $Yahwe \, S^e b\bar{a}'\hat{o}t$, once the verbal force of $yahw\hat{e}$ had been lost, for $s^e b\bar{a}'\hat{o}t$ cannot be regarded as a genitive in the shorter, more original phrase; see *Canaanite Myth and Hebrew Epic* (Cambridge, Mass.: Harvard University Press, 1973), pp. 69-70. Cf. Matitiahu Tsevat, "Studies in the Book of Samuel," IV, *HUCA*, XXXVI (1965):49-58, espec. pp. 51-55.

[7]B. N. Wambacq's careful study, *L'épithète divine Jahve $s^eba'\hat{o}t$: Étude philologique, historique et exégétique* (Desclée: De Brouwer, 1947) is of major importance.

ship over all powers in heaven and on earth is asserted. In this later development, the title is an affirmation of the fact that YHWH is all-powerful and irresistible.

The original background of the title is compared with the time of Samuel and of David. Here the military context is clearly established. For example, the youthful David says to Goliath, "I come to you in the name of the Lord of hosts, the God of the armies of Israel" (1 Sam.17:45). A similar example is to be found when Nathan the prophet is instructed to say to David, "Thus says the Lord of hosts, I took you from the pasture . . . and have cut off all your enemies from before you" (2 Sam.7:8,9). So also, the ark of the covenant was taken from Shiloh by the sons of Eli to the camp of the Israelites as a war palladium, when they were engaged in battle against the Philistines (1 Sam.4:4). The extent of the castrophe for Israel when the ark was taken by the Philistines is emphasized by the dirge-like five-fold repetition of the phrase, "the ark of God has been captured" (1 Sam.4:11,17,19,21,22). The cultic significance of the ark is in evidence in the statement in 1 Sam.1:3 that Elkanah "used to go up year by year from his city to worship and to sacrifice to the Lord of hosts at Shiloh." Hannah, making a vow that if she is given a son he will be dedicated to the service of YHWH, addresses her prayer to the Lord of hosts (1 Sam.1:11). The destruction of Shiloh is alluded to by Jeremiah in his temple sermon. Shiloh is described as the place "where I made my name dwell at first" (Jer.7:12). In the century or so before the establishment of the monarchy in Israel, cities were frequently destroyed. W. F. Albright aptly comments on the fact that Bethel was destroyed four times between 1200 and 1000 B.C.: "One can hardly be surprised if under such conditions, Israel became martially minded and Israel's God became 'Yahweh, God of (the) Hosts (of Israel).'"[8]

"YHWH of hosts," then, appears to be a usual title for God in the period when Samuel served at the sanctuary. Otto Eissfeldt, acknowledging the cultic significance of the title, indicates that a wider interpretation of $s^e b\bar{a} \dot{o} th$ was implicit.[9] He draws attention to the fact that when the ark of the covenant of the Lord of hosts is mentioned in 1 Sam.4:4, a descriptive phrase follows, "who is enthroned on the cherubim." Likewise, when David makes Jerusalem his political and religious capital, he goes to Baale-judah, "to bring up from there the ark of God, which is called by the name of the Lord of hosts who sits enthroned on the cherubim" (2 Sam.6:2; cf. 2 Kings 18:15 = Isa.37:16). The Priestly passage, Exod.25:10-28, describes the construction of the ark, in which the cherubim are to overshadow the *kapporeth*, "mercy-seat." This finds a parallel in the description of the inner sanctuary of Solomon's temple, 1 Kings 6:23-28; 8:6-9. These descriptions are in keeping with the view that the ark was

[8]W. F. Albright, *From the Stone Age to Christianity*, 2nd ed. (Baltimore: The Johns Hopkins Press, 1946), p. 219.

[9]O. Eissfeldt, "Jahwe Zebaoth" in *Miscellanea Academica Berolinensia* II, 2 (Berlin: 1950), pp. 128-150, reprinted in *Kleine Schriften*, III (Tübingen: J.C.B. Mohr, 1966), pp. 103-123.

considered as the pedestal of YHWH's throne, an idea which may well be present also in Ps.24:7-10, where the gates of the temple are to be lifted up so that those who bear the ark in procession may come in, and to the question, "Who is the King of glory?" the triumphant reply is given, "The Lord of hosts, he is the King of glory!" Eissfeldt reminds us that Ps.18:10 - H11, with its parallel in 2 Sam.22:11, says of YHWH, "He rode on a cherub and flew." Cosmic dimensions are implicit in this imagery. The God who sits like an earthly king upon his throne but who also, in vivid imagery, rides on a cherub and comes swiftly upon the wings of the wind, exercises the cosmic might of one who dwells above the clouds. Indeed, in Isaiah's vision in the temple, one of the seraphs calls out, "Holy, holy, holy is the Lord of hosts, the whole earth is full of his glory" (Isa.6:2). Isaiah trembles because his eyes have seen "the King, the Lord of hosts" (Isa.6:5). The Priestly writer concludes his account of the creation with the statement, "Thus the heavens and the earth were finished, and all the host of them" (Gen.2:1), implying once again, a cosmic dimension.

The concepts of kingly majesty and creative power are very much in the forefront in the prophetic literature, where the title, "YHWH of hosts," occurs so frequently. Although Amos speaks of the "Lord God, the God of hosts" as about to punish Israel for his transgressions (Amos 3:13,14), and one might surmise that foreign "hosts" are now the agents of YHWH's judgment, in the poetic passage, Amos 4:13, it is "he who forms the mountains and creates the wind," about whom it can be said, "the LORD, the God of hosts, is his name."[10] So also, he of whom it may be said, "YHWH is his name" (Amos 5:8), the one who brings destruction, is he who made Pleiades and Orion. Specifically, he is again described as "YHWH, God of hosts" in Amos 9:5, where his control of the world of nature is evidence of his power to control the movements and the destinies of the peoples of the earth.

At the end of Psalm 103, various beings are called upon to bless YHWH, "angels," "mighty ones," "all his hosts," "his ministers," "all his works" (Ps. 103:20-22). Some support may be found here for the view that "the hosts" are celestial beings that surround YHWH, ready to do his bidding. In Isa.40:26, Deutero-Isaiah cries out, "Lift up your eyes on high and see: who created these? He who brings out their host by number, calling them all by name." Just as in the Song of Deborah, where in poetic imagery, the very stars from their courses fought against Sisera (Judges 5:20), the stars may be seen in Isa.40:26 as called out by YHWH, as a military commander calls out his troops to follow him in battle. But the force of this passage is to be found in the use of the verb $b\bar{a}r\bar{a}'$, "create," in the penetrating question, "Who created these?" God's initial act of

---

[10]For the view that the doxologies in Amos 4:13; 5:8-9; 9:5,6 are part of a hymn, see F. Horst, "Die Doxologien in Amosbuch," *ZAW*, XLVIII (1929):45ff.; J. D. Watts, "An old hymn preserved in the Book of Amos," *JNES*, XV (1956):33-39; A. Kapelrud, *Central Ideas in Amos* (Oslo University Press, 1961), pp. 38-39; James Ward, *Amos & Isaiah* (N.Y.: Abingdon Press, 1969), pp. 112-125.

creation of the heavens and the earth, in the Priestly account (Gen.1:1), emphasizes the divine creativity by the use of the verb *bārā'*. Indeed, this verb is reserved for divine creative action and is not used otherwise. Isa.40:26, then, surely contains a polemic against the astral powers. C. R. North comments, "The Prophet of the exile makes bold to affirm that the God of his captive people 'created' the stars whom their captors worshipped as gods."[11]

In Psalm 46, the refrain, "the Lord of hosts is with us; the God of Jacob is our refuge," is preceded in the final strophe by an appeal to behold the power of God in bringing warfare to an end; his universal sovereignty is proclaimed, "I am exalted among the nations, I am exalted in the earth!" (Ps.46:9-11; H10-12). Occasionally, the military connotation is uppermost in the prophets (e.g., Isa.13:4; 31:4), but the idea of sovereign power predominates, as in the use of the title in such a passage as Isa.54:5, where other names are also given, "Maker," "Holy One of Israel," "Redeemer," "the God of the whole earth." In Malachi 1:11, the worship of the nations is envisaged, "for my name is great among the nations, says the Lord of hosts." Nevertheless, the frequency of the occurrence of the title and its variations (e.g., in Isaiah 1-39, 53 times; Jeremiah, 76 times;[12] Deutero-Isaiah, 6 times; Haggai, 14 times; Zechariah, 52 times; Malachi, 24 times) suggests that it is used somewhat loosely as a stock phrase which nevertheless evokes in hearers a sense of the all-encompassing majesty of YHWH.

This emphasis on "YHWH of hosts" as sovereign lord, supreme in his legitimate control of nations and of all powers in heaven and on earth, is aptly reflected both in the uniform use of *kyrios*, "lord," as a translation of the Tetragrammaton in the LXX, and also in the substitution of *ᵃdōnāy*, "lord" in the reading of the Hebrew text, so as to avoid the pronunciation of the divine name.

The divine name is frequently used in the Old Testament in liturgical phrases, such as "I am YHWH," "I am He." The introduction of the Tetragram-

[11]C. R. North, *The Second Isaiah* (Oxford: Clarendon Press, 1964), p. 88. Cf. James D. Smart, *History and Theology in Second Isaiah* (Philadelphia: The Westminster Press, 1965), p. 60, "Some people may worship the stars as gods, but Israel's God is the Creator and Ruler of the stars."

[12]Apart from the translation of "YHWH of Hosts" in the LXX as *Kyrios Sabaōth*, the usual LXX translation in the Prophets is *Kyrios Pantokrator*. Yet in most cases in Jeremiah, *Kyrios* alone is used. The problem of the relationship between the LXX and MT of Jeremiah is well known, e.g., H. St. John Thackeray, *The Septuagint and Jewish Worship*, The Schweich Lectures 1920 (London: Oxford University Press, 1923), p. 29, "The Greek Jeremiah has probably provoked more inquiry than any other Septuagint book, owing to its exceptionally wide divergence from the Hebrew." Eissfeldt, *op. cit.*, p. 122, expresses the opinion that the Hebrew Vorlage of the LXX contained the Tetragrammaton only in most cases, not "YHWH of hosts." Certainly, J. Ziegler's critical text of the LXX of Jeremiah, *Septuagint Vetus Testamentum Graecum*, XV (Göttingen: Vandenhoeck & Ruprecht, 1957) indicates that *Kyrios* is well attested as the reading in most cases where MT reads "YHWH of hosts."

maton in the Priestly account (Exod.6:2,3) is set in a convenantal context. The covenantal formula, "I will take you for my people, and I will be your God" (Exod.6:7) is here closely related to the redemptive act by which YHWH has brought his people out "from under the burdens of the Egyptians" (Exod.6:6,7). Twice over in this passage, in Exod.6:2,6, the phrase *^anî YHWH,* "I am YHWH" occurs. The phrase "I am *El Shadday"* appears in another Priestly passage, Gen.17:1. As Umberto Cassuto has indicated, "Such a formula was customary in the ancient East in the declarations of kings, when proclaiming their deeds and might."[13] A case in point is the Moabite inscription, with the proud declaration, "I am Mesha." In a directly religious context, the "I am" formula was used in such affirmations as "I am Ishtar of Arbela," "I am the god Nabu."[14]

Although the phrase "I am YHWH" occurs principally in the Priestly source in the Pentateuch, and especially in the "Holiness" (H) Code, it is found also in other strata. The Yahwist employs the phrase in Gen.15:7 and again in Gen.28:13, in each case in connection with the promise of the land which is to be the possession of the posterity of the patriarchs. The Elohistic account of the Decalogue (Exod.20:2ff)[15] begins with the solemn phrase, "I am YHWH your God," and as in Exod.6:6,7, associates the proclamation with the redemption from Egypt. Other passages within the Pentateuch in which the *^anî YHWH* is followed by a declaration of the deliverance from Egypt include Exod.29:46; Lev.11:45; and in the Holiness Code, Lev.19:36; 25:38 and 26:13. Outside of the Pentateuch, Hosea twice uses the expression "I [*^anōkhî*] am YHWH your God from the land of Egypt," in Hos.12:9 - H10 and 13:4.[16] There is no suggestion that Hosea thinks of Israel's relationship to YHWH as beginning only with deliverance from Egypt, for the references to Jacob in Hos.12:2-5 and 13:12 preclude this. Nevertheless, for Hosea, an important landmark was reached when "by a prophet the Lord brought Israel up from Egypt and by a prophet he was preserved" (Hos.12:13). Ezekiel, like Hosea, relates the phrase

---

[13]U. Cassuto, *A Commentary on the Book of Exodus* (Jerusalem: The Magnes Press, The Hebrew University, 1967), p. 76.

[14]S. Mowinckel, "The Name of the God of Moses," *HUCA,* XXXII (1961):123.

[15]The longer form of the personal pronoun, *^anōkhî,* is used here and in Exod. 20:5, as well as in the parallel version of the Decalogue in Deut. 5:6,9. Other occurrences of *^anōkhî YHWH* are to be found in Ps.81:10 - H11; Hos.12:10; 13:4; Isa.43:11; 44:24 and 51:15.

[16]J. L. Mays, *Hosea: A Commentary,* OTL (London: S.C.M. Press, Ltd., 1969), p. 167, "With a solemn proclamation of his own name (13:4), Yahweh sets his own identity over against Canaanized Ephraim. . . . He is 'your God,' God of the election and covenant, to whom they are inseparably bound by the historic deed of the Exodus (11:1)." If the MT of Hosea 1:9 is correct, there may be a reference here to the tradition found also in Exod.3:14 regarding the name *'Ehyeh,* "I am"; J. L. Mays, *op. cit.,* p. 29, draws attention to the literal translation of Hosea 1:9b, "and I am not your I-AM (*'ehyeh*)"; cf. James M. Ward, *Hosea: A Theological Commentary* (N.Y.: Harper & Row, 1966), pp. 7-8.

ᵃni YHWH to the tradition of the exodus from Egypt (Ezek.20:5-7), in what amounts virtually to a historical Credo.[17] A similar historical Credo occurs in Judges 6:8-10, where the phrase "I am YHWH your God" is preceded by an assertion that YHWH delivered his people from Egypt. So also in Ps.81:10 - H11, the references to the deliverance from Egypt and the prohibition of worship of any strange god are reminiscent of the opening words of the Decalogue.

Zimmerli rightly maintains that the formula *ᵃnî YHWH* in the prophetic writings has no special *Sitz im Leben*.[18] Hosea and Ezekiel use a Credo-form; Jeremiah in 17:10 and 32:27 is employing a type of *māshāl*, or proverbial saying, although the covenantal formula is present in Jer.24:7. Deutero-Isaiah, on the other hand, with his *ᵃnōkhî ᵃnōkhî YHWH* (Isa.43:11), is expressing a sublime monotheism, as also in the *ᵃnî YHWH* of Isa.45:5. In the declaration that YHWH is the "Holy One of Israel" (Isa.45:11), Deutero-Isaiah is using a title already found in Isaiah of Jerusalem (e.g., Isa.1:4; 10:20; 12:6). In the "Holiness" Code, frequently *ᵃnî YHWH* is followed by the phrase "who sanctify you (them)," e.g., Lev.20:8; 21:8,15,23; 22:9,16,32. Norman Snaith claims, "It is likely that here we have traces of a liturgy in which each section concluded with a response which in its full form was 'I am the LORD your God (or 'I am the Lord who sanctifies . . .'), who brought you out of the land of Egypt . . . ,' 22.32f. and 19.36."[19] In Leviticus, chs. 18, 19, and 22, in some twenty instances, the phrase *ᵃnî YHWH* is used without any qualification. Sheldon Blank regards the formula in these cases as much less significant than the phrase in Deutero-Isaiah. Indeed, the formula "appears to be merely the asseveration that the words to which it is appended are Yahweh's words. It identifies the speaker so that no one may be misled into thinking that the preceding sentiments are of mere human origin."[20] Although this may be the case, the importance of the legislation in these chapters should not be underestimated. Especially is this true of Lev.19, with its many parallels to the Decalogue and its humanitarian concerns. The insistence on high ethical standards and social justice is validated by the recurring solemn refrain, *ᵃnî YHWH*.

From this brief survey of the use of the fomula, "I am YHWH," it can be readily seen that most of the occurrences are to be found in passages with priestly associations. This suggests a rich cultic and liturgical background for the formula. In the prophetic passages, the *Heilsgeschichte* ("Salvation- history") tradition is clearly present. YHWH has redeemed Israel from Egypt and has established a convenantal relationship with them. In the Decalogue, we have an

---

[17]See W. Zimmerli, "Ich bin Jahwe," in *Geschichte und altes Testament* (Alt Festschrift, 1953), reprinted *Gottes Offenbarung* (München: Chr. Kaiser Verlag, 1963), p. 19.

[18]W. Zimmerli, *op. cit.*, p. 34.

[19]N. H. Snaith, *Leviticus and Numbers*, The Century Bible (London: Nelson, 1967), p. 23.

[20]S. H. Blank, "Studies in Deutero-Isaiah," *HUCA*, XV (1940):33.

assertion of the exclusive claim of YHWH upon his people. This in Deutero-Isaiah has become a lofty monotheism, in which the sovereignty of YHWH is especially proclaimed. Claus Westermann, commenting on Isa.43:11a, states, "The so-called 'formula of revelation,' 'I am Yahweh,' plays an important part in the Old Testament. It expresses the idea that in the name Yahweh, which was revealed along with Yahweh himself at the beginning of the nation's encounter with him, his relationship with Israel is laid down in its two aspects; the name stands for God's words and God's deeds, which have their unity in it; at the same time, the name also stands for that to which Israel clung, in past and present, as she invoked it in supplication when she was in sore straights or rendered it in exultant praise."[21]

Ezekiel's use of the phrase *^{a}nî YHWH* is frequently included in a longer formula, "that they may know that I am YHWH." This formula, with minor variations, occurs about seventy times in Ezekiel.[22] Zimmerli draws attention to the parallel phrase in 1 Kings 20:28, when during the wars with the Syrians, a "man of God" declares to the king of Israel, "Thus says the LORD, 'Because the Syrians have said, "the Lord is a god of the hills but he is not a god of the valleys" therefore I will give all this great multitude into your hand, and you shall know that I am the LORD.'"[23] Sheldon Blank's summation of Ezekiel's use of the formula is instructive, "An inspection of these passages reveals that in a little more than half of the instances of its occurrence the subject of the verb is the *people of Israel*; in the remaining instances it is *foreign nations*. Also that, in more than two-thirds of the instances, it is some national *disaster* which will produce the indicated conviction. That is to say: Israel 'shall know' when Yahveh wreaks destruction in Israel; Ammon, Moab, Edom, Egypt, the land of God, etc., 'shall know' when Yahveh wreaks destruction in Ammon, Moab, Edom, etc. In the remaining passages it is the *restoration of Israel* to peoplehood after the national disaster which will produce conviction—in Israel for the most part, but, according to a few passages, also among the other nations."[24] Blank regards the formula as serving much the same function as Deutero-Isaiah's argument from prophecy to monotheism. The intention in both Ezekiel and Deutero-Isaiah is to declare the sovereignty of YHWH over history.

To summarize, the formula, "I am YHWH," points to the covenantal aspect

[21]C. Westermann, *Isaiah 40-66*, OTL (London: S.C.M. Press, Ltd., 1969), p. 123.

[22]S. H. Blank, *op. cit.* See Appendix II for this formula in Ezekiel, pp. 34-41.

[23]For Zimmerli's treatment, see his 1954 article, "Erkenntnis Gottes nach dem Buche Ezekiel," reprinted in *Gottes Offenbarung* (München: Chr. Kaiser Verlag, 1963), espec. pp. 112-119.

[24]S. H. Blank, *op. cit.*, p. 34. W. Eichrodt, *Theology of the Old Testament*, I, trans. by J. A. Baker (Philadelphia: Westminster Press, 1961), p. 191, points out "the oft-recurring phrase 'Ye shall know that I am Yahweh!' which may be uttered as a threat as well as in consolation, in either case is a constant reminder of the *real presence* of God, whether this be to afflict or bless."

of God; relationship to Israel in his saving acts, coupled with the realization in the prophetic books that YHWH is the supreme deity, sovereign in his control of events. The use of the formula is largely cultic, expressing Israel's acknowledgement of the supremacy of YHWH, to whom allegiance and worship are rightly due.

Another phrase, largely restricted to Deutero-Isaiah, is "I am He," *ʾanî hûʾ*. The personal pronoun *hûʾ* is vertually a surrogate for the divine name. The phrase requires investigation, as a self-asseveration of YHWH, and also because of its implications for the study of the Fourth Gospel. In the ancient "Song of Moses," YHWH is declared to be unique, "See now that I, even I am he, and there is no god beside me" (Deut.32:39). As Labuschagne asserts, "the saving events caused by Yahweh's judging activity serve to indicate Him not only as the incomparable God, but also as the sole God. When Yahweh intervenes, the rival gods will be eliminated, being no match for Him, and He will emerge triumphantly as the only true God."[25]

Passages such as Isa. 41:4; 43:10,13,25; 46:4 and 48:12 are especially interesting. The pericope, Isa. 41:2-4, has to do with the victorious progress of Cyrus, and concludes with a question and answer, "Who has performed and done this, calling the generations from the beginning? I, YHWH, the first, and with the last; *ʾanî hûʾ*" (Isa.41:4). In this context, *ʾanî hûʾ* is more than a monotheistic formula. YHWH is in control of the events of history. C. Westermann aptly states, "What is expressed here is not the permanence of an always existent divine being, but the contrast between God and history in its totality ('and with the last I am still he')."[26]

The oracles of Isaiah 43 are instructive. The subject is the vocation of Israel to witness to the reality of YHWH as the divine ruler of history. YHWH is uniquely Israel's God (Isa.43:3); Israel is called by his name (43:7). In a trial scene (43:8-13), the surrounding nations are challenged to bring forward any who can equal YHWH's power to declare, and determine the future. Israel, though blind and deaf, is YHWH's main witness to a continuity of history in which the acts of YHWH confirm his divinity. YHWH who has guided in the past, creates the future. The past history of YHWH's dealings with Israel and the future which he is able to create provide the basis whereby "you may know and believe me and understand that *ʾanî hûʾ*" (Isa.43:10). Comparing this statement with the *wᵉʾattāh hûʾ* of Ps.102:28, S. Mowinckel comments, "It can scarcely be denied that *hûʾ* is here very close to a sort of divine 'name.'"[27] Ethelbert Stauffer claims that "the theophanic formula *ANI HU* in God's speeches in Deutero-Isaiah can be understood as a combination of the liturgical *Ani* with the

[25]C. J. Labuschagne, *The Incomparability of Yahweh in the Old Testament* (Leiden: E. J. Brill, 1966), p. 115; cf. Deut. 32:12.

[26]C. Westermann, *Isaiah 40-66*, OTL (London: S.C.M. Press Ltd., 1969), p. 65.

[27]S. Mowinckel, "The Name of the God of Moses," *HUCA*, XXXII (1961):128.

liturgical *Hu.*"²⁸ The phrase, 'I am He,' recurs in Isa.43:13,25, although in verse
25, the longer form of the personal pronoun is repeated, with emphasis, *ᵃnōkhî*
ᵃnōkhî hû' (cf. Isa.51:12). Isa.43:13 reads, "I am God, and also henceforth I am
He." This is not so much the assertion of the eternal nature of the being of God
(although in the LXX it is understood in this way); it is rather a declaration that
YHWH remains unchangeably the same in his relation to Israel and in his sovereign command over the future events of history. The solemn repetition of the
personal pronoun in Isa.43:25 introduces the subject of YHWH's forgiveness of
Israel: "I, I am He who blots out your transgressions for my own sake, and I will
not remember your sins." James Smart observes, "In v.25 God's grace and mercy
break through again. The forgiveness of God does not depend upon the worthi-
ness of Israel. God forgives 'for his own sake,' i.e., because he is not willing that
the sins of Israel should defeat his purpose for mankind."²⁹

Two other passages also call for comment, Isa.46:4 and 48:12. In Isa.46, a
vivid word-picture is painted of the fall of Babylon, and in particular, the humili-
ation of the Babylonian gods, Bel and Nebo, whose images are taken from the
city not in triumphant procession as on festal occasions, but in the ignominy of
captivity. With a brilliant word-play on the verb *nā'sā*, "to carry" (the Babylonian idols will be carried on the backs of cattle; YHWH, who has carried Israel
from the womb, will continue to bear them), and with the cumulative use of the
first personal pronoun, the remnant of YHWH's people receive assurance that
YHWH will continue to sustain them. "Hearken to me, O house of Israel, all the
remnant of the house of Israel, who have been borne by me from your birth,
carried from the womb; even to your old age *ᵃnî hû'*, and to gray hairs I will
carry you. I have made, and I will bear; I will carry and will save" (Isa.46:4).
Claus Westermann interprets the metaphor of the life-span from birth to the gray
hairs of old age as pointing in analogy to the history of Israel, "Great faith was
needed to look beyond the fall of Jerusalem, the final destruction of Israel as a
political power, and the downfall and end of the house of David, and see the
history of the people of Israel as an interrupted life-span in which God's bearing
of her was a matter of past and future alike."³⁰ Finally, in Isa.48:12, in the
declaration, "I am He, I am the first, and I am the last," there is a repetition of
41:4 and 44:6. Once again, the emphasis is placed on YHWH as Creator, Creator
of the heaven and earth (48:13), Creator and Lord of future history (48:14ff).

G. A. F. Knight claims that the *ᵃnî hû'* passages in Deutero-Isaiah express
the prophet's "great theme of God as the self-revealing 'I am' (Exod.6:2-3;

²⁸E. Stauffer, *Jesus and His Story*, trans. by Dorothea M. Barton (London: S.C.M.
Press Ltd., 1960), p. 144. For the liturgical *ᵃnî* and *ᵃnōkhî*, he cites Deut. 5:6 (introducing
the Decalogue); Ps.46:10; 50:7; 81:10; for the liturgical *hû'*, Ps.115:9ff.

²⁹James Smart, *History and Theology in Second Isaiah* (Philadelphia: The Westminster
Press, 1965), p. 108.

³⁰C. Westermann, *op. cit.,* p. 181.

Deut.32:39)."[31] This theme is given a specific application in the New Testament, especially in the Fourth Gospel. The Johannine usage is significant in the light of the fact that in the LXX the *^{a}nî hû'* of Deutero-Isaiah is translated as *egō eimi*, "I am."

We are indebted to both Raymond Brown and Philip B. Harner for impressive studies of the predicateless *egō eimi* in the Fourth Gospel.[32] The evidence for the use of the phrase in John's Gospel is as follows. In nine passages, Jesus makes statements concerning himself which involve the use of *egō eimi* without a predicate noun following: Jno.4:26; 6:20; 8:24,28,58; 13:19; 18:5,6,8. Although in some of these occurrences, a suitable predicate drawn from the context may be implied, this is scarcely possible in 8:24,28,58 and 13:19. Harner regards the phrase as a theophanic formula reflecting the usage in the Deutero-Isaianic passages already cited.[33] He concludes that there are six important characteristics of *^{a}nî hû'* in Deutero-Isaiah: (1) It is always spoken by YHWH; (2) It signifies that YHWH alone is God; (3) YHWH is presented as lord of history and as redeemer of Israel; (4) YHWH is creator of the world; (5) Israel's perception of the reality of YHWH is in faith, within the context of witness and service to YHWH; (6) It is closely related to other expressions of divine self-predication, especially the phrase, "I am YHWH."[34] He concludes that the *^{a}nî hû'* of Deutero-Isaiah is an abbreviation of longer forms of self-predication such as *^{a}nî YHWH*, serving also a polemical function in making a contrast to the similar bold claims of other deities in Near Eastern hymns of self-praise.[35]

Harner has investigated the possibility that the Hellenistic world may provide the background for the absolute use of the *egō eimi* formula in the Fourth Gospel, particularly in the light of studies by G. P. Wetter and Adolf Deiss-

[31]G. A. F. Knight, *Deutero-Isaiah* (N.Y.: Abingdon Press, 1965), p. 171.

[32]R. Brown, *The Gospel According to John (i-xii)*. The Anchor Bible (N.Y.: Doubleday, 1966), Appendix IV; EGO EIMI—"I AM," pp. 533-538; Philip B. Harner, The "I AM" *of the Fourth Gospel: A Study in Johannine Usage and Thought* (Philadelphia: Fortress Press, 1970). Two earlier studies are also of particular importance: E. Schweizer, *Ego Eimi: Die religionsgeschichtliche Herkunft und theologische Bedeutung der johanneischen Bildreden, Zugleich ein Beitrag zur Quellenfrage des vierten Evangeliums*, FRLANT, 45 (Göttingen: 1965); K. Zickendraht, "EGO EIMI," *Theologische Studien und Kritiken*, 94 (1922).

[33]P. Harner, *op. cit.*, pp. 6-15. Cf. J. H. Bernard, *A Critical and Exegetical Commentary on the Gospel According to St. John*, I, ICC (Edinburgh: T. & T. Clark, 1928) p. cxxi, "To get an illustration of this absolute use, we must go to the prophetic *^{a}nî hû'*, *Ego Ipse* (Isa.46:4), which by its studied avoidance of the Name revealed in Ex.3:14, suggests its mystery and awe. Probably that Name did not connote *self-existence* (which is a later metaphysical conception), so much as *changelessness* and so *uniqueness* of being, 'He that IS.'"

[34]P. Harner, *op. cit.*, p. 7.

[35]*Ibid.*, p. 15.

mann.[36] There is little support for the absolute use of the phrase in the Hermetic literature, in Philo, and in the various gnostic writings. He concludes that "we cannot look to the Hellenistic religious milieu as the source for an absolute use of *egō eimi* in the Fourth Gospel."[37] R. H. Strachan has come to a similar conclusion, "The 'I am' form of speech is the appropriate language of deity both in the Hermetic books and in magical papyri. . . . The whole conception, however, of the speaker and of the worshippers' relation to the deity is different. Most often these 'I am' utterances of pagan deities, thus written down, are no more than a charm recited by the worshipper. By repetition of it he identifies himself with some potent deity, and thus vanquishes the 'demons' who threaten him."[38]

In Jno.8:24, Jesus, in contention with his hearers, makes the claim, "I told you that you would die in your sins, for you will die in your sins unless you believe that *egō eimi*." Sir Edwyn Hoskyns comments, "The absolute claim of Jesus is denoted by the majestic *I am*: majestic, and numinous, because of its Old Testament background (Exod. iii 14; Deut. xxxii 39; Isa. xliii 10). No predicate is expressed or provided by the context."[39] In the immediate reply to Jesus' statement in Jno.8:24, his hearers ask, "Who are you?" The question is essentially a demand that a predicate be supplied. In the immediate context, Jesus goes on to say (Jno.8:28), "When you have lifted up the Son of man, then you will know that *egō eimi*." Raymond Brown writes, "When Jesus himself is lifted up (v.28) in crucifixion, resurrection, and ascension, he draws all men to him (xii 32); and in that moment it will be clear to those who have the eyes of faith that he truly bears the divine name ('I AM') and that he has the power of raising men to the Father."[40] The words "then you will know that *egō eimi*" are reminiscent of Isa.43:10 (LXX).[41] E. M. Sidebottom points out that Jesus is addressing the Pharisees (Jno.8:13).[42] However, as C. K. Barrett has observed, in

---

[36]*Ibid.*, pp. 26-30. See G. P. Wetter, "Ich bin es." *Theologische Studien und Kritiken*,)9 (1915):232-235; Adolf Deissmann, *Light From the Ancient East* (N.Y.: George H. Doran 1927), pp. 136-142.

[37]P. Harner, *op. cit.*, p. 29.

[38]R. H: Strachan, *The Fourth Gospel*, 3rd ed. (London: S.C.M. Press, 1941), p. 20.

[39]E. C. Hoskyns, *The Fourth Gospel*, edited by F. N. Davey, 2nd ed. revised (London: Faber and Faber Limited, 1947), p. 334. Cf. G. H. C. MacGregor, *The Gospel of John*, The Moffatt New Testament Commentary (London: Hodder and Stoughton, 1928), p. 215, "It seems better here to take the words 'I am' in an absolute sense and see in them a 'mystic formula' (Loisy) complete in itself . . . and hinting at Christ's participation in the deity of the Father." Cf. also C. K. Barrett, *The Gospel According to St. John* (London: S.P.C.K., 1955), pp. 282-283.

[40]R. Brown, *op. cit.*, p. 350.

[41]Cf. C. H. Dodd, *The Interpretation of the Fourth Gospel* (Cambridge: Cambridge University Press, 1953), p. 95, "It is difficult not to see here an allusion to the divine name, *ᵃnî hû*'.

[42]E. M. Sidebottom, *The Christ of the Fourth Gospel* (London: S.P.C.K., 1961), p. 141.

the use of *gnōsesthe*, John is really addressing his readers.[43] The repetition of the "I am" of 8:24 in 8:28 and the use of the title "Son of man" makes 8:28 intentionally ambiguous according to Rudolf Bultmann.[44] The Son of Man was to come as a future Messianic figure, but in this saying, the event is already taking place; Jesus is identified with the Son of Man. The lifting up of the Son of Man also has a double significance; he will be lifted up on the cross, and he will be glorified.

Jno.8:31-59 consists of a long dialogue on the subject of the true descendants of Abraham. The climax comes in 8:58 in the astounding claim of Jesus, "Truly, truly, I say to you, before Abraham was, I am." Since the contrast is between the verbs *ginesthai* and *einai*, Raymond Brown translates, "I solemnly assure you, before Abraham even came into existence, I AM."[45] R. H. Lightfoot's comment is apt, "Whereas Abraham (like the Baptist; cf. 1[6]) 'came into existence' at a definite moment, He, the Lord, the Word of God, is above and beyond time."[46] This sense of transcending time is an important element in patristic understanding, as Hoskyns indicates in his exegesis of the passage: "The contrast is between an existence initiated by birth and an absolute existence (i.1-3, viii.28, xiii.19; for the form of the sentence cf. Ps.xc.2 LXX). The Son of God is not merely antecedent in time to Abraham; if so the Saying would have been, *Before Abraham came into being, I was.* The Being of the Son is continuous, irrespective of all time (Chrysostom). As Cyril of Alexandria comments, 'He therefore is not rivalling Abraham's times; But since He is above all time and o'erpasseth the number of every age, He says that He is before Abraham.'"[47]

Jno.13 recounts the events of the evening prior to the crucifixion of Jesus, and washing of the disciples' feet, the departure of Judas Iscariot after the meal to betray His Master, and the beginning of the discourse which continues throughout chapters 14 to 16. Ps.41:9 - H10 is quoted in 13:18, "He who ate my bread has lifted his heel against me." In this context of the treachery of a friend, Jesus says, "I tell you this now, before it takes place, that when it does take place you may believe that *egō eimi.*" This prophetic saying finds its counterpart in such passages as Isa.43:10 and Ezek.24:24, where the declaration of impending events will lead to the knowledge that "I am," "I am YHWH."[48] R. H. Strachan observes that in this, and the Johannine texts 8:24,28,58, "Jesus speaks the language of divinity."[49]

[43]C. K. Barrett, *op. cit.,* p. 284.

[44]R. Bultmann, *The Gospel of John: A Commentary,* trans. by G. R. Beasley-Murray (Oxford: Basil Blackwell, 1971), p. 349.

[45]R. Brown, *op. cit.,* p. 354.

[46]R. H. Lightfoot, *St. John's Gospel: A Commentary* (Oxford: Clarendon Press, 1956), p. 195.

[47]E. Hoskyns, *op. cit.,* p. 349.

[48]R. Brown, *op. cit.,* p. 571.

[49]R. Strachan, *op. cit.,* p. 20.

The remaining five texts in which *egō eimi* without a predicate is used are Jno. 4:26; 6:20; 18;5,6,8. In Jno.4:26 a predicate is implied. At the well of Samaria, the Samaritan woman says to Jesus, "I know that Messiah is coming (he who is called Christ); when he comes, he will show us all things" (4:25). Jesus replies, "*Egō eimi*, he who is speaking to you" (4:26). The predicate "Christ" is certainly implied, but nevertheless a *double entendre* may also be implicit, in view of the similarity to Isa.52:6, *ᵃnî hû' hamᵉdabber* (LXX *egō eimi autos ho lalōn*), "I am he, he who speaks," where the reference is to YHWH.[50]

The other sayings occur in the context of the account of the walking on the water (6:16-21) and the arrest in the garden of Gethsemane (18:1-8). To the frightened disciples toiling in their boat at night, Jesus appears,[51] coming towards them and saying, "*Egō eimi*; do not be afraid" (Jno.6:20; cf. Mark 6:50; Matt.14:27). Once again, both in the Johannine and Synoptic accounts, Harner regards the "I am" as conveying a double meaning. In a direct sense, it is simply the assertion in popular idiom, "It is I," but indirectly it may carry overtones of the *ᵃnî hû'* of Deutero-Isaiah, where "Yahweh's self-predication 'I am He' was associated with his sovereignty over the world of nature and, in particular, with the mythological motif that depicted creation itself as a victory over the unruly, chaotic forces represented by the sea."[52] In Jno.18:1-8, in reply to the officers and soldiers who have come to arrest him, the phrase *egō eimi* is used by Jesus three times (verses 5, 6 and 8). Certainly, in verses 5 and 8 this can be understood as meaning, "I am Jesus of Nazareth."[53] But verse 6 states, "When he said to them '*Egō eimi*,' they drew back and fell to the ground." According to Raymond Brown, "we have here a Johannine theological construction rather than a historical reminiscence";[54] nevertheless, Harner may well be right that "John wishes to express his belief that such an attitude of awe and reverence is the only fitting response to Jesus' words, *egō eimi*."[55]

The problem of dating is acsute in relation to Jewish sources, yet there remains a possibility that some clues regarding the divine name may be found which throw further light on the predicateless "I am" which we have been discussing. In connection with the feast of Tabernacles, the Mishnah records that the priests as they processed about the altar, recited Ps.118:25, "Save us, we beseech thee, O Lord" (the entreaty begins with the words *'annā YHWH)*.

---

[50]P. Harner, *op. cit.,* p. 47.

[51]According to Rudolf Otto, *The Kingdom of God and the Son of Man,* trans. by F. V. Filson and B. Lee-Woolf (London: Lutterworth Press, 1938, rev. 1943), p. 370, "The charismatic 'appears,' although he himself is in a distant place . . ." "a phantom-like 'apparitio' was originally meant, which tradition materialized into a bodily walking on the water."

[52]Harner, *op. cit.,* p. 34.

[53]Cf. Codex Vaticanus, "I am Jesus."

[54]R. Brown, *op. cit.,* II, p. 811.

[55]P. Harner, *op. cit.,* p. 45.

According to R. Judah, in order to avoid the Tetragrammaton, the words *'anî w^ehû'* were used.[56] Both "I" and "He" may be regarded as surrogates for the divine name, perhaps based on an understanding of Isa.42:8, "I [*^ani*] am YHWH, that [*hu'*] is my name."[57]

David Daube claims that in the use of "I am" in such passages as Jno.4:26; 8:24,28,58; 18:6; Mark 13:6; Lk.21:8; a Rabbinic model is followed by the evangelists, that of the Passover Haggadah.[58] The authors of the Passover Haggadah, drawing on the Credo from Deut.26 (especially verses 7 and 8) and referring explicitly to Exod.12:12, state, "For I will pass through Egypt—this means, I and not an angel; and I will smite all the firstborn—this means, I and not a seraph; and I will execute judgement—this means, I and not the messenger; I the Lord—this means, *I am and no other.*"[59] This last phrase, *I am and no other,* is in the spirit of the *^anî hû'* passages of Deutero-Isaiah and may be understood in the sense that God acted alone. *Egō eimi* in the Gospels carries the equivalent sense of "the Divine Presence."

An additional reference to the Fourth Gospel requires consideration, so far as the Tetragrammaton in the Bible is concerned. Jno.17, the prayer of Jesus to the Father, completes the farewell speech of chs. 13 following. Raymond Brown observes, "Functionally xvii has a role in John's account similar to that played by the hymn which Mark xiv 26 reports as having been sung at the end of the Last Supper (presumably a Hallel hymn terminating the Passover meal)."[60] Especial interest attaches to Jno.17:6,26. In 17:6, Jesus declares, "I have manifested thy name to the men whom thou gavest me out of the world"; in 17:26, "I made known to them thy name, and I will make it known." C. H. Dodd finds in these verses the very purpose of the coming of Christ. "According to John xvii.6,26, the mission of Christ in the world was to make known the Name of God."[61] "The Name" (*hashshēm*) in Judaism became a reverential substitute for the Tetragrammaton.[62] Although R. H. Strachan believes that the name specifically revealed by Jesus was the name 'Father,'[63] Raymond Brown, in keeping with his understanding of the use of the predicateless "I am" in the Fourth Gospel, tentatively suggests that "the divine name that the Johannine

---

[56]*Sukkah* 4:5; see H. Danby, *The Mishnah* (London: Oxford University Press, 1933), p. 178.

[57]P. Harner, *op. cit.,* p. 20.

[58]D. Daube, "The 'I am' of the Messianic Presence," in *The New Testament and Rabbinic Judaism* (University of London: The Athlone Press, 1956), pp. 325-329.

[59]Quoted from the Passover Haggadah by David Daube, *op. cit.,* p. 326.

[60]R. Brown, *op. cit.,* II, p. 745.

[61]C. H. Dodd, *The Interpretation of the Fourth Gospel* (Cambridge: Cambridge University Press, 1958), p. 96.

[62]E.g., *Sanhedrin* 7:5; see H. Danby, *op. cit.,* p. 392.

[63]R. H. Strachan, *op. cit.,* p. 301.

Jesus made known to man was 'I AM.'"[64] Indeed, for Brown, "the Jesus of the Last Discourse transcends time and space";[65] "divinity and timelessness are the mark of the Johannine prayer."[66] Revealing the Name means revealing the very reality of YHWH himself.

[64]R. Brown, *op. cit.,* II, p. 755-756.

[65]*Ibid.,* II, p. 747.

[66]*Ibid.,* II, p. 748.

VI

THE TETRAGRAMMATON WITHIN JUDAISM

The precise pronunciation of the Tetragrammaton is by no means easily recovered, although the view most widely accepted today is that the divine name was pronounced *Yahweh*. The literature on the subject is very extensive.[1] In the sixteenth century. Genebrardus suggested the pronunciation, *Jahve,*[2] largely on the strength of Theodoret's assertion that the Samaritans used the pronunciation *'Iabe*, subsequent to the time when pronunciation of the Tetragrammaton was forbidden to the Jews.[3] The question as to the date when pronunciation of the divine name was no longer permitted finds no certain answer. In only comparatively recent times has the pronunciation *Yahweh* been widely acknowledged. Even though Gesenius gave the pronunciation as *Yahweh* in his lexicon of 1815, scholars continued to employ the customary *Jehovah*, out of deference to tradition, until Ewald began to use *Jahveh* (= *Yahweh*) regularly in his writings.

Of the various alternative forms that have been proposed, the most probable is *Yāhō* or *Yāhū*. A. Lukyn Williams[4] has argued for such a pronunciation on the basis of theophorous names in the Old Testament ending in YHW, the Elephantine evidence, the attestation of Diodorus Siculus to a form *'Iao*,[5] various passages drawn from patristic sources, and charms and amulets which use the form

---

[1]Some of the more important contributions on the subject are: George F. Moore, "Notes on the Name YHWH," *AJSL*, XXV (1909):312-318; D. D. Luckenbill, "The Pronunciation of the Name of the God of Israel," *AJSL*, XL (1924):277-283; W. F. Albright, "The Name Yahweh," *JBL*, XLIII (1924):370-378; Leroy Waterman, "Method in the Study of the Tetragrammaton," *AJSL*, XLIII (1927):1-7; A. Lukyn Williams, "Yaho[h]," *JTS*, XXVIII (1927):276-283; F. C. Burkitt (in rejoinder to A. L. Williams), "Yahweh or Yahoh: Additional Note," *JTS*, XXVIII (1927):407-409; G. R. Driver, "The Original Form of the Name Yahweh: Evidence and Conclusions," *ZAW* XLVI (1928):7-25; B. D. Eerdmans, "The Name Jahu," *OTS*, V (1948):2-29 (the article was written in 1942); G. J. Thierry, "The Pronunciation of the Tetragrammaton," *OTS*, V (1948):30-42; B. Alfrink, "La Pronunciation 'Jehova' du Tétragramme," *OTS*, V (1948):43-63; A. Murtonen, *A Philological and Literary Treatise on the Old Testament Divine Names* (Helsinki: 1952), espec. pp. 54-61; Z. Ben-Hayyim, "On the Pronunciation of the Tetragrammaton by the Samaritans," *Eretz-Israel*, III (1954):147-154 (in Hebrew); M. Reisel, *Observations* (1957), pp. 41-61; George W. Buchanan, *The Consequences of the Covenant* (Leiden: E. J. Brill, 1970), Appendix I, "The Pronunciation of the Tetragrammaton," pp. 316-317.

[2]Genebrardus, *Chronologia* (1567); ed. Paris, 1600, pp. 79f.

[3]Theodoret, *Quaestiones XV* on Exodus (Exod.3:14).

[4]A. Lukyn Williams, "Yaho[h]," *JTS*, XXVIII (1927): espec. p. 280. Leroy Waterman reached similar conclusions, *op. cit.*, pp. 3-4. B. D. Eerdmans, *op. cit.*, p. 13, finds support also in Jer.5:12, by regarding *lo' hu'*, "he is not," as a play on the name *Jahu*. G. J. Thierry, *op. cit.*, p. 32, rejects this argument as unconvincing.

[5]Diodorus Siculus, *Hist.*, I, 94.

'Iao. Sachau, Grimme, and Leander had earlier made similar claims. W. F. Albright acknowledges the arguments for such a pronunciation, when he refers to "*Yâhû*, which appears beside *Yahwêh*, especially in the Elephantine Papyri, the jar-stamps from the same period found in Jericho, and as the final element in proper names."[6] However, Albright offers the explanation that *Yâhû* is a jussive form derived from the verbal form *Yahwêh*, and that the forms could be interchanged.[7]

Although *Yahweh* seems to be a probable pronunciation of the Tetragrammaton, since *Yāhū* does not really account for the final *he*, there cannot be complete certainty about it. Once pronunciation of the name was proscribed, the correct way of pronouncing it eventually was lost. We can only surmise that *Yahweh* is the correct pronunciation. Murtonen states, "The pronunciation of the tetragram was forgotten because of 1) the threat that Yhwh 'will not hold him guiltless that taketh his name in vain,' and 2) the unnaturalness of the circumstance that a god who was regarded as the only god in the whole universe had a proper name."[8]

B. D. Eerdmans claims that "the full Tetragrammaton is an onomatopoeia,"[9] imitating the sound of thunder. From Isa.30:27, "Behold, the name of the Lord comes from far, burning with his anger, and in rising smoke," he deduces that the divine name is an onomatopoeia of the thunder. He finds confirmation in such passages as Ps.29:3 and Exod.33:19. However, this view seems to be based on a very literal understanding of the texts cited. That the sound of thunder should evoke awe on the part of those who recognized in it the majesty of YHWH seems reasonable, but that the name YHWH itself should be an onomatopoeia of the thunder is questionable. In the case of Psalm 29, the word *qôl*, "voice," if drawn out, sounds much more like thunder reverberating.

Before we examine the traditions regarding the Tetragrammaton which are found in the Mishnah, some attention should be given to the forms of the divine name in the papyri from Elephantine and in the Dead Sea Scrolls.

A Jewish settlement at Elephantine existed prior to the Persian conquest, but took on the special task of acting as a military colony safeguarding the interests of the Persians at the southern border of Egypt.[10] The original reason for the settlement is not known, although it may well be that in the seventh century Manasseh sent mercenary troops to Egypt in exchange for horses (cf. Deut.17:16).[11] The Aramaic archives from the colony on the island of Elephan-

---

[6]W. F. Albright, *op. cit.*, p. 373.

[7]*Ibid.*, pp. 373-374.

[8]A. Murtonen, *op. cit.*, p. 36.

[9]B. D. Eerdmans, *op. cit.*, p. 15.

[10]See Bezalel Porten, *Archives from Elephantine* (Berkeley and Los Angeles: University of California Press, 1968).

[11]B. Porten, *op. cit.*, p. 12.

tine date from 495 B.C., down to the end of the fifth century.[12] From these archives, especially from the letters to Bagoas, governor of Judaea in the late fifth century, we learn that a Jewish Temple was erected earlier than the Persian conquest of 525 B.C., and that it was destroyed in 410 B.C. The Temple was dedicated to the god *YHW*. Oriented towards Jerusalem, its dimensions resembled those of the Jerusalem Temple. Bezalel Porten states, "Details about the Temple derive from the papyrus recording its destruction and asking assistance for its reconstruction (C30/31). It was built prior to the Persian conquest of 525 B.C.E. and contained stone pillars, five gateways of carved stone with bronze hinges, a 'cedarwood' roof and woodwork (? *'srn^c*) (C30:9ff./31:8ff.)."[13]

In all likelihood, the Temple at Elephantine was erected prior to the Deuteronomic legislation which restricted worship to the one central sanctuary at Jerusalem. The situation is not unique, however. Porten refers to other such centres of Jewish worship, "Two and perhaps three other Jewish Temples are known to have existed outside of the one in Jerusalem: the Temple of Onias at Leontopolis in Egypt, the Samaritan Temple on Mount Gerizim, and perhaps the Qaṣr el-^cAbd of Hyrcanus at ^cAraq El-Emir in Transjordan. Each of these shrines has in common a background of political rivalry, the disaffection of its priestly founders with affairs in Jerusalem, and the marked military character of its location."[14] The relationship between the priests of the Temple in Jerusalem and those in Elephantine is not altogether clear. Porten states, "Once the Jerusalem Temple was destroyed, the one at Elephantine was likely to have gained in stature. The Elephantine Jews were proud of the fact that their Temple was not harmed by Cambyses, although the Egyptian temples were 'overthrown' (C30:14/31:13). The effect on the Elephantine Temple of the reconstruction of the Jerusalem Temple is unknown, but it continued to exist, until it was destroyed at Egyptian instigation in the summer of 410 B.C.E."[15] The reason for the destruction of the Temple remains uncertain, although Porten suggests that a visit to Egypt by Hananiah regarding Passover observances may have antagonized the Khnum priests, since the festival commemorated the Exodus from Egypt and the Israelite victory over the Egyptians.[16] The members of the Elephantine community appealed to the priests of the Temple at Jerusalem for aid in recon-

[12]See A. Cowley, *Aramaic Papyri of the Fifth Century B.C.* (Oxford: Clarendon Press, 1923); H. H. Rowley, "Papyri from Elephantine" in D. Winton Thomas (ed.), *Documents from Old Testament Times* (London: Thomas Nelson and Sons Ltd., 1958), pp. 256-269; Emil G. Kraeling, *The Brooklyn Museum Aramaic Papyri: New Documents of the Fifth Century B.C. from the Jewish Colony at Elephantine* (New Haven: Yale University Press, 1953).

[13]B. Porten, *op. cit.*, p. 110. C 30:9ff., etc. refers to the numeration and translation of the papyri by Cowley.

[14]B. Porten, *op. cit.*, p. 116.

[15]*Ibid.*, pp. 121-122.

[16]*Ibid.*, pp. 280-281.

structing the Temple. At first the Jerusalem authorities were unenthusiastic, probably because of their belief that only the single sanctuary at Jerusalem was legitimate. Nevertheless, Porten writes, "Their subsequent willingness may have been due to compromise; meal offering and incense were permitted but holocaust was not. The Elephantine Jews accepted the limitation of their rights."[17] Cedars were brought from Lebanon for the roofing (C30:11/31:10). Archaeological excavation has not uncovered any trace of the Elephantine Jewish Temple, however.[18]

The Elephantine archives consist of more than thirty papyri, written in Aramaic, the diplomatic *lingua franca*. In addition to family archives, there are legal contracts and official letters. There are also a number of private notes penned on ostraca. Although the Tetragrammaton never appears, the divine name in the form YHW occurs quite frequently in the papyri. Once (C13:14) it is found in the form YHH, which is the usual form in the ostraca. Porten comments, "The spelling YHH is probably an orthographic variation of YHW; cf. *yrḥḥ* for Jericho (1 Kings 16:34). In the papyri YHH alone appears only in C13:14 but that document possesses numerous orthographic peculiarities."[19]

Cowley transliterates YHW as *Ya'u*,[20] although H. H. Rowley prefers the form *Yahu*,[21] following A. van Hoonacker's earlier proposal.[22] According to van Hoonacker, perhaps *Jah* was the primitive form of the divine name, of which *Jahou* was a development.[23] He regards the Tetragrammaton as a secondary formation, "C'est par. une modification, une adaptation du nom Jahou préexistant, qu'une forme nouvelle fut forgée en vue de faire exprimer au nom divin l'idée d'être."[24] The form YHW poses no problem for Albright, who regards it as the jussive form of *Yahweh*.[25]

The deity is referred to as "God of heaven" in the papyri, and as "YHH of hosts" in the ostraca. There are also many theophorous names. Porten com-

---

[17]*Ibid.*, p. 292.

[18]Stanley A. Cook, "The Significance of the Elephantine Papyri for the History of the Hebrew Religion," *AJT*, XIX (1915):379. Cf. B. Porten, *op. cit.*, p. 110, "Neither the German, French, nor Italian expeditions succeeded in locating the site of the Temple though each of the excavators held certain views as to its possible site."

[19]B. Porten, *op. cit.*, p. 105, n. 5.

[20]A. Cowley, *op. cit.*, p. xviii.

[21]H. H. Rowley, *op. cit.*, p. 257.

[22]A. van Hoonacker, *Une Communauté Judéo-Araméenne à Éléphantine, en Égypte, aux VIe et V^e siecles av.J-C.*; The Schweich Lectures, 1914 (London: Oxford University Press, 1915), pp. 67ff.

[23]*Ibid.*, p. 69, n. 1.

[24]*Ibid.*, p. 71.

[25]W. F. Albright, "The Names 'Israel' and 'Judah' with an Excursus on the Etymology of Todah and Torah," *JBL*, XLVI (1927):175. See also n. 6, above.

ments, "The devotion of the Elephantine Jews to YHW is revealed by the over-whelming proportion of names which contain the element YHW/H. Of the more than 160 different names borne by Elephantine Jews, including hypocoristica, only a handful were non-theophorous."[26] These names express confidence in God: "He is a refuge and a fortress, a source of hope and trust, and a covert. He is the source of warmth, light and dew, wealth and welfare. He is just, working on behalf of the individual as well as the group."[27] The largest category of theophorous names takes the form of a verbal sentence, emphasizing what the deity does: "He takes note of human conduct, judges, mediates, and requites. He shelters the needy and comforts the bereaved. He hearkens unto those who call to Him, has pity on them and answers them. He listens to prayers, draws up from Sheol, and heals the sick. He supports the righteous and honors the honorable. He is generous in giving but occasionally holds in reserve. He is able to protect, deliver, rescue, and save, help, liberate and redeem his devotees. He strives for those loyal to him and He gladdens the heart of his worshippers."[28]

A problem of interpretation is raised by the mention in the papyri of other deities. A. E. Cowley remarks, "It would seem that besides Ya'u they recognized ^cAnath, Bethel, Ishum and Herem. There may have been others, but it is at least a coincidence that we have the names of five gods and that there were five gates to the temple (30:9)."[29] If these are separate deities, what is their relationship to one another? Were syncretizing tendencies at work? Cowley concludes, "It was not a case of falling away from a monotheistic ideal, but a continuation of the pre-exilic popular beliefs."[30] According to W. F. Albright, "the three divine names *Eshem-bêth'el, Herem-bêth'el, ^cAnath-bêth'el* (= ^c*Anath-Yahu*), meaning respectively 'Name of the House of God' (= God), 'Sacredness of the House of God,' and 'Sign(?) of the House of God' would reflect pure hypostatizations of deity, probably influenced by contemporary Canaanite-Aramaean theological speculation, in which Bêth'el frequently appears as the name of a god (from the seventh to the fourth century B.C.)."[31] Porten, on the other hand, finds the evidence for hypostatization "not sufficiently decisive"[32] and looks rather to pagan influences resulting from intermarriage as the occasion for the introduction of these names of foreign deities.[33] The process of syncretism can be seen in the compound name of the deity, *Anathyahu*. Porten makes the

[26]B. Porten, *op. cit.*, p. 134.

[27]*Ibid.*, p. 137.

[28]*Ibid.*, pp. 138-139,

[29]A. E. Cowley, *op. cit.*, p. xviii.

[30]*Ibid.*, p. xix.

[31]W. F. Albright, *From the Stone Age to Christianity*, 2nd. ed. (Baltimore: The Johns Hopkins Press, 1946), p. 286.

[32]B. Porten, *op. cit.*, p. 179.

[33]*Ibid.*, p. 178.

observation, "YHW was still God, but Anath was added assurance. Anathyahu was that aspect of YHW which assured man's well-being. Although the Arameans had a shrine to the Queen of Heaven, the name Anath appears only twice among the many personal names from Elephantine and Syrene (C22:108; BK 4:3). If the goddess' cultic importance may be judged from her onomastic absence, it would seem that she did not play a major role in the communal religious life of the Jews."[34]

The Qumran scrolls contain some items of interest in relation to the use of the divine name. In describing the biblical manuscripts found in Cave 4, Patrick Skehan draws attention to a number of unusual features.[35] For example, 4QIs^c "contains such names as *Yhwh, Yhwh ṣb'wt, 'lwhynw*, and the like in paleo-hebrew script. This is almost unique among square-letter manuscripts in Qumran 4."[36] Nevertheless, the Fouad papyrus No. 266 of Deuteronomy in Greek, consisting of Deut. 31:28-32:7, appears to be the oldest witness to a differentiation in script for the Tetragrammaton, which is written in Aramaic characters.[37] A Greek papyrus MS of Leviticus (4QLXX Lev.^{b}), in a hand similar to that of the Fouad papyrus of Deuteronomy (first century B.C.), employs *'IAO* instead of *Kyrios*, which nowhere occurs in the document.[38] David Diringer mentions the fact that both the Tetragrammaton and the name *'ēl* (= God) are written in early Hebrew characters in certain of the Qumran MSS which are otherwise written in square-letter Hebrew script.[39] Some Greek codices of the Christian era contained the Tetragrammaton in early Hebrew script; e.g., P. Oxy. vii 1007, a third century papyrus fragment of Genesis, abbreviates as ZZ, probably to

---

[34]*Ibid.*, p. 177. The symbol BK 4:3 is based on the numeration and translation of the ostraca by E. Bresciani and M. Kamil, "Le lettire Aramaiche di Hermopoli" in *Atti della Accademia Nazionale dei Linci, Classe di Scienze, Morale, Memorie*, Ser. VIII, 12 (1966), pp. 357-428.

[35]P. W. Skehan, "The Qumran Manuscripts and Textual Criticism," *Supplements to Vetus Testamentum*, IV (Leiden: E. J. Brill, 1957), pp. 148-160.

[36]P. W. Skehan, *op. cit.*, p. 151. For a photographic facsimile of the Tetragrammaton in paleo-Hebrew script, see Col. x, 1.6 of the Habakkuk (*pesher*) scroll in Plate LIX of *The Dead Sea Scrolls of St. Mark's Monastery*, I, ed. M. Burrows (New Haven: A.S.O.R., 1950). "The Temple Scroll," so-named by Yigael Yadin, contains the Tetragrammaton written in full and always in the same script as the text, similar to the practice of the Qumran scribes when copying biblical texts. The *pesharim*, however, and the Cave 11 Psalm scroll utilize the paleo-Hebrew script for the Tetragrammaton. Cf. Y. Yadin, "The Temple Scroll," *Biblical Archaeologist*, XXX (1967):136.

[37]P. W. Skehan, *op. cit.*, p. 151. Cf. W. G. Waddell, "The Tetragrammaton in the LXX," *JTS*, XLV (1944):158-161, in which a photographic facsimile of the P. Fouad No. 266 is given, with the Tetragrammaton appearing in Col. ii, lines 7 and 15.

[38]P. W. Skehan, *op. cit.*, p. 157.

[39]D. Diringer, "The Biblical Scripts" in *The Cambridge History of the Bible*, Vol. 1, ed. P. R. Ackroyd & C. F. Evans (Cambridge University Press, 1970), p. 15. A case in point is the Habakkuk scroll.

represent a doubled *yodh*; in Origen's *Hexapla* (third century), the Greek versions of Aquila and Symmachus represented the divine name by pi, iota, pi, iota, capitalized,[40] obviously intended to approximate to the Hebrew characters for the Tetragrammaton in the LXX, almost always abbreviated to *ks* as in the case of the Chester Beatty papyrus of Numbers and Deuteronomy. This evidence suggests that *ᵃdônāy* may have been read as a substitute for the divine name as early as the time that the Hebrew Bible was being translated into Greek, i.e., from the third century B.C. onward.[41]

Among the Qumran manuscripts, *The Manual of Discipline* is unique in attesting a five-letter name for God, *hw'h'* (1QS VIII.13). In an allusion to Isa.40:3, the phrase *'t drk hw'h'* corresponds to *drk YHWH* of the MT, which is represented by *drk* followed by four dots where the Tetragrammaton occurs. The passage in context reads, "And when these become members of the Community in Israel according to all these rules, they shall separate from the habitation of ungodly men and shall go into the wilderness to prepare the way of Him (*hw'h'*); as it is written 'Prepare in the wilderness the way of . . . ,' 'make straight in the desert a path for our God' (Isa. xl.3)."[42] In S. Mowinckel's opinion, "As the scribe does not write *drkw* his *hw'h'* certainly means something more than an ordinary suff. 3rd. pers. masc.; it is meant to be a real compensation for the divine name."[43] This he takes as evidence that the pronoun "He" (*hû'*) was used as a name or surrogate for God, a view shared by such scholars as del Medico, S. Zeitlin and G. Lambert. The final *aleph* is an obstacle to this interpretation, however, although the fact that the pronoun *hw'h* appears in 1QS III:17, 25; 4:25, strengthens the supposition. W. H. Brownlee surmises that *hw'h'* is a periphrasis for God which originated as an abbreviation of the combined form *hû' h'lhym*.[44]

Traditions incorporated in the Mishnah and the Talmud indicate that the

---

[40]W. G. Waddell, *op. cit.*, pp. 158-159

[41]P. van Imschoot, *Theology of the Old Testament*, I (N.Y.: Desclée Company, 1965), p. 25. Cf. B. Lindars, "Is Psalm II an Acrostic Poem?" *JBL*, XVII (1967):65.

[42]Following the translation of G. Vermes, *The Dead Sea Scrolls in English* (Harmondsworth, Middlesex: Penguin Books, 1962), pp. 85, 86. M. Burrows, *The Dead Sea Scrolls* (N.Y.: The Viking Press, 1955), p. 382, translates *hw'h'* as "the Lord." Cf. P. Wernberg-Møller, *The Manual of Discipline* (Grand Rapids, Michigan: Wm. B. Eerdmans, 1967), p. 129, n. 44, for a summary of views of other scholars; and p. 44, n. 3, "The Tetragrammaton is constantly avoided in 1QS, in the commentary part of 1QpHab, and in CD."

[43]S. Mowinckel, "The Name of the God of Moses," *HUCA*, XXXII (1961):132.

[44]W. H. Brownlee transliterates the name as HUHA. In his opinion, "The surrogate may have been suggested by the recurring combination *YHWH hû' haᵉlôhîm* (Yahweh, he is the God)"; see *BASOR*, Supplementary Studies, *The Dead Sea Manual of Discipline: Translation and Notes* (New Haven, Conn.: ASOR, 1951), p. 33, n. 29. See also A. R. C. Leaney, *The Rule of Qumran and Its Meaning* (London: S.C.M. Press Ltd., 1966), p. 222, "Its spelling here suggests that it is formed from the first five letters of the Hebrew phrase 'He is God' (cf. Deut. 4.35,39; 7.9; 1 Kings 18.39)."

Tetragrammaton was avoided as being too sacred to pronounce. In the oldest manuscripts of the Cairo Geniza, the divine name in· the Mishnah is represented by two *yodhs*, which in printed editions were pointed by vocalic sh^ewa followed by *qamets* (i.e., the pointing of $sh^em\bar{a}$', the Name). According to the Babylonian Talmud (Pes. 50a), the Rabbis read $l^call\bar{e}m$ ("to conceal") rather than $l^c\bar{o}l\bar{a}m$ ("forever") in Exod.3:15 and understood this as an injunction to keep the divine name secret.[45] The cultic use of the Tetragrammaton in the daily priestly bless-ing and by the High Priest on the Day of Atonement (Yom Kippur) continued for some time as the last vestige of its legitimate use. M. Reisel, although uncriti-cally following Garstang in setting a fifteenth century date for Moses and for such cultic practices as the use of the Aaronic blessing (Numb.6:24-27), stands on surer ground when he regards the *terminus ad quem* for the use of the divine name to be as early as 198 B.C.E., i.e., the death of the High Priest, Simeon the Just.[46] He claims that "since the death of the High Priest Simeon the Just the other priests no longer considered themselves worthy to pronounce the Tetra-grammaton distinctly and completely in the daily priestly blessing."[47] Accord-ing to the Mishnah, on the Day of Atonement, "when the priests and the people which stood in the Temple Court heard the Expressed Name come forth from the mouth of the High Priest, they used to kneel and bow themselves and fall down on their faces and say, 'Blessed be the name of the glory of his kingdom for ever and ever!'" (*Yoma* 6:2).[48] G. W. Buchanan claims, "The divine name was pronounced so that people could hear it every Day of Atonement even as far as Jericho."[49] In M. Reisel's view, "The death of the venerated High Priest Simeon the Just formed the occasion for changing its pronunciation in the daily priestly blessing in such a manner that it yet remained approximately equal to the original pronunciation. The High Priest continued to use the original pronun-ciation on the Day of Atonement, but reduced its sonority. Eventually, after the destruction of the Second Temple, this pronunciation lost its audibility alto-gether."[50]

According to *Tamid* 7:2 and *Sotah* 7:6, when the blessing of the priests was given, "in the Temple they pronounced the Name as it was written, but in the

---

[45]See G. F. Moore, *Judaism*, I (Cambridge: Harvard University Press, 1927), p. 428. However, it is clear from the context of *Pes.* 50a that the Talmudists were familiar with the usual MT rendering of Exod.3:15.

[46]M. Reisel, *Observations*, p. 64.

[47]*Ibid.*, p. 64. See Talmud, *Yoma* 39b.

[48]Translation by H. Danby, *The Mishnah* (London: Oxford University Press, 1933), p. 169.

[49]G. W. Buchanan, *The Consequences of the Covenant* (Leiden: E. J. Brill, 1970), p. 316, n. 5. This tradition is found in *Tamid* 3:8. Cf. I. Abrahams, *Studies in Pharisaism and the Gospels*, Second Series (Cambridge: University Press, 1924), pp. 25-27.

[50]M. Reisel, *Observations*, p. 71.

provinces by a substituted word."[51] Samuel Cohon comments, "The Tetragrammaton was originally spoken by all the priests in the Temple in pronouncing the benediction. In the synagogues the substitute name Adonai was employed in worship. . . . Following the death of Simon the Just—which was marked by the spread of Hellenism and its heretical trends—the Tetragrammaton ceased to be spoken even in the Temple by the ordinary priests. The High Priest alone pronounced it on Yom Kippur. While reciting Lev.16:30 during the confessional, R. Tarfon reports that even the high priest uttered it cautiously under his breath. The rest of the time both he and others invoked God as *Hashem* (*Ber.* 4:4; *Yoma* 3:8; 4:2; 6:2)."[52]

Undoubtedly, one of the factors operative in forbidding the use of the divine name was the avoidance of magical practices. Nevertheless, the use of the divine name in working miracles is attested in *Exodus Rabbah* I § 34, where Moses is said to have killed the Egyptian slave-master by pronouncing the Tetragrammaton.[53] Reisel observes, "Mishnah *Sanhedrin* x:1 forbids the use of the Divine Name for magical purposes, and adds as a preventive warning that those transgressing this command would forfeit their portion in the future world."[54] Belief in the wonder-working power of the name persisted over the centuries, however. G. F. Moore claims that the attempt to prevent misuse of the Tetragrammaton in incantations and magic was futile, for, "If this was the motive for secrecy, the means defeated the end; for the *secret* name of a god is a vastly more powerful spell than that which everybody knows. The Greek magical papyri show that the adepts were alive to this fact."[55] Reisel refers to an incident in the life of Rabbi Lŏw ben Bezalel of Prague (1530-1609), who placed an amulet on which was written one of God's names in the mouth of a *gōlem* (a mannikin of clay) and brought it to life."[56] Likewise, the eighteenth century

[51]H. Danby, *op. cit.,* pp. 588, 301.

[52]Samuel S. Cohon, "The Name of God, A Study in Rabbinic Theology," *HUCA,* XXIII (1951):591-592.

[53]M. Reisel, *Observations,* p. 80. O. Eissfeldt has indicated the possibilities of magical use of the divine name within the Old Testament itself through blessing and cursing "in the name of YHWH," i.e., in 2 Sam.6:18; Ps.129:8; 2 Kings 2:24; see "Jahwe—Name und Zauberwesen" in *Kleine Schriften I* (Tübingen: J. C. B. Mohr, 1962), pp. 150-171. The use made of divine names in the semi-Jewish magical papyri of the first four or five centuries is evidence of the way in which potential magical tendencies within the divine name found expression. The sixth century also yields similar evidence; see J. A. Montgomery, *Aramaic Incantation Texts from Nippur* (Philadelphia: The University Museum, 1913), p. 226, where incantation No. 32 contains the words, "charmed and sealed and counter-sealed in this ban-writ by the vittue of YHYHYHYHYH, YHYH, YHYH."

[54]M. Reisel, *Observations,* p. 67.

[55]G. F. Moore, *op. cit.,* I, p. 426.

[56]M. Reisel, *Observations,* p. 3. For the concept of the *gōlem,* see Gershom G. Scholem, *On the Kabbalah and Its Symbolism,* trans. by Ralph Mannheim (N.Y.: Schocken Books, 1965), Ch. 5.

founder of Hasidism, Israel ben Eliezer, was known to certain Polish Jews as a worker of miracles and "master of the Name."[57]

Both Philo and Josephus witness to the reticence in uttering the divine name which was so characteristic of Rabbinic theology. According to Philo, when Moses requested the name of God at the burning bush, God replied, "First tell them that I am He Who is, that they may learn the difference between what is and what is not, and also the further lesson that no name at all can properly be used of Me, to whom all existence belongs."[58] Josephus, commenting on the same incident in Exod.3, suggests that God was reluctant to reveal his name, but at the urging of Moses, "Then God revealed to him His name, which ere then had not come to men's ears, and of which I am forbidden to speak."[59] Josephus, in *Contra Apion* II:80 refers to the desecration of the Temple by Antiochus Epiphanes: "Apion has the effrontery to assert that within this sanctuary the Jews kept *an ass's head,* worshipping that animal, and deeming it worthy of the deepest reverence; he maintains that this fact was disclosed on the occasion of the spoilation of the Temple by Antiochus Epiphanes, when the head, made of gold and worth a high price, was discovered." Norman Walker speculates that what Antiochus Epiphanes saw was the Tetragrammaton, embossed on the gold-plated altar of incense, written in a symmetrical form with the *yodh* above the remaining three letters, and that he mistakenly took this to be an ass's head.[60]

Frequently in the Targums, *mêmrâ,* "Word," is substituted for the divine name.[61] Sometimes *mêmrâ* is simply an addition, as, for example, when the Targum of Onkelos reads for Gen.3:8, "They heard the voice of the *mêmrâ* of the Lord God." But usually the purpose is to avoid anthropomorphisms, so that in Deut.3:22 it is the *mêmrâ* of God which fights for the Israelites; in Deut.4:24, his *mêmrâ* is a consuming fire. In W. F. Albright's judgment, "the targumic *Mêmrâ* is simply a fossilized expression surviving from a period when influential Jewish groups were engaged in 'building a fence' around the holiness of God, by substituting words denoting aspects or qualities of Him, such as Divine Wisdom, the Divine Word, the Divine Presence (*Panîm* in earlier times, *Yeqârâ* in later), for his Divine Name."[62] E. M. Sidebottom claims that the *raison d'être* of the

[57]M. Reisel, *Observations,* p.3.

[58]Philo, *De Vita Mosis,* I section 75, trans. by F. H. Colson, Loeb edition (Cambridge: Harvard University Press, 1956).

[59]Josephus, *Antiq.II,* sections 275-76, trans. by H. St. J. Thackeray, Loeb edition (Cambridge: Harvard University Press, 1950).

[60]N. Walker, "The Riddle of the Ass's Head and the Question of a Trigram," *ZAW,* LXXV (1963):225-226.

[61]Strack-Billerbeck, "Exkurs über den Memra Jahves" in *Kommentar zum neuen Testament aus Talmud und Midrash* (München: Oskar Beck, 1924), pp. 302-333; G. F. Moore, *Judaism,* I (Cambridge: Harvard University Press, 1927), pp. 417ff.

[62]W. F. Albright, *From the Stone Age to Christianity,* 2nd ed. (Baltimore: The Johns Hopkins Press, 1946), p. 285.

term *Mêmrâ* "is the sense of the numinous which surrounds the person of God himself, the Name."[63]

In the post-Talmudic period, speculation regarding the divine name grew apace in Jewish mysticism, as reflected in the Kabbalah, "that great body of Hebrew literature that sprang up and grew parallel to the traditional writings of rabbinical literature, for a period of over a thousand years."[64] Next to the Hebrew Bible and the Talmud, the Kabbalah is the third major source of Jewish faith. From the eleventh century onward, mysticism exercised a growing appeal. Jewish mysticism finds its classical expression in the *Sepher ha-Zohar*, "The Book of Splendor," which is written in the form of a commentary to the Torah. Moses ben Shemtov de Leon, a thirteenth century Jewish mystic of Granada in Spain, compiled and composed the *Zohar*, which purports to be a series of discourses between the second century Rabbi Simeon ben Yohai and contemporary Jewish mystical exegetes. Much of the mystic lore which the *Zohar* contains is very ancient. According to the Kabbalists, "The External Law and the Secret Doctrine were both revealed on Mount Sinai, and as Moses transmitted the one to his nation at large, so he communicated the other to certain elders, by whom it was handed on."[65] Mystical beliefs represent a protest against formalism, by keeping alive the inward, experiential aspects of faith. Gershom Scholem expresses the essential difference between the mystic and the prophet when he writes, "the mystic's experience is by its very nature indistinct and inarticulate, while the prophet's message is clear and specific. Indeed, it is precisely the indefinable, incommunicable character of mystical experience that is the greatest barrier to our understanding of it."[66] Although Jewish mysticism stands over against tendencies towards formalism, the very term *Kabbalah* means "tradition," i.e., "that which is received." The mystic stands with the Biblical and Talmudic tradition; indeed, "all his thinking and above all his imagination are still permeated with traditional material."[67]

Because the Kabbalah rests on materials drawn from different dates, there is nothing systematic about Jewish mystical beliefs. So far as systematic presentation is possible, it may be said that *En-Soph* (literally, "without end," i.e., the Infinite) stands for Divine Thought, God as unknown and unknowable in essence, "elevated above the comprehension of man."[68] From *En-Soph*, four

---

[63]E. M. Sidebottom, *The Christ of the Fourth Gospel* (London: S.P.C.K., 1961), p. 45.

[64]Dagobert D. Runes, *The Wisdom of the Kabbalah* (N.Y.: Philosophical Library, 1957), p. 9.

[65]A. E. Waite, *The Secret Doctrine in Israel: A Study of the Zohar and Its Connections* (London: William Rider & Son, Limited, 1913), p. 22.

[66]Gershom G. Scholem, *On the Kabbalah and Its Symbolism*, trans. by Ralph Mannheim (N.Y.: Schocken Books, 1965), pp. 9-10.

[67]G. Scholem, *op. cit.* p. 15.

[68]*Zohar*, I, 21a. References are to *The Zohar*, 5 vols., trans. by Harry Sperling and Maurice Simon (London: The Soncino Press, 1933).

worlds emanated, representing four stages of creation. They are subdivided by the Kabbalists into ten spheres, or *sephirôth*, speculative mystical-philosophical modes of action of God: The Crown, Wisdom, Understanding, Mercy, Severity, Beauty, Victory, Glory, Foundation, the Kingdom.[69] The *Sepher Yezirah* (Book of Formation, i.e., Creation), a Kabbalistic text earlier than the *Zohar*, is one of the sources of this information. It teaches that the world was created through the combination of the letters in the divine name.[70] The twelfth century *Masecheth Aziluth* (The Treatise on Emanation) by Jacob ha-Nazir expounds the doctrine of the four worlds through which God, who is infinite, makes himself known in the finite.

A. E. Waite summarizes the teaching of the *Zohar* on Gen.1:2 in this way, "When the world of manifest things was in the state of *Tohu*, God revealed Himself therein under the Hypostasis, *Shaddai*; when it had proceeded to the condition called *Bohu* He manifested as the Hypostasis *Sabaoth*; but when the darkness had disappeared from the face of things He appeared as Elohim. Hereto appertain the words: 'And the spirit of God moved upon the face of the waters,' understood as a reference to the sweet and harmonious voice heard by Elijah and termed: 'The voice of the Lord is upon the waters.' This signifies the completion of the Sacred Name Jehovah."[71] In Elijah's experience of the still small voice was found the name YHWH.[72] But the Tetragrammaton existed before the material world. A. E. Waite states that "the Holy One engraved in the ineffable world those letters which represent the Mystery of Faith, being *Yod, He, Vau, He*, the synthesis of all worlds above and below. *Yod* represents the central point and the cause of all things, concealed and unknown for ever, being the Supreme Mystery of the Infinite."[73]

Gershom Scholem enunciates three principles of the Kabbalists regarding the nature of Torah: the principle of God's name; the principle of the Torah as an organism; the principle of the infinite meaning of the divine word.[74] Spanish Kabbalists put forward the radical view that "the Torah is not only made up of the names of God but is as a whole the one great Name of God."[75] According to *Zohar, IV, 36a*, "the Torah is all one holy supernal name." Joseph Gikatila, a leading thirteenth century Spanish Kabbalist, regarded the Torah rather as an explanation of the Name of God. He wrote (*Sha^care 'Orah*, 2b), "The whole

---

[69] A. E. Waite, *op. cit.*, ch. 3; Isidore Epstein, *Judaism* (Harmondsworth, Middlesex: Penguin Books, 1959), espec. pp. 232-237.

[70] S. Cohon, *op. cit.*, p. 595.

[71] A. E. Waite, *op. cit.*, p. 32; *Zohar*, I 16a.

[72] *Zohar*, I, 16a.

[73] A. E. Waite, *op. cit.*, p. 56; *Zohar*, III, 126b, 127a.

[74] G. Scholem, *op. cit.*, p. 37.

[75] *Ibid.*, p. 39; cf. *Zohar*, V, 80b, "the Torah is the supernal holy Name."

Torah is a fabric of appellatives, *kinnuyim*—the generic term for the epithets of God, such as compassionate, great, merciful, venerable—and these epithets in turn are woven from the various names of God. But all these holy names are connected with the tetragrammaton YHWH and dependent upon it. Thus the entire Torah is ultimately woven from the tetragrammaton."[76]

By Gematria, or numerical equation, some correspondence was found between God and Adam, for the numerical value of the four letters of the Tetragrammaton is 45, as is also the value of the letters in the name Adam.[77] On Gen.2:7, "And the Lord God formed man," the *Zohar* comments, "'Man' here refers to Israel, whom God shaped at that time both for this world and for the future world. Further, the word *vayizer* (and he formed) implies that God brought them under the aegis of His own name by shaping the two eyes like the letter *Yod* and the nose between like the letter *Vau*."[78] Yet, God himself cannot be imagined to possess any form or to be depicted in any manner; for "in the beginning, before shape and form had been created, He was without form and similitude. Therefore it is forbidden to one who apprehends Him as He is before creation to picture Him under any form or shape whatsoever, not even by his letters *He* and *Vau*, nor by the whole of His Holy Name, nor by any letter or sign soever. The words 'For ye saw no manner of similitude' thus mean, 'Ye saw nothing which could be represented by any form or shape, nothing which ye could present or simulate by any finite conception.' But when He had created the form of supernal Man it was to Him a chariot, and He descended on it, to be known according to the style, 'YHVH, in order that He might be known by His attributes and perceived in each attribute separately."[79]

In Ps.46:8 -H9, "Come, behold the works of the LORD, who hath made desolations in the earth," the *Zohar* reads Elohim rather than YHWH, and comments, "As R. Hiya says, if the world had been created through the name which connotes mercy (YHVH), it would have been indestructible; but since it has been created through the name which connotes justice (*Elohim*), 'desolations have been placed in the earth,' and rightly so, since otherwise the world would not be able to endure the sins of mankind."[80] The matter of attributes is pursued again in the exegesis of Exod.6:2: "AND ELOHIM SPAKE UNTO MOSES AND SAID TO HIM I AM YHVH. It is written above (5:22): 'And

---

[76]G. Scholem, *op. cit.*, p. 42. Similar views were held by Nachmanides, also of the thirteenth century.

[77]G. Scholem, *op. cit.*, p. 104.

[78]*Zohar*, I, 26a.

[79]*Zohar*, III, 42b.

[80]*Zohar*, I, 58b. Although YHWH was adopted by the Massoretes as the correct reading in Ps. 46:9, many MSS read 'Elohim,' the name which appears seven times elsewhere in the Psalm. Psalm 46 belongs to the collection of Psalms (42-83) which have undergone Elohistic redaction, unless R. G. Boling's thesis of stylistic patterns is accepted in place of the more usual redaction hypothesis.

Moses said, Lord (Adonai), wherefore hast thou evil entreated this people?' What prophet could speak with such boldness as this save Moses, who knew that another and superior degree (viz. YHVH) was awaiting him? R. Isaac said: 'Moses, who was "faithful in God's house," addressed Him without fear and trembling, like a steward who has charge over the household.' According to another explanation, the words 'And God spake and said unto him, I am YHVH' mean that the manifestation was in both attributes, in Justice and Mercy, both fitly framed and joined together. R. Simeon said that they were manifested not unitedly but successively, as is indicated by the expression, 'And Elohim spake ... and said unto him "I am YHVH"': stage after stage."[81] The revelation of God to the patriarchs as El Shaddai (Exod.6:3) is also commented upon. The distinction between Jacob and Moses, for instance, is this: "The former experienced the Divine manifestations as 'El Shaddai,' but God did not speak with him in the higher grade designated by YHVH."[82]

The wearing of the phylacteries, which contained four sections of the Torah, each representing one of the four letters of the divine name, is associated with the statement in Deut.28:10, "And all the peoples of the earth shall see that you are called by the name of YHWH, and they shall be afraid of you."[83] According to Zohar I, 14a, "The phylacteries are thus literally the counterpart of the letters of the Divine Name."

The Tetragrammaton is also related to the Passover. "Said R. Abba: 'In how many ways does the Holy One show his loving kindness to His people! A man builds a house; says the Holy One to him: 'Write My Name and put it upon thy door (mezuzah), and thou wilt sit inside thy house and I will sit outside thy door and protect thee!' And here, in connection with the Passover, He says: 'You inscribe on your doors the sign of the mystery of My Faith and I shall protect you from the outside!' They inscribed the likeness of the Holy Name in the form of the letter He'. As the Holy Name was then turned from Mercy to Judgement, chastisement came into (God's) view at that time. Everything was turned into red, as a symbol of vengeance on Israel's enemy."[84]

The rite of circumcision is also associated with the divine name. "That circumcision is of such significance can be seen from Abraham: before he was circumcised he was, as it were, a closed vessel, impervious on all sides, but when he was circumcised, and the sign of the letter yod of the Holy Name was manifested in him, he became open to supernal influences, this being the inner meaning of the words, 'he sat at the door of the tent in the heat of the day' (Gen. XVIII, 1), i.e. of the supernal holy Tent. R. Eleazar said that when the yod was manifested he received the glad tidings that Grace was confirmed with

---

[81]Zohar, III, 22b.

[82]Zohar, III, 23a.

[83]Zohar, I, 13b.

[84]Zohar, III, 36a.

Righteousness. R. Abba said, it refers to the tenth crown (that of Grace), with which he was then endowed, as indicated by the words 'in the heat of the day,' namely at the time when Grace predominates."[85]

Moses Gaster has made a translation of a thirteenth or fourteenth century Rabbinical manuscript, entitled on the basis of Deut.33:29 *The Sword of Moses*.[86] The "Sword" was regarded as "a peculiar form of the divine Name, excellent and all-powerful, which served as a shield and protection."[87] The document, written in a mixture of Hebrew and Aramaic, is "a complete encyclopaedia of mystical names, of eschatological teachings, and of magical recipes."[88] This particular work shows some indebtedness to Gno'stic beliefs. A variety of divine and angelic names is given, including *Sabaôth*, and names ending with *-ēl*. There are affinities with the thaumaturgical "magic" of the Gnostics. The names have certain curative properties, can heal pain in the ear, cataract, paralysis, and bring relief from a variety of afflictions. Other magical uses are itemized for those who wish to know whether their journey will be lucky, or who intend to send dreams to their neighbours, or kill a lion, or make a man ill.[89] An appendix at the end of Section II states, "Verily, this is the ('Sword of Moses') with which he accomplished his miracles and mighty deeds, and destroyed all kinds of witchcraft; it had been revealed to Moses in the bush when the great and glorious Name was delivered to him. Take care of it and it will take care of thee. If thou approachest fire, it will not burn thee, and it will preserve thee from every evil in the world."

Various combinations of letters and words based on the Tetragrammaton were believed to have mystical and magical significance, according to the Talmud.[90] Gaster writes, "The Ineffable Name of God and the fear of pronouncing it can be traced to a comparatively remote antiquity. We find in those ancient writings that have retained the traditions of the centuries before the common era, the idea of a form of the Ineffable Name composed of 22, 42, or 72 parts, or words, or letters, of which that consisting of 72 was the most sacred. It is still doubtful what those 22, 42 and 72 were—either different *words* ex-

---

[85]*Zohar*, III, 36a.

[86]M. Gaster, *The Sword of Moses: An Ancient Book of Magic* (London: 1896), repr. (N.Y.: Samuel Weiser, Inc., 1970).

[87]*Ibid.*, p. 22.

[88]*Ibid.*, p. 18.

[89]*The Sword of Moses*, Section III.

[90]E.g., Babylonian Talmud, *Ḳid.* 71a. Two quotations from the Soncino edition are interesting; "Our Rabbis taught: At first (God's) twelve-lettered Name used to be entrusted to all people. When unruly men increased, it was confided to the pious of the priesthood, and these 'swallowed it' during the chanting of their brother priests"; "Rab Judah said in Rab's name: The forty-two lettered Name is entrusted only to him who is pious, meek, middle-aged, free from bad temper, sober, and not insistent on his rights."

94   The Divine Name in the Bible

pressing the various attributes of God, or *letters* in a mystical combination; but
whatever those may have been they took the place of the Ineffable mystical
name and were credited with the selfsame astounding powers. By means of these
every miracle could be done and everything could be achieved."[91] Arthur Waite
claims that a nine-lettered name was produced by combining YHWH with
Elohim and alternating the consonants: Yodh, Aleph, He, Lamedh, Waw, He,
He, Yodh and Mem.[92] According to the Kabbalistic book of *Bahir*, the sacred
name of twelve letters consisted of a three-fold repetition of the Tetragrammaton.[93] S. Cohon claims, "The twelve lettered Name is supposed to be composed of the three words *'ehyeh* in Ex.3:14. The forty-two lettered Name is
represented by the abbreviations of the forty-two word prayer ascribed to the
first century tanna, R. Nehunya b. Hakaniah. The seventy-two lettered Name is
derived from the three verses, Ex.14:19-21 . . . each of which contains seventy-
two letters."[94] Another view of the seventy-two lettered name is that the Tetragrammaton was written three times, then in the following line three times less
the initial *yodh*, omitting one more letter in the following lines until the final
line contained simply YHWH: this gives a total of seventy-two letters altogether.
In M. Reisel's view, "The recitation of this protracted Tetragrammaton was a
descrescendo with regard to the fulness of sound, as appears from its graphical
representation,"[95]

H. J. Franken claims that Jewish mysticism has its experiential basis within
the Hebrew Bible, particularly in the book of Psalms.[96] In his view, "it lies in
the very nature of the *kabōd Jhwh* to be the starting-point for mystic experi-
ences in the cultus. Being connected with the experience of God as light it
provided the pious with the pattern of the revelation on Mount Sinai."[97]
Indeed, "the oriental way of meditation, the ecstasy in the sanctuary, the per-
fect peace with the world of God expressed in praise, the lifting up of the hands
and blessings, and finally the experience of seeing God point to the mystical
tendency in the piety of the psalms."[98] The Kabbalists found mystical significance by an allegorical and theosophical approach to the Torah, claiming that
"the whole Torah can be expounded in seventy ways."[99] In spite of the many

[91]M. Gaster, *op. cit.,* pp. 7, 8.

[92]A. E. Waite, *op. cit.,* p. 191, n. 1.

[93]L. Blau, art. TETRAGRAMMATON in the *Jewish Encyclopedia,* XII (N.Y.: Funk
and Wagnalls, 1906), p. 120.

[94]S. Cohon, *op. cit.,* pp. 596-597.

[95]M. Reisel, *Observations,* p. 86.'

[96]H. J. Franken, *The Mystical Communion with Jhwh in the Book of Psalms* (Leiden:
E. J. Brill, 1954). For a more general statement of the biblical basis of Jewish mysticism, see
Epstein, *op. cit.,* p. 224.

[97]H. J. Franken, *op. cit.,* p. 46.

[98]*Ibid.,* p. 92.

[99]*Zohar,* I, 54a.

extravagances of Kabbalism, the mystical tendency within Judaism had its part to play in the rise of Hasidism; for example, in the contribution of Israel Baal-Shem, the founder of Polish Hasidism.[100] Yet, as early as the twelfth century, Moses Maimonides, who influenced subsequent Judaism more than any other single figure, favoured a more rationalistic approach. He frowned on the mystical tendencies of some of his contemporaries and, in particular, was opposed to the use of the divine name as a basis for speculation or for purposes of magic or healing.[101] In *The Guide of the Perplexed*, I, 61-67, Maimonides writes at length about the Tetragrammaton. From Zech.14:9, "On that day YHWH will be one and his name one," he deduces that the four-lettered name is indicative of the essence of God without associating any other notion with it.[102] In a careful exposition of Exod.3 (*I*, 63), he maintains that "I am what I am" includes the idea of the negation of attributes. The verb "to be" is indicative of existence, and the fact that in the phrase "I am that I am" the subject is identical with the predicate leads on to the conclusion that "there is a necessarily existent thing that has never been, or ever will be, nonexistent."[103] The name *Yah* "refers similarly to the notion of the eternity of existence."[104] All other names for deity are derivative and equivocal. The influence of Aristotelian philosophy cannot be dismissed, although a primary purpose of Maimonides was to give a valid exegesis of the crucial phrase "I am that I am" with careful attention to the grammatical structure. Nevertheless, his emphasis on reasoning faith provided the basis for later developments in Jewish philosophical thought just as Thomas Aquinas may be said to have laid the groundwork for the theology of subsequent Catholic theologians, so influential within the Christian Church.

This survey of the way in which the Tetragrammaton has been regarded within Judaism has placed emphasis on the avoidance of the divine name in speech, out of motives of reverence and the desire to avoid profanation. Philo, and later, Maimonides, saw clearly that to attach a name at all to God is to delimit him and to set boundaries, for God is more than the sum of his attributes. Mystical contemplation has viewed the Tetragrammaton as the agent of creation, the Ineffable name which carries within it the qualities of power and love.

Modern Jewish theologians have made a significant contribution to our understanding of the divine name. Martin Buber has drawn attention to the pervasive influence of the concept of YHWH as the Present One, based on his

[100]G. Scholem, *op. cit.*, p. 26.

[101]Moses Maimonides, *The Guide of the Perplexed*, trans. by Shlomo Pines (The University of Chicago Press, 1963), I, 61, 62.

[102]*Ibid.*, I, 61.

[103]*Ibid.*, I, 63.

[104]*Ibid.*, I, 63.

understanding of Exod.3:12-15. He summarizes, "YHVH is 'He who will be present' or 'He who is here,' he who is present here; not merely some time and some where but in every now and in every here. Now the name expresses his character and assures the faithful of the richly protective presence of their Lord."[105]

Yehezkel Kaufmann affirms the lofty monotheistic concept which dominates the Hebrew Scriptures. He refuses to accept the view that "the religion of YHWH began as henotheism or monolatry, recognizing him as sole legitimate god in Israel, but acknowledging the existence of other national gods."[106] YHWH is the only active divine being. The real threat to Israel is idolatry, the worship of an anonymous idol, a fetish. During the early period, Israel was being consolidated as the people of YHWH, a covenant people with an obligation to destroy idolatry. The protest against idolatry was a major concern of the prophets. But after the great watershed in Israel's history, the fall of Jerusalem and the Babylonian exile, Israel has a mission to the gentile nations; Israel's god, YHWH. We may debate the question as to whether or not Judaism ever consciously accepted this missionary role, but it cannot be denied that the monotheistic beliefs and high ethical standards of Judaism drew many "fearers of God" to the synagogues that were established throughout the Mediterranean world, especially in the two centuries before the Common Era, and the two succeeding centuries.

Abraham Heschel brings forward the penetrating insight that the prophets knew YHWH as possessing a hidden "pathos." By his participation in existence, by his attentiveness and concern for mankind, God reveals himself always as a Subject, and not an object. The prophets did not, and could not, understand the mystery of God's essence, but were caught up in the mystery of God's relation to man. Heschel writes, "For biblical theology these ideas are as basic as the ideas of being and becoming are for classical metaphysics. They mark the difference between pagan and prophetic experience. There, existence is experiencing being; here, existence is experiencing concern. It is living in the perpetual awareness of being perceived, apprehended, noted by God, of being an object of the divine subject. This is the most precious insight: to sense God's participation in existence; to experience oneself as a divine secret (See Ps. 139:7-18)."[107]

The dynamic presence of YHWH with his people, especially from the time of Moses and throughout history, the uniqueness of YHWH, the "pathos" of YHWH, combine as the priceless legacy which Judaism shares with the world.

[105]M. Buber, *Moses: The Revelation and the Covenant* (N.Y.: Harper and Brothers, 1958), p. 53.

[106]Y. Kaufmann, *The Religion of Israel: From its Beginnings to the Babylonian Exile*, trans. and abridged by Moshe Greenberg (London: George Allen & Unwin Ltd., 1961), p. 8.

[107]A. J. Heschel, *The Prophets* (N.Y.: Harper & Row, 1962), p. 483.

VII

THE TETRAGRAMMATON WITHIN CHRISTIANITY

The historical problem of the origin and meaning of the Tetragrammaton has by no means found a solution which can be accepted with any degree of confidence. Jewish and Christian scholars alike have investigated questions of origins without any one view commanding more than a degree of probability. The Kenite hypothesis has the virtue of helping to explain the divergence between the Yahwist's assertion of continuity with the past and the emphasis of the Elohist and Priestly sources on the novelty of the name in the time of Moses. This hypothesis, however, offers no assistance in the recovery of the meaning of the divine name.

Even although the original meaning of the name remains a matter for speculation, the modern exegete is fascinated by the hermeneutical possibilities within the biblical tradition, i.e., with interpretation that has contemporary significance. Kornelis Miskotte, for example, states categorically that "YHWH is an anonymous Name" and then goes on to assert: "The primary meaning is that the God of Israel withdraws himself from all conjuration: he cannot be conjured up with this nameless name and be made subservient to an ulterior purpose. But more specifically . . . Israel is referred to the *action* that proceeds from YHWH, to what he undertakes to do, the long journey he takes with Israel from Egypt to the Promised Land and from there into the exile and the Diaspora, the 'days' and the 'deeds' which are the days and the deeds of God."[1] We are not dealing here with philological or etymological considerations, but rather with the totality of the Old Testament witness to YHWH as the covenant God of Israel, known and recognized in those events within history which are perceived to be revelatory. In the particularity of theophanic disclosure and in the light of God's mighty deeds on behalf of Israel, the divine name acquires meaning. For Miskotte, "God's 'being-one-with' and God's 'being-with' human life are revealed simultaneously in the theophany."[2] He concludes that "the omnipresence of the one true God cannot be known in any other way except on the basis of his special presence, that his universal love is perceived only in a very special election, his omnipotence in a very special redemptive power."[3] God's revelation in Israel's history, so concrete and so particular, prepares the way for the unique revelation in the birth, death and resurrection of Jesus Christ, in whom the name (the character, the nature) of God is seen to be universal love, and who is known as Immanu-el, "God with us," God omnipresent. This revelation is also concrete

[1] Kornelis H. Miskotte, *When the Gods are Silent* (London: Collins, 1967), p. 121.

[2] *Ibid.*, p. 131.

[3] *Ibid.*, p. 129.

5000

and particular. A new Israel (Gal.6:16) comes into being, the Christian Church, the firstfruits of a new humanity, declaring the reality, the presence, and the redemptive power of God to the whole world.

A study of Exodus 3 indicates that within Israel an association was found between the Tetragrammaton and the verb "to be." Whatever reservations one may have regarding the etymological correctness of this derivation, one cannot negate the fact that a connection with *hayah* gives content and meaning to the divine name, even although Exodus 3:13-15 is somewhat enigmatic. J. C. Hoekindijk has coined the term "hayyaology"[4] to represent the "-ology of the One who happens," and in so doing he has placed a particular interpretation on the passage under discussion. Bruce Boston combines the insights of W. F. Albright and J. C. Hoekindijk when he writes, "many interpreters take the Hebrew *Yahweh* form to mean 'the one bringing to pass, the creator, the performer of his promises.' We may also say that the God of Israel is the one who 'happens' with his people, the one who, when he presents himself, does so as event and in events. The chief significance and advantage of this understanding for coming to terms with revelation is that we are freed by it to develop 'hayya-logical' categories which find their correspondence in history rather than being limited by metaphysical categories."[5] God is not so much the object of philosophical inquiry (God-in-himself) as he who has acted concretely in history.

Charles West argues against the view that God can "be understood as an object of which certain attributes can be predicated and verified."[6] Rather, "He who reveals himself to Moses under the name YHWH refused to be so categorized and therefore captured. He would make himself known in the events of his continuing relation with the Hebrew people, and words which describe him would be forms of human response to the events of the relationship. Old Testament history is the continuing story of the redefinition and deeper understanding of these words: holy, righteous, jealous, merciful, and the rest."[7] In this sense, Exod.34:6,7 is a commentary on Exod.3:14, and Deutero-Isaiah brings out the theological significance of "I am YHWH," "I am he," by affirming God's creative and redemptive activity.

Ronald G. Smith, in a study entitled *The Doctrine of God,*[8] brings under review a number of theories regarding the interpretation of the Exodus passage. Étienne Gilson remains in the classic tradition of those who find in the association with the verb "to be " the basis for metaphysical, ontological categories,

[4]Bruce O. Boston, "How are Revelation and Revolution Related?" *Theology Today*, XXVI (1969):143, n. 1.

[5]*Ibid.*, p. 143.

[6]Charles C. West, "The Problem of Ethics Today," *Theology Today*, XXV (1968):357.

[7]*Ibid.*, p. 358.

[8]Ronald Gregor Smith, *The Doctrine of God* (London: Collins, 1970), espec. pp. 92-100.

i.e., God as pure being, the essence of deity. Ronald Smith points out that if indeed Exodus has to do not with the giving of the name, but with withholding it, "then the way towards the classic doctrine of God's aseity, his being from, for and of himself, would be unambiguously clear."[9] However, he refers with approval to a private communication from William McKane, who states, "Approaching 'I am as I am' more positively, we should have to say that it points to the freedom of YHWH or, perhaps, to his transcendence. He is the God who comes to his people when he chooses to come. In so far as the life of his people is open to this coming God (i.e., in so far as they are that kind of community) they will recognize him whenever he comes. . . . In so far as they are open to Yahweh their existence will be a historical existence. He is then a God who makes history and who gives his people a history by coming to them."[10]

Ronald Smith traces the influence of Franz Rosenzweig on Martin Buber's thought from 1923 (*Ich und Du*) to a position in the third and subsequent editions of *Königtum Gottes* (1956; English translation, 1967), which is not unlike that of Gerhard von Rad.[11] From the translation "I am that I am," Buber moved to "I am there as I am there," and finally to "I shall be there as I Who will always be there." This is the reality of the "being" of YHWH; the promise of his unfailing presence with his people. God belongs not so much to the realm of ideas as to the realm of relationships.

The emphasis on the active existence of YHWH is made strongly by Walther Eichrodt and is representative of modern scholarship.[12] Smith comments as follows, "at the moment we are not entitled to say more than that the consensus among Old Testament scholars provides a strong basis for an understanding of the God of biblical faith in historical and dynamic terms, and not in conceptions of timeless and static entities, whether eternity or God's aseity."[13]

The "theologians of hope" have incorporated similar insights in their interpretation of the divine name. For example, Jürgen Moltmann maintains, "YHWH, as the name of the God who first of all promises his presence and his kingdom and makes them prospects for the future, is a god 'with future as his essential nature,' a God of promise and of leaving the present to face the future, a God whose freedom is the source of new things that are to come."[14] Here the imperfect *'ehyeh* is understood primarily as a future tense. So also, the Roman

[9]*Ibid.*, p. 93.

[10]*Ibid.*, p. 94.

[11]*Ibid.*, p. 96.

[12]W. Eichrodt, *Theology of the Old Testament*, I, trans. by J. A. Baker (Philadelphia: The Westminster Press, 1961), espec. Chs. V-VII.

[13]R. G. Smith, *op. cit:*, p. 99.

[14]J. Moltmann, *Theology of Hope*, trans. by James W. Leitch (London: S.C.M. Press Ltd., 1967), p. 30.

Catholic theologian, J. B. Metz, abandons the traditional Thomist metaphysic of being and makes this comment on the meaning of Exod.3:14, "According to this version God revealed himself to Moses more as the power of the future than as a being dwelling beyond all history and experience. . . . His transcendence reveals itself as our 'absolute future.'"[15]

The Old Testament witness to YHWH brings with it a change in the meaning of other terms for deity which are used in place of the Tetragrammaton. Charles West observes, "The other concepts for deity in the Old Testament, *Elohim* and *Adonai*, the former of which was rooted in pagan polytheism and the latter in everyday social experience of power and authority, were used and redesigned, emptied of their previous significance, and made to demonstrate the absolute subordination of human and divine powers to this one lord."[16] The eventual substitution of *ᵃdōnây* for YHWH within Judaism as a mark of veneration for the divine name which could no longer be uttered with propriety, had far-reaching consequences. Among Jews of the Diaspora, *kyrios* was the Greek equivalent for the Tetragrammaton in the LXX version of the Hebrew scriptures, reflecting the fact that *ᵃdōnây* was understood as a substitute for the Tetragrammaton. Inevitably the emphasis had shifted to the concept of sovereignty, lordship.

The use of *ᵃdōnây* in the Hebrew Bible and *kyrios* in the LXX has very wide ramifications for New Testament scholarship, especially in relation to Christological formulation. The content of the term *kyrios* in the declaration of I Cor.12:3, "Jesus is Lord [kyrios]," requires to be determined, in order to arrive at an adequate understanding of a most important aspect of the person of Christ. Gustaf Dalman summarized the historical situation in this way: "The significant transition from the divine name 'Jahve' to the divine name 'Lord' did not take place in the region of Hebraic Judaism. It is rather a peculiarity of Jewish-Hellenism, and from that source found its way into the language of the Church, even of the Semitic-speaking part of it."[17] This, indeed, is the thesis of William Bousset in his monumental study, *Kyrios Christos.*[18] He claims that "the title *kyrios* spans an area in the history of religions which can still be fairly precisely delimited. It penetrated Hellenistic-Roman religion from the East; Syria and Egypt are its actual home territories."[19] Although *kyrios* was used in the ordinary secular sense of "master" or "owner," the use of the specific religious sense

---

[15]J. B. Metz "The Church and the World" in *The Word in History*, ed. by T. Patrick Burke (N.Y.: Sheed and Ward, 1966), p. 76, quoted by R. G. Smith, *op. cit.,* p. 86.

[16]Charles C. West, *op. cit.,* p. 358.

[17]G. H. Dalman, *The Words of Jesus*, trans. by D. M. Kay (Edinburgh: T. & T. Clark, 1902), pp. 179-180.

[18]W. Bousset, *Kyrios Christos* (Göttingen: Vandenhoeck & Ruprecht, 1913), trans. by John E. Steely (N.Y.: Abingdon Press, 1970). References are to the English edition.

[19]*Ibid.,* p. 145.

can be fully documented from the Hermetic literature and the writings of the Gnostic sects.[20] "It was in this atmosphere," Bousset writes, "that Antiochene Christianity and that of the other primitive Christian Hellenistic communities came into being and had their growth."[21]

In Bousset's view, the Gentile Christian Church at Antioch, recognizing Jesus as a cult-hero, and coming under Hellenistic influences, began to apply the title *Kyrios* to him. This was the situation within the church to which Paul was introduced. The Pauline epistles give abundant evidence that the designation *kyrios* was the title which now became normative for Jesus, since *Christos* had now become virtually a proper name. The affirmation of faith, "Jesus is *kyrios*" (I Cor. 12:3), perhaps originally an ecstatic cry of prophetic rapture, became a baptismal confession (1 Cor. 6:11; Acts 19:5).

Rudolf Bultmann, in the foreword to the fifth edition of Bousset's *Kyrios Christos* (1964) and in his *Theology of the New Testament*,[22] has adopted this position without reservation. However, Oscar Cullmann in *The Christology of the New Testament* is by no means persuaded that the concept of Jesus as Lord was lacking in the primitive Jewish-Christian community in Palestine, with its eschatological outlook.[23] Although within the Palestinian church Christological titles such as "Messiah" and "Son of Man" referred mainly to the future work of Jesus, such titles as *Kyrios* ("Lord") and *Soter* ("Saviour"), referring primarily to the present work of Jesus, also have a Hebraic background. In particular, he claims that the use of the ancient prayer *Maranatha* (1 Cor.16:22) belongs originally to the worship of the primitive Church in Palestine. For him, this oldest liturgical formula "is an expression of the cultic veneration of Christ by the original Aramaic-speaking Church."[24] The eschatological orientation, pointing to the end of the age, is to be seen if the formula is understood as *marana tha,* "Our Lord, come!" (cf. Rev.22:20).[25] Cullmann quotes with approval the *dictum* of A.E.J. Rawlinson, that the formula is the "Achilles heel" of

[20]*Ibid.*, espec. pp. 138ff. See also Werner Foerster and Gottfried Quell, *Lord*, Bible Key Words from Gerhard Kittel's *TWNT*, trans. by H. P. Kingdon (London: Adam & Charles Black, 1958), Ch. 11 (by Werner Foerster).

[21]W. Bousset, *op. cit.*, p. 146.

[22]R. Bultmann, *Theology of the New Testament*, I (N.Y.: Charles Scribner's Sons, 1954), pp. 51ff., 121ff.

[23]O. Cullmann, *The Christology of the New Testament* (London: S.C.M. Press Ltd., 1959), espec. Ch. 7.

[24]*Ibid.*, p. 214.

[25]*Ibid.*, pp. 209-210. See James Moffatt, *The First Epistle of Paul to the Corinthians*, The Moffatt New Testament Commentary (London: Hodder & Stoughton, 1938), pp. 282-286, for a full discussion; cf. Jean Héring, *The First Epistle of Saint Paul to the Corinthians*, trans. from the Second French Edition by A. W. Heathcote and P. J. Allcock (London: The Epworth Press, 1962), p. 186.

Bousset's thesis.[26] Indeed, the Aramaic prayer *Maranatha* "forms both a factual and philological link between *Mari* and *kyrios.*"[27]

The question that is being raised for historical and theological investigation is that of the relationship between the primitive Palestinian church of Jerusalem and the Gentile Christian church throughout the Mediterranean world. Bousset readily grants that *Maranatha* is a very old cultic formula. However, for him "the possibility cannot be dismissed that the Maranatha formula could have been developed not on the soil of the Palestinian primitive community but in the bilingual region of the Hellenistic communities of Antioch, Damascus, and even Tarsus."[28] That *Maranatha* is a eucharistic prayer is to be seen from its occurrence in the *Didache* (10:6). The question for historical investigation is this: At what point in the early life of the Church did the breaking of the bread carry with it the eschatological hope of the *parousia* ("appearance," i.e. final coming) of Jesus as *kyrios*? I Cor. 11:3 makes it clear that this hope was very early indeed.

The conclusion which seems best to satisfy the evidence is that *kyrios* was indeed used in the primitive Palestinian Church, but was a title readily acceptable in the Gentile Christian church, in view of the religious associations which the term had already acquired in a Hellenistic milieu.

Another question has to do with the use of the Old Testament within the Christian Church. The LXX certainly paved the way in the Christian communities of the Diaspora for the *kyrios* title (used in translation of *ʾadōnây*, the surrogate of YHWH) to be applied directly to Christ himself. Bousset argues against the view that *kyrios*, used of God in the LXX, was simply transferred to Christ in the Palestinian Church. "They would hardly have dared without further ado," he claims, "to make such a direct transferral of this holy name of the almighty God—actually almost a deification of Jesus."[29] Rather, "such proceedings take place in the unconscious, in the uncontrollable depths of the group psyche of a community; this is self-evident, it lay as it were in the air, that the first Hellenistic Christian communities gave the title *kyrios* to their cult hero."[30] In the Mediterranean world, with its "many 'gods' and many 'lords'" (1 Cor.8:5), Paul makes the claim, "yet for us there is one God, the Father, from whom are all things and for whom we exist, and one *Kyrios* Jesus Christ, through whom are all things and through whom we exist" (1 Cor.8:6). In this statement, Bousset asserts, "the spirit of unconquerable and stalwart Old Testa-

---

[26] A. E. J. Rawlinson, *The New Testament Doctrine of the Christ*, The Bampton Lectures for 1926 (London: Longmans, Green and Co., 1926), p. 235.

[27] O. Cullmann, *op. cit.*, p. 203.

[28] W. Bousset, *op. cit.*, p. 129.

[29] *Ibid.*, p. 146.

[30] *Ibid.*, p. 146.

ment monotheism is transferred to the Kyrios worship and the Kyrios faith."[31]

In the early Christian preaching, Jesus was proclaimed as both *kyrios* and *christos* (Acts 2:36). Again the question forces itself upon us as to the way in which the Old Testament was used in the earliest preaching. The sermons in the Acts of the Apostles may well represent the preaching of the church in the last decade or so of the first century.[32] Were the earliest sermons concerned primarily with demonstrating from the Old Testament testimonia that Jesus was indeed the Messiah?

C. H. Dodd[33] has argued persuasively that the *kerygma* ("proclamation," i.e. "the message preached") as stated in these sermons, rests on earlier tradition, proceeding from the Aramaic-speaking church at Jerusalem. Dodd summarizes the content of the early *kerygma* in this way: The Messianic age of fulfilment has dawned in the ministry, death and resurrection of Jesus of Nazareth, of Davidic descent, who is now exalted at the right hand of God as Messianic head of the new Israel, and whose present power and glory are to be seen in the activity of the Holy Spirit, prior to the final return of Christ at the end of the age. Jesus is declared to be the holy and righteous "Servant" (Acts 13:13,14) of Deutero-Isaiah, as well as "Lord and Christ" in this re-interpretation of the title "Messiah" (cf. the prayer in Acts 4:24-30, especially the use of the title "Anointed" in verse 26).

The Johannine confession of faith, in the mouth of Thomas, "My *kyrios* and my God!" (Jno.20:28) constitutes a declaration of the deity of Christ. At what point within the life of the Church could such a confession be made? Bousset traces the process of deification of Jesus within the New Testament writings and throughout the first two centuries. He argues that "the deification of Jesus develops gradually and with an inner necessity out of the veneration of the Kyrios in earliest Christianity. The Kyrios becomes the *theos Iesous Christos*."[34] By the end of the second century, Ignatius was freely using the term *theos* (God) of Jesus. "The first literary document in which the half-instinctive, half-traditional reluctance to speak without embarrassment of the deity of Christ is abandoned, not merely occasionally but throughout and fundamentally is the body of *Ignatian epistles*."[35]

Special interest attaches to the way in which Old Testament passages such as Joel 2:32 - H3:5 and Isa.40:13 are used in the New Testament. Joel 2:32 (LXX) reads, "all who call upon the name of the *kyrios* shall be delivered." In Rom.10:13, Paul quotes from this passage in Joel, with application to Christ,

[31]*Ibid.,* p. 151.

[32]See M. Dibelius, *Studies in the Acts of the Apostles*, trans. by Mary Ling (London: S.C.M. Press, Ltd., 1956), pp. 72, 180, 213.

[33]See C. H. Dodd, *The Apostolic Preaching and Its Developments* (London: Hodder & Stoughton, 1936), espec. Ch. 1.

[34]W. Bousset, *op. cit.,* p. 317.

[35]*Ibid.,* p. 321.

especially in the light of Rom.10:9, "if you confess with your lips that Jesus is *kyrios* and believe in your heart that God raised him from the dead, you will be saved." Similarly, in the context of Perer's sermon at Pentecost, the quotation from Joel 2:32 (Acts 2:21) leads on to the statement that "God has made him both *kyrios* and *christos*, this Jesus whom you crucified" (Acts 2:36). Isa.40:13 in the LXX version is quoted with some freedom by Paul in Rom.11:34, where the entire context indicates that the *kyrios* is God, but in 1 Cor.2:16 the phrase "the mind of Christ" interprets the phrase "the mind of the *kyrios.*"[36] Isa.45:23 strikes a universalistic note, "To me every knee shall bow, every tongue shall swear." This passage is applied to God by Paul in Rom.14:11, but in the Christological hymn, Phil.2:5-11, the application is made to Jesus, and again, the key phrase is "Jesus Christ is *kyrios*" (Phil.2:11). It was inevitable that by using the title *kyrios* of Christ and by appealing to passages from the Old Testament in which God receives the title *kyrios*, the direction in which doctrinal formulation would lead would be the assertion of the deity of Jesus.

The New Testament not only refers to Jesus as *kyrios* but also lays special emphasis upon the "name" of the *kyrios* Jesus. Bousset boldly asserts, "As the cohesiveness and the knowledge of God of the old covenant were conditioned and determined by the sacred name of Yahweh, so is the unity of the new religious fellowship dominated by the name of Jesus. In this sense it is meant that the Father has given his name to the Son."[37] In the prayer of John 17, Jesus prays, "Holy Father, keep them in thy name, which thou hast given me" (Jno.17:11; cf. 17:6,26). According to the letter to the Ephesians, Christ is "above every name that is named" (Ephes.1:21), and in the letter to the Hebrews, he has obtained a name more excellent than any angelic name (Heb.1:4). Baptism was "in the name of the *kyrios* Jesus Christ" (1 Cor.6:11; Acts 19:5). Bousset, in reviewing the patristic evidence for baptism in the name of the *kyrios*, seeks to relate the practice to the religious branding in the milieu surrounding Christianity. "The uttering of the name is probably only a weakened sacramental form for the more original, more robust custom of branding or etching upon the person being initiated the sign (name, symbol) of the appropriate god, to whom he was consecrated."[38] Bousset's interpretation of the *stigmata* which Paul bears (Gal.6:17, "I bear on my body the *stigmata* of Jesus"), follows along such lines.[39]

---

[36]E.g., W. G. H. Simon, *The First Epistle to the Corinthians*, Torch Bible Commentaries (London: S.C.M. Press, Ltd., 1959), p. 69, "In v. 16 St. Paul moves directly from the thought of THE MIND OF THE LORD, that is, of Almighty God (Isa.41:13) to THE MIND OF CHRIST seen as its equivalent."

[37]W. Bousset, *op. cit.*, p. 293.

[38]*Ibid.*, p. 295.

[39]*Ibid.*, p. 298, n. 188. E. D. W. Burton, *A Critical and Exegetical Commentary on the Epistle to the Galatians*, ICC (Edinburgh: T. & T. Clark, 1921), p. 361, refers to the practice of branding slaves, and sees this as the metaphor by which Paul, as a slave of Jesus, is marked by the scars of his sufferings.

The wonder-working propensities of the name are to be seen in the healings and exorcisms so frequently recounted in the Acts of the Apostles. The lame man who is healed at the temple gate responds to the words "in the name of Jesus Christ of Nazareth, walk" (Acts 3:6); in Peter's sermon which follows, the crowd learns that "his name, by faith in his name, has made this man strong" (Acts 3:16, cf. 4:10). At Philippi, a slave girl with a spirit of divination is exorcised when Paul calls out, "I charge you in the name of Jesus Christ to come out of her" (Acts 16:18). At Corinth, "itinerant Jewish exorcists undertook to pronounce the name of the *kyrios* Jesus over those who had evil spirits" (Acts 19:13). The persistence of belief in the efficacy of the name of Jesus is to be seen in the longer ending of Mark's Gospel (Mark 16:17,18).

In the Gnostic "Gospel of Truth," the name of the Father is given to the Son: "And this is the Father, He from whom proceeded the Beginning and to whom all who have proceeded from Him and who have been manifested for the Glory and for the Joy of His Name will return. And the Name of the Father is the Son. He it is who at the first gave the Name to him who proceeded from Him and who was Himself. And He has begotten him as Son. He has given him His name. . . . And the Sons of the Name are those in whom the Name of the Father rests. And they for their part rest in His Name."[40]

One may surmise that the emphasis placed upon the name of Jesus by the early Christian Church, together with the recognition of him as *kyrios*, stood in the way of any use of the Tetragrammaton in mystical or magical fashion. Christian mysticism has been more concerned with the name of Jesus than with the name YHWH.[41]

A modern writer who has made some use of the Tetragrammaton as symbolic is Charles Williams. In his novel, *Many Dimensions*, the focus of attention is "a cubical stone measuring about half an inch every way, and having apparently engraved on it certain Hebrew letters," "the letters of the Tetragrammaton."[42] A further description follows, "But they are not engraved on the Stone; they are in the centre—they are, in fact, the Stone."[43] Possession of the stone, which has creative and curative properties, gives the power to transcend space and time.

---

[40]H. C. Puech, G. Quispel and W. C. van Unnik, *The Jung Codex*, trans. and edited by F. L. Cross (London: A. R. Mowbray, 1955), pp. 73-74. Although the Codex is dated in the fourth century, Quispel believes that "the Gospel of Truth" goes back to the second century, and is probably the work of Valentinus, *ibid.*, p. 50.

[41]Cf. the influence of the *Philokalia* in Eastern Orthodoxy; e.g. in the case of the nineteenth century Russian pilgrim who learns that, "The continuous Prayer of Jesus is a constant uninterrupted calling upon the divine name of Jesus, with the lips, in the spirit, in the heart," *The Way of a Pilgrim*, trans. by R. M. French (London: Philip Allan, 1930), p. 19.

[42]Charles Williams, *Many Dimensions* (Victor Gollancz, 1931). This quotation is from a later edition (London: Feber & Faber Limited, 1947), p. 7.

[43]*Ibid.*, p. 7.

The stone is a talisman, but is also dangerous in the hands of unbelievers.[44] It can multiply itself without any diminution of the original. Charles Williams is able to convey a sense of the numinous in the way in which he brings the characters in his novel into encounter with the divine name. Questions of divine sovereignty and the limitations and potentialities of human free will are never far beneath the surface. In the death of Sir Giles Tumulty we are given an illustration of the fact that "our God is a consuming fire" (Heb.12:29), for "It is a fearful thing to fall into the hands of the living God" (Heb.10:31). The use of the Tetragrammaton in his novel is a means by which Charles Williams arouses the interest and curiosity of the reader, who finds himself engaged in asking questions regarding human motivations and personal relationships, the meaning of life, the presence of God.

Theologians of the nineteenth and twentieth centuries have been deeply involved in the question of the relationship between the Jesus of history and the Christ of faith.[45] There are limitations on the extent to which historical inquiry can lead us behind and beyond the Gospels to a biographical reconstruction of the life, deeds and teaching of Jesus. The Gospels are not primarily biographies, but represent rather the traditions regarding Jesus, treasured by the Church and reflecting the faith of the Church. The theological orientation of the Gospels points to the Christ of faith, Jesus proclaimed as the Christ in preaching and teaching. Jesus is already recognized as "The Lord," even in the Gospel of St. Mark, the earliest of the four Gospels (e.g. Mark 11:3; cf. also the frequent use of "Lord" as a title of address or as a designation of Jesus; Matt.16:22, 17:4; Luke 13:15, 17:5, 24:34, etc.). Clearly the Christian Church in its kerygmatic proclamation of a risen and exalted *kyrios* precipitated theological questions regarding the nature of Christ as both human and divine and of the relationship between Father, Son and Holy Spirit. These questions were of crucial importance in the formulation of Christological and Trinitarian doctrinal beliefs, in the fourth century of the life of the Church. At the Council of Nicaea in 325 A.D., Jesus was understood to be truly divine and truly human, in the phrases, "being of one substance with the Father," and "became man," avoiding a one-sided view that would do less than justice to either aspect of the person of Christ. The

---

[44]*Ibid.*, p. 9.

[45]Various aspects of the subject are treated in the following: A. Schweitzer, *The Quest of the Historical Jesus*, trans. by W. Montgomery, 1910 (London: Adam & Charles Black, 1952); Rudolf Bultmann, *Jesus and the Word*, trans. by Louise Pettibone Smith & Erminie Huntress Lantero (N.Y.: Chas. Scribner's Sons, 1958); Günther Bornkamm, *Jesus of Nazareth*, trans. by Irene and Fraser McLuskey with James M. Robinson (London: Hodder and Stoughton, 1960); James M. Robinson, *A New Quest of the Historical Jesus*, SBT No. 25 (London: S.C.M. Press, Ltd., 1960); John MacQuarrie, *The Scope of Demythologizing*, (London: S.C.M. Press, Ltd., 1960); Schubert M. Ogden, *Christ Without Myth* (N.Y.: Harper, 1961); Gerhard Ebeling, *Theology and Proclamation*, trans. by John Riches (Philadelphia: Fortress Press, 1962); Wolfhart Pannenberg, *Jesus—God and Man*, trans. by Lewis L. Wilkins and Duane A. Priebe (Philaddphia: The Westminster Press, 1968).

influence of Athanasius may be seen in the formulation of Trinitarian doctrine, especially at the Council of Constantinople in 381 A.D. Father, Son, and Holy Spirit were declared to be co-equal and co-eternal, yet without denying the genuine humanity of Jesus Christ.

The rise of biblical critical methodology in the nineteenth century also brought into prominence the question of the interpretation of the person of Christ. Literary analysis of the Gospels, for instance, led on to a close examination of the form and function of the individual units of the traditions, e.g., the parables, the narratives of healing, the teaching passages, the use of the Old Testament in the New. Areas of theological concern which continue to be debated at length include the question of the relationship between the Old and the New Testament and the extent to which the latter may be said to fulfil the former.[46] Is it legitimate to regard Jesus of Nazareth as the supreme revelation of God, in whom "all the fulness of God was pleased to dwell" (Col.1:19)? Christian theologians rightly find in the themes of divine lordship and sovereignty continuity between the Old and New Testaments.

The key question in the historical interpretation of the Gospels is, how did Jesus view himself and his mission, in relation to God? Psychological interpretations which concentrate attention on the self-awareness and vocational consciousness of Jesus are limited by the paucity of evidence within the Gospels. Although the incident when Jesus at the age of twelve remained in the temple among the teachers (Luke 2:41-51), and the accounts of the temptation (Mark 1:12, 13; Matt.4:1-11; Luke 4:1-13), suggest stages in a growing "Messianic" consciousness, interpretation on psychological lines is somewhat subjective, and therefore precarious. The consensus of much recent writing on the interpretation of the Gospels is that Jesus did not openly claim to be the Messiah, principally because first century Jewish concepts of Messiahship were political and nationalistic in orientation.[47] Yet the gospels, particularly in their treatment of the trial scenes before Jewish and Roman authorities are somewhat ambiguous as to whether or not Jesus admitted that he was the Messiah.[48] According to Mark 14:61,62, in response to the question of the high priest, "Are you the Christ, the

[46]See, for example, Rudolf Bultmann's essay, "Prophecy and Fulfillment" in *Essays on Old Testament Hermeneutics*, ed. Claus Westermann, Eng. trans. ed. by J. L. Mays (Richmond, Virginia: John Knox Press, 1963), pp. 50-75; W. Zimmerli, "Promise and Fulfillment," in *ibid.*, pp. 89-122; C. Westermann, "The Way of Promise Through the Old Testament" in *The Old Testament and Christian Faith*, ed. B. W. Anderson (N.Y.: Harper & Row, 1963), pp. 200-224.

[47]For illuminating treatments of the Messiahship of Jesus, see William Manson, *Jesus the Messiah* (London: Hodder & Stoughton, Limited, 1943); T. W. Manson, *The Servant-Messiah* (Cambridge University Press, 1953); O. Cullmann, *The Christology of the New Testament*, trans. by Shirley C. Guthrie and Charles A. M. Hall (London: S.C.M. Press, Ltd., 1959), Ch. 5.

[48]Recent studies of the Jewish and Roman trials of Jesus include: Josef Blinzler, *The Trial of Jesus*, trans. by Isabel and Florence McHugh (Cork: The Mercier Press, Ltd., 1959);

Son of the Blessed?" Jesus replied, *"ego eimi* (I am), and you will see the son of man sitting at the right hand of Power, and coming with the clouds of heaven." The theme of "the Messianic secret"[49] finds a partial resolution in this declaration regarding the apocalyptic Son of Man of Daniel 7. However, in the Matthaean version of this incident, the reply of Jesus to the high priest's question is "You have said so" (Matt.26:64; cf. Luke 23:70, "You say that I am"). Again, when Pilate questioned Jesus, "Are you the King of the Jews?" the reply was, "You have said so" (Mark 15:2; cf. Matt.27:11; Luke 23:3). There is a studied ambiguity about these replies. Yet, as Raymond Brown observes, "It is difficult to avoid the impression created by all the Gospels, that the Jewish authorities saw something blasphemous in Jesus' understanding of himself and his role."[50]

There is a reticence in the Synoptic Gospels in ascribing to Jesus himself statements concerning his identity and the nature of his person. The evangelists, however, are fascinated by the mystery of the person of Jesus, and are at times explicit in their declarations regarding him (e.g. Mark 1:1; Matt.1:20-23; Luke 4:41). The remarkable fact is that the Synoptic Gospels are so objective in their treatment. The author of the Fourth Gospel has no reservations in proclaiming the divinity of Jesus (Jno.1:1; 1:34: 20:31).

Especially interesting in the Fourth Gospel are the *egō eimi* ("I am") sayings. Philip Harner is skeptical of any attempt to establish a direct connection between the use of *egō eimi* in the Synoptic tradition and the absolute use in the Fourth Gospel.[51] The more basic question is not whether there is a link between Synoptic and Johannine traditions regarding the use of *egō eimi* in the mouth of Jesus but whether Jesus actually used the absolute *egō eimi* regarding himself. Most Johannine scholars would understand the Fourth Gospel as an inspired commentary on the theological meaning of the incarnation, death, and resurrection of Jesus. W. F. Howard claims, "It is the Evangelist's manner to take a saying of Jesus and render it into an idiom that is rich in meaning for his own contemporaries."[52] In Harner's view, "the absolute *egō eimi* probably represents an early Christian attempt to formulate and depict the significance of Jesus."[53]

Paul Winter, *On the Trial of Jesus* (Berlin: Walter de Gruyter & Co., 1961); Ernst Bammel, ed., *The Trial of Jesus: Cambridge Studies in Honour of C. F. D. Moule,* SBT, 13 (London: S.C.M. Press, Ltd., 1970).

[49]The seminal work is that of W. Wrede, *Das Messias-geheimnis in den Evangelien* (Göttingen: 1901), trans. by J. C. G. Greig, *The Messianic Secret* (London: James Clarke & Co., Ltd., 1971).

[50]Raymond Brown, *The Gospel According to John, i-xii,* The Anchor Bible (N.Y.: Doubleday, 1966), p. 368.

[51]P. Harner, *The "I am" of the Fourth Gospel* (Philadelphia: Fortress Press, 1970), pp. 30-36.

[52]W. F. Howard, *The Fourth Gospel in Recent Criticism and Interpretation* (London: The Epworth Press, 1931, 4th ed., revised, 1955), p. 219.

[53]P. Harner, *op. cit.,* p. 64.

By attributing to Jesus himself the use of the "I am" sayings, with their background ultimately in Deutero-Isaiah, the essential unity of Jesus with God is
being asserted. At the same time, the Son is recognized as subordinate to the
Father (Jno.14:28). Monotheistic faith is not to be undermined by the "I am"
sayings; rather, the intention is to express the role of the Son in his oneness with
the Father in carrying out the will and purpose of God. It remained for the
theologians of the Church subsequently to wrestle with the implications of such
assertions in attempting to arrive at viable Christological and Trinitarian formula-
tions. In the process, attention shifted from any preoccupation with the Tetragrammaton or meaning of the divine name *per se*, to the person and work of
Christ, whose sovereign lordship becomes an expression of the lordship of
YHWH. Cullmann's summation provides a fitting conclusion to this study, "The
designation of Jesus as *Kyrios* has the further consequence that actually all the
titles of honour for God himself (with the exception of 'Father') may be transferred to Jesus. Once he was given the 'name which is above every name,' God's
own name ('Lord,' *Adonai, Kyrios*), then no limitations at all could be set for
the transfer of divine attributes to him."[54]

---

[54]O. Cullmann, *op. cit.*, pp. 236-237.

SELECT BIBLIOGRAPHY

Abba, Raymond. "The Divine Name Yahweh." *JBL*, LXXX (1961):320-328.

——————. "Name." *IDB*, III. New York: Abingdon Press, 1962, 500-508.

Abrahams, Israel. *Studies in Pharisaism and the Gospels*, II. Second Series. Cambridge University Press, 1924. Reprinted New York, 1967, 26-27; 174-176.

Albrektson, Bertil. "On the Syntax of *'ehyeh ᵃsher 'ehyeh* in Exod.3:14." *Words and Meanings*. Edited by Peter R. Ackroyd and Barnabas Lindars. Cambridge University Press, 1968, 15-28.

Albright, William Foxwell. "The Name Yahweh." *JBL*, XLII (1924):370-378.

——————. "Further Observations on the Name Yahweh and its Modifications in Proper Names." *JBL*, XLIV (1925):158-162.

——————. "The Names 'Israel' and 'Judah' with an Excursus on the Etymology of Tôdâh and Tôrâh." *JBL*, XLVI (1920):151-185.

——————. "The Names Shaddai and Abram." *JBL*, LIV (1935):173-204.

——————. "The Oracles of Balaam." *JBL*, LXIII (1944):207-233.

——————. *From the Stone Age to Christianity*. 2nd ed. Baltimore: The Johns Hopkins Press, 1946.

——————. "Jethro, Hobab and Reuel in Early Hebrew Tradition (With Some Comments on the Origin of 'JE')." *CBQ*, XXV (1963):1-11.

Alfrink, Bern. "La Prononciation 'Jehova' du Tétragramme." *OTS*, V (1948):43-63.

Allegro, John Marco. *The Sacred Mushroom and the Cross*. London: Hodder and Stoughton, 1970.

Alt, Albrecht. "Ein Ägyptisches Gegenstück Zu Ex 3^{14}." *ZAW*, LVIII (1940):159-160.

——————. "Der Gott Der Väter." *BWANT*, III, 12 (1929). Stuttgart: W. Kohlhammer. Trans. by R. A. Wilson and reprinted in *Essays on Old Testament Religion*. Oxford: Basil Blackwell, 1966, 3-77.

111

Anderson, Bernard W.   "God, Names of." *IDB*, II. New York: Abingdon Press, 1962, 407-417.

Arnold, William R.   "The Divine Name in Exodus iii.14." *JBL*, XXIV (1905):107-165.

Auerbach, Elias.   *Moses*. Amsterdam: G. J. A. Ruys, 1953.

Barr, James.   *The Semantics of Biblical Language*. Oxford University Press, 1961.

Barton, George Aaron.   *Semitic and Hamitic Origins, Social and Religious*. Philadelphia: University of Pennsylvania Press, 1934.

Ben-Ḥayyim, Z.   "On the Pronunciation of the Tetragrammaton by the Samaritans." *Eretz-Israel*, III (1954):147-154.

Berkovits, Eliezer.   *Man and God*. Detroit: Wayne State University Press, 1969.

Blank, Sheldon H.   "Studies in Deutero-Isaiah." *HUCA*, XV (1940):1-46.

Blau, L.   "Tetragrammaton." *The Jewish Encyclopedia*, XII. Edited by I. Singer. New York: Funk and Wagnall's, 1906, 118-120.

Boling, Robert G.   "'Synonymous' Parallelism in the Psalms." *JSS*, V (1960):221-255.

Boman, Thorlief.   *Hebrew Thought Compared with Greek*. Trans. by Jules L. Moreau. London: S.C.M. Press Ltd., 1960.

Bowman, Raymond A.   "Yahweh the Speaker." *JNES*, III (1944):1-8.

Brekelmans, Chr. H. W.   "Exodus XVIII and the Origins of Yahwism in Israel." *OTS*, X (1954):215-224.

Buber, Martin.   *Königtum Gottes*. Berlin: 1932, 3rd ed., 1956. Trans. by Richard Scheimann, *Kingship of God*.

————————.   *Moses: The Revelation and the Covenant*. New York: Harper and Brothers, Torchbook Edition, 1958.

————————.   *The Prophetic Faith*. MacMillan, 1949. New York: Harper & Row, Torchbook Edition, 1960.

Burkitt, Francis Crawford. "On the Name Yahweh." *JBL*, XLIV (1925):353-356.

————————. "Yahweh or Yahoh: Additional Note." *JTS*, XXVIII (1927):407-409.

Childs, Brevard S. *The Book of Exodus*. OTL. Philadelphia: The Westminster Press, 1974.

Cohon, Samuel S. "The Name of God." *HUCA*, XXIII, Pt. 1 (1951):579-604.

Cook, Stanley A. "The Significance of the Elephantine Papyri for the History of Hebrew Religion." *AJT*, XIX (1915):346-382.

Cowley, Arthur Ernest. *Aramaic Papyri of the Fifth Century, B.C.* Oxford: Clarendon Press, 1923.

Cross, Frank Moore, Jr. "Yahweh and the God of the Patriarchs." *HTR*, LV (1962):225-259.

————————. *Canaanite Myth and Hebrew Epic*. Cambridge, Mass.: Harvard University Press, 1973.

Dalman, Gustaf Hermann. *The Words of Jesus*. Translated by D. M. Kay. Edinburgh: T. & T. Clark, 1902.

Danby, Herbert. *The Mishnah. Translated from the Hebrew with Introduction and Brief Explanatory Notes*. London: Oxford University Press, 1933.

Daube, David. *The New Testament and Rabbinic Judaism*. London: The Athlone Press, 1956.

Delitzsch, Friedrich. *Babel and Bible*. Translated by G. H. W. Johns. London: Williams and Norgate, 1903.

Della Vida, G. Levi. "El Elyon in Genesis 14:18-20." *JBL*, LXIII (1944):1-9.

Dentan, Robert C. *The Knowledge of God in Ancient Israel*. New York: The Seabury Press, 1968.

Dhorme, Édouard. "Le Nom du Dieu d'Israel." *RHR*, CXLI (1952):5-18.

Driver, Godfrey Rolles. "The Original Form of the Name Yahweh: Evidences and Conclusions." *ZAW*, XLVI (1928):7-25.

————————. "The Interpretation of *Yhwh* as a Participial Form." *JBL*, LXXIII (1954):125-131.

Eerdmans, B.D. "The Name Jahu." *OTS*, V (1948):2-29. The article was written in 1942.

Eichrodt, Walther. *Theology of the Old Testament*, I. Translated by J. A. Baker. Philadelphis: The Westminster Press, 1961.

Eissfeldt, Otto. "Jahwe–Name und Zauberwesen." *Zeitschrift für Missionskunde*, XLII (1927):161-186. Reprinted in *Kleine Schriften*, I. Tübingen: J.C.B. Mohr, 1962, 150-171.

————————. "Jahwe als König." *ZAW*, XLVI (1928):81-105. Reprinted in *Kleine.Schriften*, I. Tübingen: J.C.B. Mohr, 1962, 172-193.

————————. "Neue Zeugnisse für die Aussprache des Tetragramms als Jahwe." *ZAW*, LIII (1935):59-76. Reprinted in *Kleine Schriften*, II. Tübingen: J.C.B. Mohr, 1963, 80-96.

————————. "Baalshamem und Jahwe." *ZAW*, LVII (1939):1-31. Reprinted in *Kleine Schriften*, II. Tübingen: J.C.B. Mohr, 1963, 171-198.

————————. "Jahwe Zebaoth." *Miscellanea Academica Berolinensia*, II.2. Berlin: 1950, 128-150. Reprinted in *Kleine Schriften*, III. Tübingen: J.C.B. Mohr, 1966, 103-123.

————————. "El und Jahwe." *JSS*, I (1956):25-37. Reprinted in *Kleine Schriften*, IIII. Tübingen: J.C.B. Mohr, 1966, 386-397.

————————. "Jahwe, der Gott der Väter." *Theologische Literaturzeitung*, LXXXVIII (1963): cols. 481-490. Reprinted in *Kleine Schriften*, IV. Tübingen: J.C.B. Mohr, 1968, 79-91.

————————. "Jakobs Begegnung mit El und Moses Begegnung mit Jahwe." *Orientalistische Literaturzeitung*, LVIII (1963): 325-331. Reprinted in *Kleine Schriften*, IV. Tübingen: J.C.B. Mohr, 1968, 92-98.

————————. "'äh^{e}yäh ^{a}sär 'äh^{e}yäh und 'El ôlām." *Forschungen und Fortschritte*, XXXIX (1965):298-300. Reprinted in *Kleine Schriften*, IV. Tübingen: J.C.B. Mohr, 1968, 193-198.

Fitzmyer, J.A. *The Aramaic Inscriptions of Sefire*. Rome: The Pontifical Biblical Institute, 1967.

Franken, Hendricus Jacobus. *The Mystical Communion with Jhwh in the Book of Psalms*. Leiden: E. J. Brill, 1954.

Freedman, David Noel. "The Name of the God of Moses." *JBL*, LXXIX (1960):151-156.

Gardner, W. R. W. "The Name 'Yahweh'." *The Expository Times*, XX (1908/9):91-92.

Gaster, Moses. *The Sword of Moses: An Ancient Book of Magic*. London, 1896. Reprinted in New York: Samuel Weiser, Inc., 1970.

Giveon, Raphael. "Toponymes Ouest-Asiatiques à Soleb." *VT*, XIV (1964):239-255.

Gleason, R. W. *Yahweh the God of the Old Testament*. New Jersey: Prentice-Hall, Inc., 1964.

Goitein, S. D. "YHWH the Passionate: The Monotheistic Meaning and Origin of the Name YHWH." *VT*, VI (1956):1-9.

Gray, George Buchanan. *Studies in Hebrew Proper Names*. London: Adam and Charles Black, 1896.

Gray, John. "The God Yw in the Religion of Canaan." *JNES*, XII (1953):278-283.

Gressmann, Hugo. *Mose und Seine Zeit*. Göttingen: Vandenhoeck & Ruprecht, 1913.

Grether, Oskar. *Name und Wort Gottes in Alten Testament*. BZAW, LXIV. Giessen, 1934.

Grimme, Hubert. "Sind Jaho und Jahwe zwei Verschiedene Namen und Begriffe?" *Biblische Zeitschrift*, XVII (1926):29-42.

Harner, Philip B. *The "I am" of the Fourth Gospel: A Study in Johannine Usage and Thought*. Philadelphia: Fortress Press, 1970.

Haupt, Paul. "Der Name Jahwe." *Orientalistische Literaturzeitung*, XII (1909): cols. 211-214.

Heschel, Abraham J.. *The Prophets*. New York: Harper & Row, 1962.

Hillers, Delbert R.   "Paḥad Yiṣḥaq." *JBL*, XCI (1972):90-92.

Hirsch, Emil G.   "Jehovah." *The Jewish Encyclopedia*, VII. Edited by I. Singer. New York: Funk and Wagnall's, 1906, 87-88.

Hoonacker, A. van.   *Une Communauté Judéo-Araméenne à Éléphantine.* The Schweich Lectures of 1914. London: Oxford University Press, 1915.

Huffmon, Herbert Bardwell.   *Amorite Personal Names in the Mari Texts: A Structural and Lexical Study.* Baltimore, Maryland: The Johns Hopkins Press, 1965.

Hyatt, J. Philip.   "Yahweh as 'the God of my Father'." *VT*, V (1955): 130-136.

————————.   "Was Yahweh Originally a Creator Deity?" *JBL*, LXXXVI (1967):369-377.

Imschoot, Paul van.   *Theology of the Old Testament, I: God.* Translated by Kathryn Sullivan and Fidelis Buck. New York: Desclée Company, 1965.

Irwin, William A.   "Critical Note: Exod. 3:14." *AJSL*, LVI (1939):297-298.

Jacob, Edmond.   *Theology of the Old Testament.* Translated by Arthur W. Heathcote and Philip J. Allcock. London: Hodder & Stoughton, Ltd., 1958.

Kahle, Paul Ernst.   *The Cairo Geniza.* 2nd ed. Oxford: Basil Blackwell, 1959.

Kaufmann, Yehezkel.   *The Religion of Israel: From its Beginnings to the Babylonian Exile.* Translated and abridged by Moshe Greenberg. London: George Allen and Unwin Ltd., 1961.

Kittell, Gerhard and G. Friedrich, eds.   *Theologisches Wörterbuch zum Neuen Testament*, III. Articles on *kyrios* by G. Quell and W. Foerster. Stuttgart: W. Kohlhammer, 1938, 1038-1094. Translated and edited by Geoffrey W. Bromiley, *Theological Dictionary of the New Testament*, III. Grand Rapids, Michigan: Wm. B. Eerdmans Publishing Company, 1965, 1039-1095.

Knight, George A. F.   *A Christian Theology of the Old Testament.* London: S.C.M. Press Ltd., 1959. 2nd revised edition, 1964.

Köhler, Ludwig.   *Hebrew Man.* Translated by Peter R. Ackroyd. London: S.C.M. Press Ltd., 1956.

König, Ed. "Die Formell-genetische Wechselbeziehung der beiden Wörter Jahweh und Jahu." *ZAW*, XVII (1897):172-179.

Kraeling, Emil G. *The Brooklyn Museum Aramaic Papyri: New Documents of the Fifth Century B.C. from the Jewish Colony at Elephantine*. New Haven: Yale University Press, 1953.

Kuntz, J. Kenneth. *The Self-Revelation of God*. Philadelphia: The Westminster Press, 1967.

Lewy, Immanuel. "The Beginnings of the Worship of Yahweh: Conflicting Biblical Views." *VT*, VI (1956):429-435.

Luckenbill, Daniel David. "The Pronunciation of the Name of the God of Israel." *AJSL*, XL (1924):277-283.

Maclaurin, E. C. B. "Yhwh: The Origin of the Tetragrammaton." *VT*, XII (1962):439-463.

Margoliouth, David Samuel. *Relations Between Arabs and Israelites Prior to the Rise of Islam*. The Schweich Lectures, 1921. London: Oxford University Press, 1924.

May, Herbert G. "An Inscribed Jar from Megiddo." *AJSL*, L (1933):10-14.

————————. "The Patriarchal Idea of God." *JBL*, LX (1941):113-128.

————————. "The God of my Father—A Study of Patriarchal Religion." *JBR*, IX (1941):155-158, 199-200.

Mayer, R. "Der Gottesname Jahwe in Lichte der neusten Forschung." *Biblische Zeitschrift*, n.s.2 (1958):26-53.

Meek, Theophile J. "Some Religious Origins of the Hebrews." *AJSL*, XXXVII (1920-21):101-131.

————————. *Hebrew Origins*. Toronto: University of Toronto Press, 1936. 2nd revised edition, 1950.

Miskotte, Kornelis H. *When the Gods are Silent*. Translated by John W. Doberstein. London: Collins, 1967.

Moltmann, Jürgen. *The Theology of Hope*. Translated by James W. Leitch. London: S.C.M. Press, Ltd., 1967.

Montefiore, Claude J. G. and H. Loewe. *A Rabbinic Anthology.* London: MacMillan and Co., Ltd., 1938. Reprinted by Meridian Books, Cleveland: World Publishing Company, and Philadelphia: Jewish Publication Society, 1963.

Montgomery, James Alan. *Arabia and the Bible.* Philadelphia: University of Pennsylvania Press, 1934.

————————. *Aramaic Incantation Texts from Nippur.* Philadelphia: The University Museum, 1913.

————————. Some Hebrew Etymologies."*JQR*, XXV (1934-35):268-269.

————————. "The Hebrew Divine Name and the Personal Pronoun Hu." *JBL*, LXIII (1944):161-163.

Moore, George Foot. "Notes on the Name Yhwh." *AJSL*, XXV (1909):312-318.

————————. *Judaism.* Cambridge: Harvard University Press, *I*, 1927; *III*, 1930.

Morgenstern, Julian. "The Elohist Narrative in Exodus 3:1-15." *AJSL*, XXXVII (1920-21):242-262.

————————. "The Oldest Documents of the Hexateuch." *HUCA*, IV (1927):1-138.

Mowinckel, Sigmund. "The Name of the God of Moses." *HUCA*, XXXII (1961):121-133.

Murtonen, A. *A Philological and Literary Treatise on the Old Testament Divine Names.* Studia Orientalia Fennica, XVII.1. Helsinki, 1952.

Noth, Martin. *Die israelitischen Personennamen im Rahmen der gemein-semitischen Namengebung.* Stuttgart: W. Kohlhammer, 1928.

————————. *Das System den zwölf Stämme Israels.* Stuttgart: W. Kohl-hammer, 1930.

————————. *The History of Israel.* Translated by Stanley Godman. London: Adam & Charles Black, 1958.

Obermann, Julian. "The Divine Name Yhwh in the Light of Recent Dis-coveries." *JBL*, LXVIII (1949):301-323.

Ogden, G. S. "Time, and the verb *hayah* in the Old Testament Prose." *VT*, XXI (1971):451-469.

Otto, Rudolf. *The Idea of the Holy*. Translated by J. W. Harvey. London: Oxford University Press, 1923.

Pedersen, Johs. *Israel, Its Life and Culture, I-II*. Copenhagen: Povl Brannen, 1926. Reprinted, London: Oxford University Press, Geoffrey Cumberlege, 1946.

Phythian-Adams, William J. *The Call of Israel*. London: Oxford University Press, 1934.

Plastaras, James. *The God of Exodus: The Theology of the Exodus Narratives*. Milwaukee: The Bruce Publishing Company, 1966.

Pope, Marvin H., *El in the Ugaritic Texts*. Supplements to Vetus Testamentum, II, Leiden: E. J. Brill, 1955.

Porten, Bezalel. *Archives from Elephantine: The Life of an Ancient Jewish Military Colony*. Berkeley: University of California Press, 1968.

Quell, Gottfried. "The Old Testament Name for God." Chapter III in *Lord*; Bible Key Words from Gerhard Kittel's *Theologisches Wörterbuch zum Neuen Testament*. W. Foerster and G. Quell, translated with additional notes by H. P. Kingdon. London: Adam & Charles Black, 1958.

Rad, Gerhard von. *Old Testament Theology, I*. Translated by D. M. G. Stalker. London: Oliver & Boyd, 1962.

Ratschow, Carl H. *Werden und Wirken, Eine Untersuchung des Wortes Hajah als Beitrag zur Wirklichkeitserfassung des Alten Testaments*. BZAW, No. 70. Berlin: Töpelmann, 1941.

Reisel, Max. *Observations on 'ehyeh $^{\prime a}$sher 'ehyeh (Ex.III.14), hu'h' (D.S.D. VIII.13) and shem hamm^{e}phorash*. Assen: Van Gorcum & Comp. N.V., 1957.

Rowley, Harold Henry. *The Re-Discovery of the Old Testament*. London: James Clarke & Co., Ltd., 1945.

————. *From Joseph to Joshua*. The Schweich Lectures of the British Academy, 1948. London: Oxford University Press, 1950.

—————. "Moses and the Decalogue." *BJRL*, XXXIV (1951-52):81-118. Reprinted in *Men of God*. London: Thomas Nelson and Sons, Ltd., 1963, 1-36.

—————. "Papyri from Elephantine." *Documents from Old Testament Times*. Edited by D. Winton Thomas. London: Thomas Nelson and Sons, Ltd., 1958, 256-269.

—————. "Moses and Monotheism." *From Moses to Qumran*. London: Lutterworth Press, 1963.

Sandmel, Samuel. "Genesis 4:26b." *HUCA*, XXXII (1961):19-29.

Schild, E. "On Exodus iii 14: 'I am That I am'." *VT*, IV (1954):296-302.

Schmökel, Hartmut. "Jahwe und die Keniten." *JBL*, LII (1933):212-229.

Scholem, Gershom G. *On the Kabbalah and its Symbolism*. New York: Schocken Books, 1965.

Segal, Moses Hirsch. "El, Elohim, and YHWH in the Bible." *JQR*, XLVI (1955):89-115.

Skehan, Patrick W. "The Qumran Manuscripts and Textual Criticism." *Supplements to Vetus Testamentum*, IV. Leiden: E. J. Brill, 1957, 148-160.

Skinner, John. *The Divine Names in Genesis*. London: Hodder and Stoughton, 1914.

Smith, Henry Preserved. "Theophorous Proper Names in the Old Testament." *AJSL*, XXIV (1907):34-61.

Smith, Ronald Gregor. *The Doctrine of God*. London: Collins, 1970.

Spoer, Hans H. "The Origin and Interpretation of the Tetragrammaton." *AJSL*, XVIII (1901):9-35.

Thierry, G. J. "The Pronunciation of the Tetragrammaton." *OTS*, V (1948):30-42.

Thomas, David Winton. "Tetragramm." *Die Religion in Geschichte und Gegenwart*, VI. 3rd edition. Tübingen: J.C.B. Mohr, 1962, col. 703.

Tsevat, Matitiahu. "Studies in the Book of Samuel." IV. *HUCA*, XXXVI (1965):49-58.

Vaux, Roland de. "Les Textes de Ras Shamra et l'Ancien Testament." *RB*, XLVI (1937):527-555.

————. "Sur l'Origine Kénite ou Madianite du Yahvisme." *W. F. Albright Festschrift. Eretz-Israel*, IX (1969):28-32.

————. "The Revelation of the Divine Name Yhwh." *Proclamation and Presence*. Edited by John I. Durham and J. Roy Porter. London: S.C.M. Press, Ltd., 1970, 48-75.

Volz, Paul. *Mose und sein Werk*. 2nd ed. Tübingen: J.C.B. Mohr, 1932.

Vriezen, Theodorus Christiaan. "'Ehje 'ᵃšer 'ehje." *Festschrift Alfred Bertholet zum 80. Geburtstag*. Edited by W. Baumgartner, O. Eissfeldt, K. Elliger, and L. Rost, 498-512. Tübingen: J.C.B. Mohr, 1950.

Walker, Norman. *The Tetragrammaton*. West Ewell, England, 1948. Privately published.

————. "The Writing of the Divine Name in the Mishna." *VT*, I (1951):309-310.

————. "Yahwism and the Divine Name, 'Yhwh'." *ZAW*, LXX (1958):262-265.

————. "Concerning Ex. 34:6." *JBL*, LXXIX (1960):277.

————. "Concerning Hû' and 'Anî Hû'." *ZAW*, LXXIV (1962):205-206.

————. "The Riddle of the Ass's Head, and the Question of a Trigram." *ZAW*, LXXV (1963):225-226.

Wambacq, B.N. *L'Épithète Divine Jahvé Sebaoth*. Paris-Bruges: Desclée, de Brouwer, 1947.

Ward, William Hayes. "The Origin of the Worship of Yahwe." *AJSL*, XXV (1909):175-187.

Waterman, Leroy. "Method in the Study of the Tetragrammaton," *AJSL*, XLIII (1926):1-7.

West, Charles. "Art and Being in Charistian and Marxist Perspective." *Openings for Marxist-Christian Dialogue*. Edited by Thomas W. Ogletree. New York: Abingdon Press, 1968.

Wevers, John William.   "A Study in the Form Criticism of Individual Complaint
Psalms." *VT*, VI (1956):80-96.

Whitley, Charles F.   *The Genius of Ancient Israel*. Amsterdam: Philo Press,
1969.

Williams, A. Lukyn.   "Yaho[h]." *JTS* XXVIII (1927):276-283.

————————.   "The Tetragrammaton—Jahweh, Name or Surrogate?" *ZAW*,
LIV (1936):262-269.

Williams, Charles.   *Many Dimensions*. London: Victor Gollancz, 1931. New
Edition. London: Faber & Faber Limited, 1947.

Zimmerli, Walther.   "Ich bin Jahwe." *Geschichte und Altes Testament*. Beiträge
zur historischen Theologie, 16, Albrecht Alt zum 70. Geburtstag darge-
bracht, Tübingen: Paul Siebeck, 1953, 179-209. Reprinted in *Gottes Offenbarung*. Gesammelte Aufsätze zum Alten Testament. München: Chr. Kaiser
Verlag, 1963, 11-40.

————————.   "Erkenntnis Gottes nach dem Buche Ezechiel." *Eine Theologische Studie*. Abhandlung zur Theologie des Alten und Neuen Testaments,
27. Zürich: Zwingli-Verlag, 1954. Reprinted in *Gottes Offenbarung*.
Gesammelte Aufsätze zum Alten Testament. München: Chr. Kaiser Verlag,
1963, 41-119.

INDEX OF BIBLICAL REFERENCES

INDEX OF AUTHORS

INDEX OF SUBJECTS